The Princeton Review®

Workout for the New

PSAT®

275+ Practice Questions & Answers to Help You Prepare for the New Test

The Staff of The Princeton Review

PrincetonReview.com

Penguin
Random
House

The Princeton Review
24 Prime Parkway, Suite 201
Natick, MA 01760
E-mail: editorialsupport@review.com

Published in the United States by Penguin Random House LLC, New York,
and in Canada by Random House of Canada, a division of Penguin Random
House Ltd., Toronto.

Terms of Service: The Princeton Review Online Companion Tools ("Student
Tools") for retail books are available for only the two most recent editions
of that book. Student Tools may be activated only twice per eligible book
purchased for two consecutive 12-month periods, for a total of 24 months
of access. Activation of Student Tools more than twice per book is in
direct violation of these Terms of Service and may result in discontinua-
tion of access to Student Tools Services.

ISBN: 978-0-8041-2607-6
eBook ISBN: 978-0-8041-2638-0
ISSN: 2377-7265

PSAT is a registered trademark of the College Board, which does not
sponsor or endorse this product.

The Princeton Review is not affiliated with Princeton University.

Editor: Selena Coppock
Production Editor: Emily Epstein White
Production Artist: Deborah Silvestrini

Printed in the United States of America on partially recycled paper.

10 9 8 7 6 5 4 3

Editorial

Rob Franek, Senior VP, Publisher
Casey Cornelius, VP Content Development
Mary Beth Garrick, Director of Production
Selena Coppock, Managing Editor
Meave Shelton, Senior Editor
Colleen Day, Editor
Aaron Riccio, Editor
Orion McBean, Editorial Assistant

Random House Publishing Team

Tom Russell, Publisher
Alison Stoltzfus, Publishing Manager
Melinda Ackell, Associate Managing Editor
Ellen Reed, Production Manager
Kristin Lindner, Production Supervisor
Andrea Lau, Designer

Acknowledgments

Special thanks to Brian Becker, Zoe Gannon, and Cat Healey.

Thanks also to Chris Aylward, Clarissa Constantine, Lori DesRochers, Erik Kolb, Aaron Lindh, Kathryn Menefee, Amy Minster, Anne Morrow, Alexander Palmer, Garrison Pierzynski, Stephen Shuck, and Jess Thomas.

—Jonathan Chiu
National Content Director
High School Programs
The Princeton Review

Contents

Register Your

1 Go to **PrincetonReview.com/cracking**

2 You'll see a welcome page where you can register your book using the following ISBN: 9780804126076.

3 After placing this free order, you'll either be asked to log in or to answer a few simple questions in order to set up a new Princeton Review account.

4 Finally, click on the "Student Tools" tab located at the top of the screen. It may take an hour or two for your registration to go through, but after that, you're good to go.

If you are experiencing book problems (potential content errors), please contact EditorialSupport@review.com with the full title of the book, its ISBN number (located above), and the page number of the error. Experiencing technical issues? Please e-mail TPRStudentTech@review.com with the following information:

- your full name
- e-mail address used to register the book
- full book title and ISBN
- your computer OS (Mac or PC) and Internet browser (Firefox, Safari, Chrome, etc.)
- description of technical issue

Book Online!

Once you've registered, you can...

- Find any late-breaking information released about the New PSAT

- Get valuable advice about the college application process, including tips for writing a great essay and where to apply for financial aid

- Sort colleges by whatever you're looking for (such as Best Theater or Dorm), learn more about your top choices, and see how they all rank according to *The Best 380 Colleges*

- Check to see if there have been any corrections or updates to this edition

Look For These Icons Throughout The Book

- Proven Techniques
- Study Break
- Applied Strategies
- More Great Books

The Princeton Review®
Your Goals. Our Expertise.™

Part I
Orientation

Chapter 1
Your Guide to Getting the Most Out of This Book

WHAT'S INSIDE

Hello, and welcome to *Workout for the New PSAT*! In these pages you'll find 276 practice questions to help you prepare for the redesigned PSAT. These questions showcase all the features of the new PSAT, including its retooled subject areas: Reading, Writing & Language, and Math. Working through these problems in conjunction with our detailed, technique-filled explanations is a great way to familiarize yourself with the challenges of the redesigned PSAT.

What Is The Princeton Review?

The Princeton Review is the nation's leading test-preparation company. In just a few years, we became the nation's leader in SAT preparation, primarily because our techniques work. We offer courses and private tutoring for all of the major standardized tests, and we publish a series of books to help in your search for the right school. If you would like more information about how The Princeton Review can help you, go to **PrincetonReview.com** or call 800-2-Review.

HOW TO USE THIS BOOK

This book is broken apart into the respective sections that you will see in the redesigned PSAT: Reading, Writing & Language, and Math. All 276 practice questions represent the total content that you would see in two PSATs, so you could use the first Reading Test to learn about the types of passages, question types, and answer choices that would appear. Then, after you've assessed how well you did on those questions by checking the answer key and truly understanding the explanations, you could move on to the second test and time yourself to see how you would fare. The same strategy would work well for the Writing & Language and Math tests. Once these are completed, keep an eye out for our upcoming *Cracking the New PSAT* book that will be published in the near future!

Bubble Sheets
A bubble sheet for each drill can be found on the next page after the drill. You may want to rip these out of your book. Complete answers and explanations are located in the chapter after the drill.

When You Take a Drill

Here are some guidelines for taking these tests:

- Time yourself strictly. Use a timer, watch, or stopwatch that will ring, and do not allow yourself to go over time for any section. If you try to do so at the real test, your scores will likely be canceled.
- Always take a practice drill using an answer sheet with bubbles to fill in, just as you will for the real test. You need to be comfortable transferring answers to the separate sheet because you will be skipping around a bit.

- Each bubble you choose should be filled in thoroughly, and no other marks should be made in the answer area.
- As you fill in the bubble for a question, check to be sure you are on the correct number on the answer sheet. If you fill in the wrong bubble on the answer sheet, it will not matter if you worked out the problem correctly in the test booklet. All that matters to the machine scoring the test is the No. 2 pencil mark.

STAYING AHEAD OF THE REDESIGNED PSAT

Because the first official test administration for the New PSAT is October 2015, it is possible that the College Board will continue to make slight changes and tweaks to the way the test is presented. The **PrincetonReview.com/SATchanges** page of our website will always feature the most up-to-date information. You can also attend free events at the Princeton Review—both in-person and online—to learn more about the redesigned PSAT and the other college prep resources we offer. Search on our website for events taking place near you.

PRINCETON REVIEW TECHNIQUES AND STRATEGIES

Think about the last time you set out to accomplish something: whether it's taking a photo, recording a song, building a cabinet, or writing a screenplay, you probably used all the tools at your disposal to get the job done. The PSAT is no different from any other task—just as you wouldn't attempt to film a movie without a video camera or a boom mike, you wouldn't want to take this test without the skills and strategies that will best help you to succeed. This book is what we at The Princeton Review affectionately call "drill and kill" in that we are offering you gobs of practice problems and detailed answers and explanations. In some of those explanations we will use Princeton Review strategies and jargon that might sound foreign to you. So before we go any further, let's introduce some of the shorthand terms that you might see in your PSAT practice problems.

ZONEF (FROZEN)—This acronym stands for Zero, One, Negative, Extreme, and Fraction, and it refers to a few special numbers that you should test out when checking to see what will satisfy an algebraic expression.

POE—There are many more wrong answers on the PSAT than there are credited answers, so on some of the more difficult questions, you'll be well served by not trying to find the best answer, but rather finding the wrong answers and using POE, Process Of Elimination. Even if you aren't quite sure of the correct answer, you can guess strategically by eliminating a few choices that you know are incorrect and then taking your best guess.

PITA or **Plugging In the Answers**—Plugging In the Answers (PITA) converts algebra problems into arithmetic problems. No matter how good you are at algebra, you're better at arithmetic. Why? Because you use arithmetic every day, every time you go to the store, balance your checkbook, or tip a waiter. Chances are you rarely use algebra in your day-to-day activities. Plug in real numbers to make a problem concrete rather than abstract.

Ballparking—Ballparking helps you eliminate answer choices and increase your odds of zeroing in on the correct answer by eliminating any answer choices that are "out of the ballpark." For example, use quick estimations to eliminate one or two answer choices that are simply out of the ballpark.

FOIL—When faced with two sets of parentheses in a quadratic equation, use this acronym to help you remember to multiply every term in the first set by every term in the second set. FOIL stands for First, Outer, Inner, and Last. So, for example, if you see $(x + 4)(x + 3)$, you would multiply the first terms $(x \cdot x)$, the outer terms $(x \cdot 3)$, the inner terms $(4 \cdot x)$, and finally, the last terms $(4 \cdot 3)$.

GOOD LUCK!

We know that the redesigned PSAT might seem intimidating, but you're already headed in the right direction. And we'll be with you every step of the way.

Chapter 2
What You Need to Know for the New PSAT

WHAT DOES THE PSAT TEST?

First off, while the PSAT may be changing, we at The Princeton Review understand that certain fundamentals of a test always stay the same. As you begin your prep, it's useful to remember that the PSAT is not a test of aptitude, how good of a person you are, or how successful you will be in life. The PSAT simply tests how well you take the PSAT. That's it. And performing well on the PSAT is a skill, one that can be learned like any other. The Princeton Review was founded more than 30 years ago on this very simple idea, and—as our students' test scores show—our approach is the one that works.

All of these changes to tests that you hear could heavily influence your college admission strategy can be extremely daunting. However, remember that any standardized test is a coachable test. A beatable test. Just remember:

The PSAT doesn't measure the stuff that matters. It measures neither intelligence nor the depth and breadth of what you're learning in high school. It doesn't predict college grades as well as your high school grades do, and many schools are still hesitant to use the score from your essay in their application decisions at all: that's why it's now optional. Colleges know there is more to you as a student—and as a person—than what you do at a single test administered on a Saturday morning.

WHO WRITES THE PSAT?

The PSAT is written and administered by Educational Testing Service (ETS), under contract by the College Board. You might think that the people at ETS are educators, professors of education, or teachers. They are not. The people who work for ETS are average people who just happen to make a living writing tests. In fact, they write hundreds of tests, for all kinds of organizations. They are a group of "testers-for-hire" who will write a test for anyone who asks.

The folks at ETS are not paid to educate; they are paid to write and administer tests. Furthermore, even though you (or your school) will be paying ETS to take the PSAT, you are not their customer. The actual customers ETS caters to are the colleges, who get the information they want at no cost. This means that you should take everything that ETS says with a grain of salt and realize that its testing "advice" is not always the best advice. (Getting testing advice from ETS is a bit like getting baseball advice from the opposing team.)

Every test reflects the interests of the people who write it. If you know who writes the test, you will know a lot more about what kinds of answers will be considered "correct" answers on that test.

Category	Current PSAT/NMSQT	Redesigned PSAT/NMSQT (coming fall 2015)
Time	2 hours and 10 minutes	2 hours and 45 minutes
Components	• Critical Reading • Writing • Mathematics	• Evidence-Based Reading and Writing: Reading; Writing & Language • Math
Number of Questions, Time by Section	Critical Reading: 48, 50 mins Writing: 39, 30 mins Mathematics: 38, 50 mins	Reading: 47, 60 mins Writing & Lang: 44, 35 mins Math: 47, 70 mins
Important Features	• Emphasis on general reasoning skills • Emphasis on vocabulary, often in limited contexts • Complex scoring (a point for a correct answer; blank responses have no impact on scores)	• Continued emphasis on reasoning alongside a clearer, stronger focus on the knowledge, skills, understandings more important for college and career readiness and success • Greater emphasis on the meaning of words in extended contexts and on how word choice shapes meaning, tone, and impact • Rights-only scoring (a point for a correct answer but no deduction for an incorrect answer; blank responses have no impact on score)
Score Reporting	• Scale ranging from 60 to 240 • Scale ranging from 20 to 80 for Critical Reading, Mathematics, and Writing	• Some scores will be reported on the same scale used for the SAT. This scale ranges from 400 to 1600 for total score, 200-800 for two section scores, and 10-40 for test scores
Subscore Reporting	None	Subscores for every test, providing added insight for students, parents, educators, counselors

In addition to the obvious changes listed on the table above, such as the shift from five answer choices to four answer choices for multiple-choice questions, the PSAT suggests that it has increased the complexity of questions across the board. For the Reading and Writing & Language tests, this refers in part to the way in which all questions are now connected to full passages, which are themselves purportedly aligned with what introductory college courses and vocational training programs offer. This means that there will be an increase in History and Science-based reading material. More importantly, there are no longer any fill-in-the-blank Sentence Completion questions, nor stand-alone sentence-editing questions: instead, you will be tested on your ability to demonstrate a full understanding of the source's ideas.

The More You Know…
These changes may be intimidating, but as long as you adopt a careful approach after mastering your fundamentals, you will do well on the new PSAT!

The math has also shifted, and not just in the number of questions (from 38 to 48). The actual scope of the content now focuses on a more specific set of problem-solving and analytical topics, and includes higher-level content (like trigonometry). Students are also likely to encounter more grid-in questions, and will face topics that are both specifically geared to test a student's ability to use a calculator and for which calculators are not permitted.

The Math Test will be divided into two sections, one with the calculator, with 31 questions over the course of 45 minutes, and one without, with 17 questions administered in 25 minutes. Because of the tight time limit, particularly in the non-calculator section, it's important that you review the explanations for the problems in this book that you solved correctly, as you may discover techniques that help to shave seconds from your solutions. A large part of what's being tested is your ability to use the appropriate tools in a strategic fashion, and while there may be multiple ways to solve a given problem, you'll want to focus on the most efficient.

SCORING ON THE PSAT

Another major difference has to do with the way that the test is scored: the PSAT will now be scored on a scale of 400–1600 that will be the sum of the two section scores that range from 200–800. The two sections are the Evidence-Based Reading and Writing section and the Mathematics section. Wrong answers to multiple-choice questions will no longer be penalized, so you're advised never to leave a question blank—even if that means blindly picking a letter and bubbling it in for any uncompleted questions before time runs out.

In addition to the overall composite score and the section scores, there will be other subscores reported on your PSAT score report:

An **Analysis in History/Social Studies** and **Analysis in Science** cross-test score is generated based on questions from all three of the subject tests (Math included!) and these assess the cross-curricular application of the tested skills to other contexts. Relax! This doesn't mean that you have to start cramming dates and anatomy—every question can be answered from the context of a given reading passage or the data included in a table or figure. The only changes have to do with the content of the passages and questions themselves.

Additionally, the Math test is broken into several categories, as we've done in this book. The **Heart of Algebra** subscore looks specifically at how well students understand how to handle algebraic expressions, work with a variety of algebraic equations, and relate real-world scenarios to algebraic principles. **Problem Solving and Data Analysis** focuses more on interpretation of mathematical expressions, graphical analysis, and data interpretation. Your ability to not only understand what a problem is asking, but to represent it in your own words, will come in handy here. **Passport to Advanced Mathematics** questions showcase the higher-level math that's been added to the test, from quadratics and their graphs to the creation and translation of functions.

Finally, there is an **Additional Topics** domain that's filled with what you might consider wild-card material. Although these questions might not correlate directly to a subscore, six of these miscellaneous types will show up on the redesigned test. In the Verbal portions of the test, the **Command of Evidence** subscore measures how well students can translate and cite specific lines that back up their interpretation, while the **Relevant Words in Context** subscore ensures that students can select the best definition for how a word is used in a passage. The Writing & Language section additionally measures **Expression of Ideas**, which deals with revising language in order to make more logical and cohesive arguments, and **Standard English Conventions**, which assesses a student's ability to conform to the basic rules of English structure, punctuation, and usage.

Chapter 3
All About National Merit Scholarships

The NMSQT part of the name PSAT/NMSQT stands for National Merit Scholarship Qualifying Test. That means that the PSAT serves as the test that will establish whether or not you are eligible for National Merit recognition. This chapter will help you figure out what that may mean for you.

WHAT IS THE NATIONAL MERIT SCHOLARSHIP PROGRAM?

The National Merit Scholarship Program is the NMS in the NMSQT that you saw on the cover of this book. You might think that the PSAT is simply a warm-up for the SAT, but the National Merit Scholarship Program makes the PSAT an important test in its own right.

The mission of National Merit Scholarship Corporation (NMSC) is to recognize and honor the academically talented students of the United States. NMSC accomplishes this mission by conducting nationwide academic scholarship programs. The enduring goals of NMSC's scholarship programs are the following:

- To promote a wider and deeper respect for learning in general and for exceptionally talented individuals in particular
- To shine a spotlight on brilliant students and encourage the pursuit of academic excellence at all levels of education
- To stimulate increased support from organizations that wish to sponsor scholarships for outstanding scholastic talent.

The National Merit Scholarship Program is an academic competition for recognition and scholarships that began in 1955. High school students enter the National Merit Program by taking the Preliminary SAT/National Merit Scholarship Qualifying Test (PSAT/NMSQT) and by meeting published program entry and participation requirements.

How Do I Qualify for National Merit?

To participate in the National Merit Scholarship Program, a student must:

1. Take the PSAT/NMSQT in the specified year of the high school program and **no later than** the third year in grades 9 through 12, regardless of grade classification or educational pattern;
2. Be enrolled as a high school student (traditional or homeschooled), progressing normally toward graduation or completion of high school, and planning to enroll full time in college no later than the fall following completion of high school; and
3. Be a citizen of the United States; or be a U.S. lawful permanent resident (or have applied for permanent residence, the application for which has not been denied) and intend to become a U.S. citizen at the earliest opportunity allowed by law.

The Index

How does your PSAT score qualify you for National Merit? The National Merit Scholarship Corporation uses a Selection Index, which is the sum of your Math, Critical Reading, and Writing Skills scores. For instance, if your PSAT scores were 60 Math, 50 Critical Reading, and 60 Writing Skills, your index would be 170.

Math + Critical Reading + Writing Skills = National Merit Index

$$60 \quad + \quad 50 \quad + \quad 60 \quad = \quad 170$$

Note that the Selection Index qualifying scores vary from year to year and state to state. Visit **www.nationalmerit.org** for up-to-date information.

The Awards and the Process

In the fall of their senior year, about 50,000 students will receive one of two letters from NMSC: either a Letter of Commendation or a letter stating that they have qualified as semifinalists for National Merit.

Commended Students Roughly two-thirds of these students (about 34,000 total students each year) will receive a Letter of Commendation by virtue of their high scores on the test. This looks great on your college application, so if you have a reasonable chance of receiving this recognition, it is definitely worth your time to prepare for the PSAT. Make no mistake, though, these letters are not easy to get. They are awarded to students who score between the 95th and the mid-99th percentiles—that means to the top three percent in the country.

If you receive this honorable mention from NMSC, you should be extremely proud of yourself. Even though you will not continue in the process for National Merit scholarships, this commendation does make you eligible for special scholarships sponsored by certain companies and organizations, which vary in their amounts and eligibility requirements.

Semifinalists The other third of these students—those 16,000 students who score in the upper 99th percentile in their states—will be notified that they are National Merit semifinalists. If you qualify, you will receive a letter announcing your status as a semifinalist, along with information about the requirements for qualification as a finalist. These include maintaining high grades, performing well on your SAT, and getting an endorsement from your principal.

Becoming a National Merit semifinalist is quite impressive, and if you manage it, you should certainly mention it on your college applications.

What does "scoring in the upper 99th percentile in the state" mean? It means that you're essentially competing against the other people in your state for those semifinalist positions. Since some states have higher average scores than others, this means that if you're in states like New York, New Jersey, Maryland, Connecticut, or Massachusetts, you need a higher score to qualify than if you live in other states. However, the majority of the indices are in the range of 200–215. (This means approximate scores of 70 Critical Reading, 70 Math, 70 Writing Skills.)

Many students want to know exactly what score they need. Sadly, National Merit is notoriously tight-lipped about these numbers. It releases them only on rare occasions and generally does not like to announce them. However, it is not difficult to obtain some pretty reliable unofficial data on what it takes to be a semifinalist. Below you will find the most up-to-date qualifying scores for the class of 2014 National Merit semifinalists:

State	Score	State	Score
Alabama	207	Montana	206
Alaska	210	Nebraska	209
Arizona	213	Nevada	208
Arkansas	206	New Hampshire	212
California	222	New Jersey	224
Colorado	213	New Mexico	210
Connecticut	220	New York	218
Delaware	215	North Carolina	212
District of Columbia	224	North Dakota	201
Florida	211	Ohio	213
Georgia	215	Oklahoma	206
Hawaii	214	Oregon	217
Idaho	211	Pennsylvania	216
Illinois	215	Rhode Island	212
Indiana	212	South Carolina	209
Iowa	207	South Dakota	203
Kansas	213	Tennessee	212
Kentucky	210	Texas	218
Louisiana	208	Utah	208
Maine	212	Vermont	213
Maryland	221	Virginia	219
Massachusetts	223	Washington	219
Michigan	210	West Virginia	201
Minnesota	215	Wisconsin	208
Mississippi	207	Wyoming	204
Missouri	209	Territories outside U.S.	201

Note, however, that while these numbers are probably roughly the same from year to year, they do change to a certain degree. These should be used only to give you a rough idea of the range of scores for National Merit recognition.

Finalists   The majority of semifinalists (more than 90 percent) go on to qualify as finalists. Students who meet all of the eligibility requirements will be notified in February of their senior year that they have qualified as finalists. This means that they are now eligible for scholarship money, though it does not necessarily mean that they will receive any. In fact, only about half of National Merit finalists actually win scholarships. What determines whether a student is awarded money or not? All winners are chosen from that Finalist group based on their abilities, skills, and accomplishments—without regard to gender, race, ethnic origin, or religious preference. A variety of information is available for NMSC selectors to evaluate: the Finalist's academic record, information about the school's curricula and grading system, two sets of test scores, the high school official's written recommendation, information about the student's activities and leadership, and the Finalist's own essay. This year, there will be 7,600 Merit Scholarship winners and 1,300 Special Scholarship recipients. Unlike the Merit Scholarships, which are given by the NMSC, the Special Scholarship recipients will receive awards from corporate sponsors and are selected from students who are outstanding, but not National Merit finalists.

Though the amounts of money are not huge, every little bit helps, and the award itself looks very impressive in your portfolio. So if you think you are in contention for National Merit recognition, study hard. If not, don't sweat it too much, but do prepare for the PSAT because it is good practice for the SAT.

But I am Not a Junior in High School Yet…

If you are not yet a junior, and you are interested in National Merit, you will have to take the test again your junior year in order to qualify.

A certain number of schools give the PSAT to students in their sophomore year—and sometimes even earlier. These schools hope that earlier exposure to these tests will help their students perform better in later years. If you are not yet in your junior year, the PSAT will not count for National Merit scholarship purposes, so it is really just a trial run for you. However, it is still a good idea to go into the test prepared in order to feel and perform your best.

What If I am in a Three-Year or Other Nonstandard Course of Study?

If you are going to spend only three years in secondary school, you have two options for when to take the PSAT for National Merit purposes: You can take it either in your next-to-last year or in your last year of secondary school. However, our advice is this: If you are in any program other than a usual four-year high school, be sure to talk to your guidance counselor. He or she will consult with NMSC and help ensure that you take the PSAT at the right time. This is important, because not taking the PSAT at the right time can disqualify you from National Merit recognition.

What If I Miss the PSAT Administration My Junior Year?

If you are not concerned about National Merit scholarships, there is no reason to do anything in particular—except, perhaps, to obtain a few PSAT booklets to practice on, just to see what fun you missed.

However, if you want to be eligible for National Merit recognition, then swift action on your part is required. If an emergency arises that prevents you from taking the PSAT, you should write to the National Merit Scholarship Corporation *immediately* to request alternate testing dates. If your request is received soon enough, it should be able to accommodate you. (NMSC says that this kind of request must absolutely be received by March 1 following the missed PSAT administration.) You will also need a signature from a school official.

For More Information

If you have any questions or problems, the best person to consult is your school guidance counselor, who can help make sure you are on the right track. If you need further help, contact your local Princeton Review office at 800-2-REVIEW or **PrincetonReview.com**. Or, you can contact National Merit directly:

National Merit Scholarship Corporation
1560 Sherman Avenue, Suite 200
Evanston, IL 60201-4897
(847) 866-5100
NationalMerit.org

Part II
Reading Test

Chapter 4
Reading Test
Drill 1

Reading Test

60 MINUTES, 47 QUESTIONS

Turn to Section 1 of your answer sheet to answer the questions in this section.

DIRECTIONS

Each passage or pair of passages below is followed by a number of questions. After reading each passage or pair, choose the best answer to each question based on what is stated or implied in the passage or passages and in any accompanying graphics (such as a table or graph).

Questions 1–9 are based on the following passage.

The following is excerpted from the Texas Declaration of Independence, in which Texas declared its independence from Mexico in the Texas Revolution.

When a government has ceased to protect the lives, liberty, and property of the people, from whom its legitimate powers are derived, and for the
Line advancement of whose happiness it was instituted,
5 and so far from being a guarantee for the enjoyment of those inestimable and inalienable rights, becomes an instrument in the hands of evil rulers for their oppression.
When the Federal Republican Constitution of their
10 country, which they have sworn to support, no longer has a substantial existence, and the whole nature of their government has been forcibly changed, without their consent, from a restricted federal republic, composed of sovereign states, to a consolidated
15 central military despotism, in which every interest is disregarded but that of the army and the priesthood, both the eternal enemies of civil liberties, the ever ready minions of power, and the usual instruments of tyrants.
20 When, long after the spirit of the constitution has departed, moderation is at length so far lost by those in power, that even the semblance of freedom is removed, and the forms themselves of the constitution discontinued, and so far from their petitions and
25 remonstrances being regarded, the agents who bear them are thrown into dungeons, and mercenary armies sent forth to force a new government upon them at the point of the bayonet.

When, in consequence of such acts of malfeasance
30 and abdication on the part of the government, anarchy prevails, and civil society is dissolved into its original elements. In such a crisis, the first law of nature, the right of self-preservation, the inherent and inalienable rights of the people to appeal to first principles, and
35 to take their political affairs into their own hands in extreme cases, enjoins it as a right towards themselves, and a sacred obligation to their posterity, to abolish such a government, and create another in its stead, calculated to rescue them from impending dangers,
40 and to secure their future welfare and happiness.
Nations, as well as individuals, are amenable for their acts to the public opinion of mankind. A statement of a part of our grievances is therefore submitted to an impartial world, in justification of the
45 hazardous but unavoidable step now taken, of severing our political connection with the Mexican people, and assuming an independent attitude among the nations of the earth.
The Mexican government, by its colonization
50 laws, invited and induced the Anglo-American population of Texas to colonize its wilderness under the pledged faith of a written constitution, that they should continue to enjoy that constitutional liberty and republican government to which they had been
55 habituated in the land of their birth, the United States of America.
In this expectation they have been cruelly disappointed, inasmuch as the Mexican nation has acquiesced in the late changes made in the government
60 by General Antonio Lopez de Santa Anna, who having

overturned the constitution of his country, now offers us the cruel alternative, either to abandon our homes, acquired by so many privations, or submit to the most intolerable of all, tyranny.

65   It has sacrificed our welfare to the state of Coahuila, by which our interests have been continually depressed through a jealous and partial course of legislation, carried on at a far distant seat of government, by a hostile majority, in an unknown tongue, and this

70 too, notwithstanding, we have petitioned in the humblest terms for the establishment of a separate state government, and have, in accordance with the provisions of the national constitution, presented to the general Congress a republican constitution, which was,

75 without just cause, contemptuously rejected.

    We, therefore, the delegates with plenary powers of the people of Texas, in solemn convention assembled, appealing to a candid world for the necessities of our condition, do hereby resolve and declare, that our

80 political connection with the Mexican nation has forever ended, and that the people of Texas do now constitute a free, Sovereign, and independent republic.

1

The tone of the passage is best described as

A) passive.

B) inspiring.

C) hateful.

D) accusatory.

2

As used in line 6, "inestimable" most nearly means

A) worthy.

B) infinite.

C) respectful.

D) desirable.

3

The description in the second paragraph indicates that what the authors value most about their government is

A) a weak centralized government with stronger with autonomous territories.

B) a militarily strong government.

C) a government with strong moral and religious convictions.

D) a transparent government that engages in hostile behavior toward sovereign states.

4

In paragraph 6 the author explains the ways in which the Mexican government encouraged colonists in order to

A) demonstrate the positive relationship the state of Texas once shared with the government of Mexico.

B) illustrate the unethical behavior Americans have experienced from foreigners historically.

C) compare the United States government and the Mexican government

D) establish the initial understanding those who immigrated to Texas had of Mexico.

5

The passage most strongly suggests that authors of the document and recipients of the document share which of the following assumptions?

A) The state of Texas is under the rule of the Mexican government.

B) Compromise is necessary in order to repair the mistrust created by each side's actions

C) The creation and maintenance of a Federal Republican Constitution is the best way in which to insure everyone's rights are guaranteed.

D) The importance of the federal government and the priesthood cannot be overstated.

6

Which choice provides the best evidence for the answer to the previous question?

A) Lines 41-42, ("Nations . . . of mankind")

B) Lines 65-75, ("It has . . . contemptuously rejected")

C) Lines 49-56, ("The Mexican . . . United States of America")

D) Lines 1-8, ("When a . . . their oppression")

7

The position General Santa Anna takes in the seventh paragraph is best described as that of

A) a democratically appointed leader of an unstable nation.

B) a strong and fearless leader of an army.

C) an uncompromising ruler.

D) a bloodthirsty dictator.

8

The authors include the description of their grievances against the Mexican government in paragraph 8 in order to

A) explain their decision to secede from the Mexican nation.

B) begin a dialogue that results in political change within the Mexican government.

C) demonstrate to the world that the Mexican government is an illegal and unethical entity.

D) bolster their claim that they would be better fit to establish a strong federal government than those who are currently in power.

9

As used in line 77, "convention" most nearly means

A) trend.

B) habit.

C) conference.

D) contract.

THIS PAGE IS LEFT INTENTIONALLY BLANK.

Questions 10–19 are based on the following passage.

The following passage discusses some of the early, lesser-known governments, documents, and people that shaped the formation of the United States of America.

It is difficult for many to imagine an American government that does not begin with George Washington as the president. But from the moment
Line we declared independence from the rule of the British
5 Monarchy, and even before, America had to be run by someone or something. A successful revolution and construction of a country does not happen without deliberation. Hence, neither the first functioning government of the United States of America nor its
10 first president is the one we are most familiar with today. In fact, there are quite a few more governments and presidents of the United States of which many may not be aware.

For all intents and purposes, and despite the
15 contrary opinion of the British Monarchy, the governing body of the American colonies prior to and during the American Revolution was the Continental Congress. The Continental Congress was a convention of delegates from all Thirteen Colonies formed in
20 1774 when it met from September 5 to October 26. Although the Declaration of Independence would not be signed for two years, it was this Congress that wrote and issued the redress of grievances to King George and began an economic boycott of Great Britain.
25 Because of the actions entered into by the Continental Congress and the democratic approach it adopted in its function, it is viewed by some as the first active autonomous government of the United States.

There were 56 delegates in all who attended the
30 first meeting of the Continental Congress. From among the notable men in attendance, which included Benjamin Franklin, George Washington, and John Adams, a land-owner and public official from Virginia named Peyton Randolph was elected as president
35 of the Congress. Since, as was stated previously, the Continental Congress was at this point functioning as a democratic, autonomous government for the united colonies, Randolph is considered by many to be the

first president of the United States. Randolph did
40 not serve in this capacity for long. On May 5, 1775, Randolph suffered from acute apoplexy, bleeding within the internal organs, and passed away. He was succeeded as president by John Hancock. It was Hancock who served as president during the writing
45 and issue of the Declaration of Independence to the British Monarchy, which is why his signature was both first and most prominent.

The Second Continental Congress, which followed the First Continental Congress, convened on May
50 10, 1775. This Congress outlasted its predecessor as it continually met throughout the course of the American Revolution, and by issuing the Declaration of Independence on July 4, 1776, claimed sovereignty over the whole of the colonies. The Second Continental
55 Congress remained the governing body of the nascent nation until March 1, 1781, when it adopted the Articles of Confederation.

The Articles of Confederation was a type of precursor to the Constitution of the United States
60 of America. It formally established the Congress of the Confederation as the governing body of the United States of America. That body was maintained from 1781 to 1789. Although the Congress of the Confederation was paramount to the successful end of
65 the American Revolution, once peace and American freedom was attained its significance was dramatically decreased. Under the Articles of Confederation, the Congress had little control over the individual states or commonwealths, especially in regards to tax collection
70 and debt consolidation at the federal and state level.

Because such a discordant system of varying powers was unsustainable, the Congress of the Confederation drafted and enacted the modern day Constitution of the United States, laying the
75 groundwork for a stronger central government than currently existed. Under that constitution, the Congress of the Confederation became the Congress of the United States, half of the legislative branch of the three-branched government. It is this same Congress
80 that we elect today, although it now represents a few more states than its predecessors.

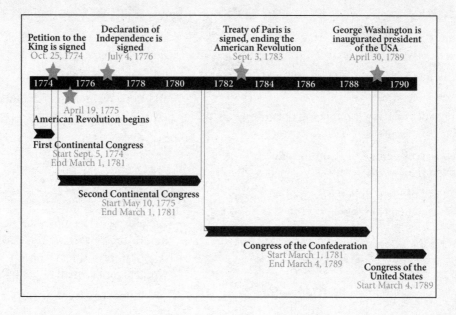

The phrase "For all intents and purposes" in line 14 serves primarily to

A) demonstrate that the Continental Congress' power was effectively recognized domestically.

B) indicate that the one true authority over the colonies was the King of England.

C) allow the author to straddle both sides of the American Revolution without preferring one to the other.

D) state the purpose of the formation of the Continental Congress.

According to the passage, it can be inferred that which of the following influenced the dissolution of the Congress of the Confederation?

A) The Congress' inability to exert a strong federal authority

B) The Articles of Confederation were not as well written as the Constitution.

C) A single legislature was deemed undemocratic by the leaders of the American Colonies.

D) It was overthrown by a group of delegates who established a three branch government and produced the Constitution.

Which of the following provides the most support for the answer to the previous question?

A) Lines 76-80 ("Under that . . . today")

B) Lines 58-60 ("The articles . . . America")

C) Lines 71-79 ("Because such . . . government")

D) Lines 48-57 ("The Second . . . Confederation")

The purpose of the third paragraph is chiefly to

A) support the assertion made earlier that George Washington is not considered by all as the first president of the United States.

B) explain the origin of the common phrase "put your John Hancock" on something when asked to sign a document.

C) demonstrate the close bond that existed between many of the founding fathers even before the start of the American Revolution.

D) assert that if it had not been for Peyton Randolph's untimely death, he would have been elected as President of the United States rather than George Washington.

14

The passage most strongly suggests which of the following is true of John Hancock?

A) He was the sole author of the Declaration of Independence.

B) He was president during the creation of two important documents in American History.

C) He served as president of the Continental Congress until his death.

D) He served as president in both the original and the second Continental Congress.

15

As used in line 45, "issue" most nearly means

A) copy.

B) delivery.

C) concern.

D) installment.

16

As used in line 16, "body" most nearly means

A) form.

B) physique.

C) entity.

D) bulk.

17

In context, the word "successful" in line 6 refers mainly to America's

A) victory over the British.

B) implementation of democracy.

C) establishment of a functioning government.

D) foreign diplomacy.

18

According to the information in the passage, the author most likely would agree that our modern-day Congress differs from the Congress of the Confederation in all of the following ways EXCEPT

A) it now represents a greater number of states.

B) its existence was established by a document.

C) it was granted a greater amount of authority over the states.

D) it lasted for a longer period of time.

19

Which claim about American History is best supported by the graphic?

A) George Washington's first act as president was to institute the Congress of the United States.

B) The Congress of the United States ended in 1791.

C) It was more than fourteen years after the American Revolution began and almost six after it ended that George Washington became president of the United States.

D) October 25, 1774, is the date the Continental Congress took power through the Petition to the King.

THIS PAGE IS LEFT INTENTIONALLY BLANK.

Questions 20–28 are based on the following passage.

The following passage discusses the issues surrounding internet regulation and the concept of net neutrality.

It is quite common that the government moves slower than the times in terms of law implementation and regulation. This is in no way a criticism; it is
Line only fitting and proper that a government, chosen
5 and guided by the people, should first examine the needs and protections of its people prior to imposing restriction on any aspect of life. Furthermore, it is often the case that a government is unable to create restriction on any given object or action until it is
10 comprehensively understood and its implications made clear.

Take the internet. When it was still a nascent technology it would have been difficult to imagine all the ways in which the internet would become involved
15 in our personal, public, and professional lives. It would also have been unimaginable to some that the internet would play such a fundamentally central role in our daily lives. The regulation of the internet has been slow in coming, progressing in fits and starts. The latest
20 topic of governmental interest is whether or not the internet constitutes a public utility, and, if so, whether or not it should be regulated as such.

The term public utility refers to a service that is consumed by the widespread public, such as
25 natural gas, electricity, water, and sewage. Generally government agencies provide such services in a monopolized way, meaning there is no competitive market for utilities. Although they can be privatized depending on the supply and demand needs of a
30 specific region, they are strictly regulated by the government. This regulation is necessary to insure that these resources are made available in an equitable and affordable fashion due to their necessity.

Up until this point, the internet has not been
35 considered a public utility by the United States government. Although restrictions have been placed on internet use by the government, this is has been limited to criminal internet activity, such as piracy, gambling, or harassment. Currently, internet is
40 provided by a small handful of internet providers, which are not strongly regulated in their provision of internet and exist for capital gain. This creates the opportunity for such providers to exploit their customers as customers try to attain internet access to

45 all available data. Regulating the internet would insure fair provision of the internet. This idea is called "net neutrality," which means that internet providers should act as a neutral gateway to internet content, as opposed to a gatekeeper that can control speed and access by
50 content demand as they so choose or based on fees.

The Federal Communications Commission, which is a separate government entity charged with regulating interstate communications by radio, television, wire, satellite, and cable, announced in 2014
55 that it is in favor of creating a net neutrality approach to regulation of the internet. The following statement was given by FCC Chairman Tom Wheeler on the matter:

"Using this authority, I am submitting to my
60 *colleagues the strongest open internet protections ever proposed by the FCC. These enforceable, bright-line rules will ban paid prioritization, and the blocking and throttling of lawful content and services. I propose to fully apply—for the first time ever—those bright-line*
65 *rules to mobile broadband. My proposal assures the rights of internet users to go where they want, when they want, and the rights of innovators to introduce new products without asking anyone's permission."*

Where this issue becomes tricky is not in the
70 decision of whether or not to regulate the provision of the internet, but how to enforce that regulation. The internet is unlike any other technology. Aspects such as internet speed and accessibility at the individual level are almost impossible to monitor, especially for a
75 government that acts many steps behind the progress of this technology.

20

The primary purpose of the passage is to

A) provide a better understanding of what government utility regulation is and the difficulty in applying it to new technologies.

B) convince the reader that net neutrality is unlikely to ever take place due to current government regulation of illegal electronic activity.

C) argue against the need for regulation of one of the few free spaces left to the American consumer.

D) explain the FCC's stance when it comes to net neutrality.

21

In the context of the passage, the author's use of the phrase "Take the internet." in line 12 is primarily meant to convey

A) the most difficult new technology the governement has attempted to regulate.

B) a technology of greater interest to the writer than television, radio, or cable.

C) an example of a technology that governement regulation has not yet caught up with.

D) an instance of a technology that has drastically transformed the average American day over the last twenty years.

22

The author mentions natural gas and sewage (line 25) in order to

A) clarify what a commonly used and regulated service is.

B) to help the reader understand why they are not overcharged for the use of these services.

C) to illustrate everyday services that were also once unregulated, like the internet.

D) to provide a comprehensive lists of the items that have been monopolized in our marketplace.

23

As used in line 43, "exploit" most nearly means

A) achieve.

B) mistreat.

C) explore.

D) utilize.

24

The quotation indicates that what the FCC values most about net neutrality is

A) the public's ability to move freely in society.

B) the creativity that the use of the internet helps to enhance.

C) the ability for broadband to be mobile.

D) the equal access to content for equivalent payment rates.

25

The passage most strongly suggests which of the following about the FCC?

A) The FCC has only recently begun to consider the need to regulate criminal activity on the internet.

B) It is unlikely the FCC will be able to convince the United States government to enforce regulating the internet as a public utility.

C) The FCC has been regulating such public utlities as natural gas, electricity, and water for some time now as those utilities are not as recent.

D) The FCC is unlikely to effectively implement and oversee the proposed regulations of the internet.

26

Which choice provides the best support for the answer to the previous questions?

A) Lines 7-11 ("Futhermore, it . . . clear")

B) Lines 72-76 ("Aspects such . . . technology")

C) Lines 23-25 ("The term . . . sewage")

D) Lines 34-36 ("Up until . . . government")

27

The passage suggests that regulation of the internet is necessary for all of the following reasons EXCEPT

A) speed.

B) equal access.

C) file protection.

D) online betting.

28

As used in line 69, "tricky" most nearly means

A) magical.

B) devious.

C) artful.

D) difficult.

Questions 29–37 are based on the following passage.

The following passage is excerpted from the article "Antarctica Yields Two Unknown Dinosaur Species" published by the National Science Foundation on June 9, 2004.

In December 2003, against incredible odds, researchers working in separate sites, thousands of miles apart in Antarctica found what they believe
Line are the fossilized remains of two species of dinosaurs
5 previously unknown to science.

One of the two finds, which were made less than a week apart, is an early carnivore that would have lived many millions of years after the other, a plant-eating beast, roamed the Earth. One was found at the sea
10 bottom, the other on a mountaintop.

Working on James Ross Island off the coast of the Antarctic Peninsula, veteran dinosaur hunters Judd Case, James Martin and their research team believe they have found the fossilized bones of an entirely
15 new species of carnivorous dinosaur related to the enormous meat-eating tyrannosaurs and the equally voracious, but smaller and swifter, velociraptors that terrified movie-goers in the film *Jurassic Park*.

Features of the animal's bones and teeth led the
20 researchers to surmise the animal may represent a population of carnivores that survived in the Antarctic long after they had been succeeded by other predators elsewhere on the globe.

Case, the dean of science and a professor of biology
25 at Saint Mary's College of California who discovered the bones said the shape of the teeth and features of the feet are characteristic of a group of dinosaurs known as theropods, which includes the tyrannosaurs, as well as all other meat-eating dinosaurs. The theropods, or
30 "beast-footed" dinosaurs, make up a large and diverse group of now-extinct animals with the common characteristic of walking on two legs like birds. Recent research has shown that birds are direct descendants of theropods.
35 The remains include fragments of an upper jaw with teeth, isolated individual teeth and most of the bones from the animal's lower legs and feet. The creature likely inhabited the area millions of years ago when the climate and terrain were similar to
40 conditions in today's Pacific Northwest and radically different than they are today.

Martin, curator of vertebrate paleontology at the South Dakota School of Mines & Technology, said the size and shape of the ends of the lower-leg and foot
45 bones indicate that in life the animal was a running dinosaur roughly 1.8 to 2.4 meters (6 to 8 feet) tall.

The team believes that the body of the dinosaur may have been scavenged by marine lizards after it died, coming to rest on the ocean bottom, where it was
50 found among the remains of creatures similar to those that feasted on its body.

At the same time, thousands of miles away, a research team led by William Hammer of Augustana College in Rock Island, Ill., was working in the
55 Antarctic interior on a mountaintop roughly 3,900 meters (13,000 feet) high and near the Beardmore Glacier. They found embedded in solid rock what they believe to be the pelvis of a primitive sauropod, a four-legged, plant-eating dinosaur similar to better-known
60 creatures such as brachiosaurus and diplodocus. Now known as Mt. Kirkpatrick, the area was once a soft riverbed before millions of years of tectonic activity elevated it skyward.

Also a veteran dino hunter known for his
65 discovery of *Cryolophosaurus ellioti* in 1991, Hammer had returned to the site of that find to continue his work, which had been halted in part because the *Cryolophosaurus* excavation had dug far into a cliff face, creating a potentially dangerous overhang.
70 Specialized workers were flown into the research camp at Beardmore Glacier to remove the overhang and make it safer to continue the excavations.

Based on field analysis of the bones, Hammer and his fellow researchers believe the pelvis—roughly one
75 meter (three feet) across—is from a primitive sauropod that represents one of the earliest forms of the emerging dinosaur lineage that eventually produced animals more than 30 meters (100 feet) long.

Basing his estimates on the bones excavated at the
80 site, Hammer suggests the new, and as-yet-unnamed creature was between 1.8 and 2.1 meters (six and seven feet) tall and up to nine meters (30 feet) long.

Characteristics of Vertebrate Groups

	Mammals	Birds	Modern Reptiles	Theropod Dinosaurs
Number of ear bones	3	1	1	1
Legs directly under body	yes	yes	no	yes
Produce milk	yes	no	no	no
Constant body temperature	yes	yes	no	yes
Live birth	yes	no	some	no
Skin covering	hair	feathers/scales	scales	feathers/scales

29

As used in line 20, "surmise" most nearly means

A) total.

B) amaze.

C) know.

D) conjecture.

30

The passage most strongly suggests that Case and Martin used which of the following to determine the species of dinosaur they discovered?

A) The location where the dinosaur remains were discovered

B) Skeletal and oral aspects of the remains.

C) The time period the dinosaur was mostly likey to have lived during

D) The pelvic measurement of the dinosuar

31

Which choices provides the best evidence for the answer to the previous question?

A) Lines 19-23 ("Features of . . . globe")

B) Lines 73-78 ("Based on . . . long")

C) Lines 37-41 ("The creature . . . today")

D) Lines 11-18 ("Working on . . . *Jurassic Park*")

32

The author refers to the film *Jurassic Park* (line 18) primarily to

A) introduce the reader to one of the author's favorite films from childhood.

B) impress upon the reader the importance of such a discovery, as it brings us one step closer to creating a real-life *Jurassic Park*.

C) associate the discovery of the scientists to a representation of dinosaurs that the reader may be familiar with.

D) help the reader better understand the time period which the dinosaur discovered was most likely to have lived.

33

According to the passage, Case, Martin, and Hammer have what in common?

A) They all specialize in carnivorous dinosaur skeletal excavation.

B) They were funded by the same grant, which accounts for their closely timed discoveries.

C) They all believe that Antarctica is the best remaining site for dinosaur excavation.

D) They are all affiliated with educational institutions.

34

The author includes the descriptions of where the remains of the dinosaur discovered by the team led by Martin and Case in paragraph 8 primarily to

A) provide a description of the primary predator of theropods.

B) account for the location where the remains of the theropod was found.

C) illustrate the dangers of working in such a remote site.

D) transition into the other discovery by Hammer of a primitive marine lizard, thereby connecting the two discoveries.

35

With which of the following statements would the author most likely agree?

A) It is uncommon for two distinct discoveries of dinosaur skeletal remains to occur not only within such close physical proximity but also time period.

B) Because the dinosaur discovered by Hammer is an older dinosaur species than that discovered by Martin and Case, it is a more scientifically important discovery.

C) Antarctica is one of the more popular sites for dinosaur excavation due to its desolate landscape.

D) We now know that dinosaurs who walked on two legs are direct descendants of birds.

36

As used in line 63, "elevated" most nearly means

A) enlightened.

B) prominent.

C) raised.

D) advanced.

37

Which of the following can be reasonably inferred from information in the passage and the graphic?

A) The newly discovered dinosaur species are more closely related to mammals than reptiles.

B) Marine lizards are direct descendants of theropods, and share the same number of ear bones.

C) Tyrannosaurs maintained a constant body temperature.

D) The newly discovered dinosaurs lived concurrently with modern birds.

THIS PAGE IS LEFT INTENTIONALLY BLANK.

Questions 38–47 are based on the following passages.

Both Passage 1 and Passage 2 discuss vaccines and relative benefits and risks of administering them to children.

Passage 1

Despite the first vaccination having been administered in the United States as long ago as 1800, it still remains one of the most divisive topics in the
Line United States today. But the fact that vaccinations
5 have continued to be administered at increasing rates despite such strong, long-held opposition is an indicator of their efficacy.

Physicians strongly encourage families to follow the prescribed vaccination schedule for their young
10 children for a variety of reasons. But there is one reason that is more prominent than others: vaccines work. According to the American Academy of Pediatrics, "most child vaccines are 90%-99% effective in preventing disease." And by "effective" these
15 physicians don't just mean that the vaccines have cut down on the rate of flu and measles infection, which is like a more severe version of the chicken pox. It is estimated that between 1994 and 2014 alone 732,000 American children were saved from death due to
20 vaccinations, and 322 million cases of childhood illnesses were prevented.

This is not to say that there are no drawbacks to vaccinations whatsoever. On the contrary, physicians are quick to acknowledge that vaccinations do not
25 come without risk. However, this risk is strictly minimal. Adverse reactions, such as anaphylaxis, illness, or even death, occur so infrequently it is difficult to determine exact numbers. The American Academy of Pediatrics estimates the number to
30 somewhere between "one per several hundred thousand to one per million vaccinations." For the sake of the general population, this number is not great enough to argue against widespread vaccination.

It is believed that if enough people were to become
35 vaccinated against any one disease, that disease could eventually be eradicated. This would work out well for both those who are pro-vaccine and anti-vaccine; because vaccines are so effective, there would no longer be a need for them. Speaking as an American
40 with children of my own, it is in our best interest to everyone around to the idea of mandatory child vaccination.

Passage 2

The Greek philosopher Socrates is credited with having said "I know that I know nothing." These are
45 wise words from a wise man, and should be kept in mind whenever dealing with "scientific fact." The truth is that despite the leaps and bounds we have made over the course of human history, especially in the medical sciences, we in truth know very little. And there is
50 never a time that this fact is as salient as when it comes to the health of the most vulnerable in our society.

This is exactly the problem with a vaccine, which is defined as a preparation of killed microorganisms, living attenuated organisms, or living fully virulent
55 organisms. There is a great deal that is unknown about vaccines, both in terms of the general public and the scientific community. The general public knows very little about what goes into vaccines and how they function, while the scientific community knows very
60 little about the range of effects vaccines may have.

Although vaccinations have been in use for some time, the composition of them has changed drastically over the last several decades. Certain flu vaccines have been found to contain trace amounts
65 of thimerosal, an organic mercury compound, which may have adverse neurological impacts on young children. Aluminum, which is found in many vaccines, can also cause neurological damage to humans in excess amounts. Because the recommended
70 vaccine schedule calls for so many vaccines to be administered in quick succession, it is difficult to tell what amount of aluminum may exist in the child's body and for how long. Some vaccines even contain the carcinogen formaldehyde, even though no studies
75 have been conducted to determine the long-term effect of its use on future health. The short term effects of formaldehyde are known, however, and can include cardiac impairment, central nervous system depression, anaphylactic shock, and comas in some
80 who receive it.

The question is not "do vaccines help?" Undoubtedly they do, that we know. The question is, or at least it should be "do vaccines harm?" The answer here is equally clear: undoubtedly they do. We just
85 don't know to what extent.

38

Passage 1 most strongly suggests that which of the following is true of the author?

A) She believes more research is needed to convince those who are anti-vaccine that vaccines are indeed safe.

B) She thinks that the worldwide use of vaccines would eliminate all instances of childhood death.

C) She herself is likely to vaccinate her own children.

D) She was vaccinated as a child.

39

Which choice provides the best evidence for the answer to the previous question?

A) Lines 17-21 ("It is . . . prevented")

B) Lines 39-41 ("Speaking as . . . mandatory")

C) Lines 4-7 ("But the . . . efficacy")

D) Lines 57-60 ("The general . . . have")

40

As used in line 66, "adverse" most nearly means

A) other.

B) contradictory.

C) confrontational.

D) undesirable.

41

What claim about vaccination is best supported by the third paragraph in Passage 1?

A) Vaccines should be used despite the fact that they do harm some individuals.

B) Sciencists give a wide range of numbers of those harmed from vaccines in order to avoid accountability for the harmful effects of vaccines.

C) Physicians are very strict regarding the vaccination schedule parents should adhere to for their children.

D) The goal of administering any vaccine is to eliminate a specific type of disease once and for all.

42

The author of Passage 2 refers to Socrates in order to

A) use a prominent scholar the reader is familiar with to validate her argument.

B) illustrate a point that discussed throughout the remainder of the passage.

C) explain how one man has greatly influenced our approach to scientific and medical research.

D) dismiss the notion that it is safe to use drugs before they are approved by the FDA.

43

As used in line 50, "salient" most nearly means

A) relevant.

B) smart.

C) related.

D) welcome.

44

The author of Passage 2 refers to formaldyhyde in order to

A) demonstrate the ways in which doctors manipulate patients and parents into accepting vaccines with harmful chemicals.

B) assert that a vaccine without formaldyhyde may be safe to use, but those that contain it should be avoided.

C) provide an example of an ingredient found in vaccines that has known and possibly unknown harmful side-affects.

D) offer proof that vaccines can kill the patients who receive them.

45

In the final paragraph of Passage 2, the author

A) undermines her argument.

B) offers a concession.

C) quotes scientific evidence.

D) compares doctors who vaccinate to those who do not.

46

The central ideas of the passages differ in that Passage 1

A) reviews the positive aspects of vaccinations while Passage 2 examines specific instances of vaccinations having been harmful after being administered.

B) is against the uninformed use of vaccinations while Passage 2 states the benefits of vaccinations far outweigh the risks.

C) offers an argument in favor of vaccines, while Passage 2 contests that our understanding of vaccines is deficient.

D) is ambivalent regarding the use of vaccinations on the recommended schedule, while Passage 2 states not enough is known of the long-term effects of vaccines.

47

Both passages contain which of the following?

A) A definition

B) A similie

C) A question

D) A quotation

The Princeton Review

Redesigned PSAT

1. Student Information

Your Name: _____
(Print)
                 Last   First   M.I.

Email Address: _____ Date: ___ / ___ / ___
(Print)   MM DD YYYY

Home Address: _____ Apartment No. _____
(Print)   Number and Street

_____
       City   State   Zip Code

High School: _____ Class of: _____

2. Your Name

First 4 letters of last name | | | | FIRST INIT | MID INIT

(Bubble columns A–Z for each of the 4 letters plus first initial and middle initial)

3. Phone Number

Area Code			Phone number						

(Bubble columns 0–9 for each digit)

Reading

SECTION 1

1. Ⓐ Ⓑ Ⓒ Ⓓ
2. Ⓐ Ⓑ Ⓒ Ⓓ
3. Ⓐ Ⓑ Ⓒ Ⓓ
4. Ⓐ Ⓑ Ⓒ Ⓓ
5. Ⓐ Ⓑ Ⓒ Ⓓ
6. Ⓐ Ⓑ Ⓒ Ⓓ
7. Ⓐ Ⓑ Ⓒ Ⓓ
8. Ⓐ Ⓑ Ⓒ Ⓓ
9. Ⓐ Ⓑ Ⓒ Ⓓ
10. Ⓐ Ⓑ Ⓒ Ⓓ

11. Ⓐ Ⓑ Ⓒ Ⓓ
12. Ⓐ Ⓑ Ⓒ Ⓓ
13. Ⓐ Ⓑ Ⓒ Ⓓ
14. Ⓐ Ⓑ Ⓒ Ⓓ
15. Ⓐ Ⓑ Ⓒ Ⓓ
16. Ⓐ Ⓑ Ⓒ Ⓓ
17. Ⓐ Ⓑ Ⓒ Ⓓ
18. Ⓐ Ⓑ Ⓒ Ⓓ
19. Ⓐ Ⓑ Ⓒ Ⓓ
20. Ⓐ Ⓑ Ⓒ Ⓓ

21. Ⓐ Ⓑ Ⓒ Ⓓ
22. Ⓐ Ⓑ Ⓒ Ⓓ
23. Ⓐ Ⓑ Ⓒ Ⓓ
24. Ⓐ Ⓑ Ⓒ Ⓓ
25. Ⓐ Ⓑ Ⓒ Ⓓ
26. Ⓐ Ⓑ Ⓒ Ⓓ
27. Ⓐ Ⓑ Ⓒ Ⓓ
28. Ⓐ Ⓑ Ⓒ Ⓓ
29. Ⓐ Ⓑ Ⓒ Ⓓ
30. Ⓐ Ⓑ Ⓒ Ⓓ

31. Ⓐ Ⓑ Ⓒ Ⓓ
32. Ⓐ Ⓑ Ⓒ Ⓓ
33. Ⓐ Ⓑ Ⓒ Ⓓ
34. Ⓐ Ⓑ Ⓒ Ⓓ
35. Ⓐ Ⓑ Ⓒ Ⓓ
36. Ⓐ Ⓑ Ⓒ Ⓓ
37. Ⓐ Ⓑ Ⓒ Ⓓ
38. Ⓐ Ⓑ Ⓒ Ⓓ
39. Ⓐ Ⓑ Ⓒ Ⓓ
40. Ⓐ Ⓑ Ⓒ Ⓓ

41. Ⓐ Ⓑ Ⓒ Ⓓ
42. Ⓐ Ⓑ Ⓒ Ⓓ
43. Ⓐ Ⓑ Ⓒ Ⓓ
44. Ⓐ Ⓑ Ⓒ Ⓓ
45. Ⓐ Ⓑ Ⓒ Ⓓ
46. Ⓐ Ⓑ Ⓒ Ⓓ
47. Ⓐ Ⓑ Ⓒ Ⓓ

Chapter 5
Reading Test
Drill 1: Answers
and Explanations

ANSWERS AND EXPLANATIONS

Section 1—Reading Test

1. **D** The people of Texas are declaring their independence because they feel they have been misled by the Mexican government. In the passage, the people charge the Mexican government with wrongdoing, so the tone of the passage is one of blaming. The best answer is choice (D), *accusatory*, since that is the only answer choice that is synonymous with blaming.

2. **B** The first paragraph of the passage uses the words *inestimable* and *inalienable* to describe the rights of the people. By using these adjectives, the authors of this declaration are stating that these rights have a value unable to be estimated and that these rights should be guaranteed. In context, the word *inestimable* means something similar to "immeasurable." Choices (A), (C), and (D) do not mean "immeasurable," which leaves choice (B). *Infinite* is the most similar word to "immeasurable" and is, therefore, the best answer.

3. **A** In the second paragraph, the people of Texas claim that *their government has been forcibly changed… from a restricted federal republic, composed of sovereign states, to a consolidated central military despotism*. The authors of this declaration are upset by this and believe that a tyrannical government now governs them. Therefore, the authors of this passage would not value a *militarily strong government* since that would be reflective of a *consolidated central military despotism* (eliminate choice (B)). Furthermore, they would not value a government that *engages in hostile behavior towards sovereign states* (eliminate choice (D)). Since they are upset that *their government has been forcibly changed, without their consent*, the authors would value the government they had before—one that was a *restricted federal republic, composed of sovereign states*. This makes choice (A) the best answer. There is no mention that they desire for their government to have strong *religious convictions—priesthood* is mentioned negatively in the passage as *an eternal enemy of civil liberties* (eliminate choice (C)).

4. **D** The sixth paragraph states that the Mexican government wanted the *Anglo-American population of Texas to colonize its wilderness* and lists the things the government used to induce the colonists to come: they would ensure constitutional liberty for the colonists and a government of the type the colonists were used to having in the USA. Therefore, the purpose of this paragraph is to explain why the colonists came (i.e. the expectations the colonists had once they immigrated to Texas. The next paragraph reveals that they were *cruelly disappointed* when their expectations were not met). Therefore, choice (D) is the correct answer. There is no evidence in the passage to support choice (A). The previous relationship the state of Texas had with the government of Mexico is never revealed. The sixth paragraph does not contain historical examples of how Americans have experienced *unethical behavior* from foreigners, so the purpose of this paragraph would not be to illustrate unethical behavior (eliminate choice (B)). The colonists are being assured that they should continue to enjoy the liberty and government they're used to having, but the purpose of this paragraph is not to compare the two governments (eliminate choice (C)).

5. **A** The only choice that would be an assumption shared by both the authors of the document and the recipients of it is the idea that the state of Texas is under Mexican rule (choice (A)). The Mexican government invited and induced these people to colonize their land and promised a government like the one they had in the USA (lines 57-66), and the authors wrote the document to formally declare the end of their political connection with the Mexican nation (lines 76-82). All other answer choices can be eliminated: based on the seventh paragraph the Mexican government does not desire to ensure everyone's rights (choice (C)), and based on the whole passage neither side would share the assumptions made in choices (B) or (D).

6. **B** The answer to the previous question is best supported by choice (B) since these lines contain support for an assumption that both the authors and recipients of the document would share—that the state of Texas is under the rule of the Mexican government. Choices (A) and (D) are incorrect because neither mention the Mexican government. Choice (C) is incorrect since these lines suggest that the people will enjoy the same liberties they had in their nation of origin.

7. **C** In the seventh paragraph, General Santa Anna is described as someone who has *overturned the constitution of his country* and has declared two options (*either to abandon our homes…or submit to… tyranny.*). Choice (A) is incorrect because the general is not described in the passage as a leader who was democratically appointed—he *overturned the constitution of his country*. There is no mention of an actual army, so even though his title is *General*, there is no support in the passage for choice (B). Killing people is not mentioned in this paragraph, so there is not textual support that he is *bloodthirsty*, which eliminates choice (D). Therefore, the best answer is choice (C). He is *uncompromising* since he gave the people *the cruel alternative*—either leave or submit to tyranny.

8. **A** The authors have listed their grievances against the Mexican government in order to support the decision they have come to in the final paragraph of the passage: *we* [the people of Texas]…*do hereby resolve and declare that our political connection with the Mexican nation has forever ended.* Therefore, choice (A) is the correct answer. The people of Texas are not interested in beginning a dialogue—their petitions have already been *contemptuously rejected* (eliminate choice (B)). Their purpose is not to expose the Mexican government as illegal and unethical to the world—this declaration is intended for the Mexican government not the world (eliminate choice (C)). Finally, choice (D) is incorrect because the authors are not trying to claim that they themselves would be better rulers; they are using the grievances to establish why they are now declaring themselves as a free, sovereign, and independent republic.

9. **C** The authors state in the last paragraph of the passage that the people of Texas have *assembled* or come together in a serious discussion and have to decide to declare the end of their political connection with Mexico. In context, the word *convention* means something similar to "discussion" or the idea of coming together. Choices (A), (B), and (D) do not mean "discussion," which leaves choice (C). *Conference* is the most similar word to "discussion" and is, therefore, the best answer.

10. **A** The paragraph describes the formation and actions of the Continental Congress. The paragraph also states that the Continental Congress was the governing body of the colonies *despite the contrary opinion of the British Monarchy* and that only *some* view it as the first government of the United States. This information taken together indicates that the Continental Congress was acting as a governing body, but was technically not the recognized government by all at the time. The phrase *for all intents and purposes* accounts for the functional role of the Continental Congress in enacting policies such as the boycott, while allowing for its lack of official authority. Therefore, choice (A) is the best answer. Choice (B) contains the extreme language *solely* and refers to the King of England, which is not being described by this phrase. Choice (C) refers to the American Revolution, which had not yet occurred during the time this passage discusses. Choice (D) is a deceptive answer, as it contains words from the phrase but does not explain the reason for the phrase. Although the passage does discuss the formation of the Continental Congress, the phrase *intents and purposes* refers to the Congress itself, not its formation.

11. **A** The Congress of the Confederation is discussed in the last two passages. The author states the Congress had *little control over the states and commonwealths* and that it *drafted and enacted the modern day Constitution* because *such a discordant system was unsustainable.* Based on these lines, it is clear that the Congress of the Confederation purposefully created a stronger federal Congress in order to consolidate authority over the states, which it had previously lacked. Choice (B) is deceptive as it names both of the documents discussed in this area of the passage, but refers to the quality of the documents rather than their purpose/function. Choices (C) and (D) are not supported by the passage, and are deceptive based on the later discussion of our current model of government. Choice (A) is the correct answer, as it addresses the lack of centralized power held by the Congress of the Confederation.

12. **C** The statement in choice (A) refers to the transformation of the Congress of the Confederation into the Congress of the United States, but does not indicate what lead to the dissolution of the Congress of the Confederation. Choice (B) refers only to the Articles of Confederation, not to the Congress of the Confederation or its dissolution. Choice (D) refers to formation of the Congress of the Confederation, not to its dissolution. Choice (C) correctly references the lack of a strong, centralized power that lead to the dissolution of the Congress of the Confederation, making it the best answer choice.

13. **A** The third paragraph focuses primarily on the delegates and the president of the initial Continental Congress, Peyton Randolph, who is described as *considered by many to be the first president of the United States.* This discussion references the earlier statement made by the author in the first paragraph that the first president of the United States is not *the one we are most familiar with today*, who is referenced earlier as George Washington. Choice (A) is the best answer as correctly states the paragraph is included to support that earlier statement. Choice (B) is incorrect as it focuses on John Hancock, who is not the chief purpose of this paragraph. Choice (C) is not supported by the paragraph as there is no indication that there was a *close bond* among the founding fathers, only a

political one. Choice (D) is not supported because it goes too far; the paragraph does not indicate anything about the likelihood of subsequent election results.

14. **D** The passage states that John Hancock succeeded Randolph as the president of the initial Continental Congress, during which time the Declaration of Independence was signed and sent, and that he was the first to sign that document. Choice (A) contains extreme language and is not supported by the passage; it states that Hancock *oversaw the writing* of the Declaration of Independence, not that he was the sole author of it. Since the passage states that he *oversaw the writing* of the Declaration of Independence only, choice (B) can be eliminated. Hancock's death is not discussed in the passage, only Randolph's is, so eliminate choice (C) as well. That leaves choice (D). The passage clearly states that Hancock served as president of the first Continental Congress, but it may seem unclear whether or not Hancock served as president of the Second Continental Congress. However, since the author says Hancock was president during the *writing and issue* of the Declaration of Independence and that the document was written during the Second Continental Congress, it can be reasonably inferred that choice (D) is correct.

15. **B** In this sentence the author is discussing the writing of the Declaration of Independence and the subsequent step taken with it, saying that something was done with it *to the British Monarchy*. Since the Declaration of Independence was sent to the British monarchy, the best word will mean something close to "sent" or "given." Since choices (A), (C), and (D) all have meanings that differ from the meaning of the word "given," they can be eliminated. The choice that best matches this meaning is choice (B), delivered.

16. **C** In this sentence, *body* refers to the Second Continental Congress. Since the Continental Congress is a group that acts a single thing, *body* in this context refers to something that means unit or object. Choices (A) and (B) are physical descriptions, those can be eliminated. Choice (D) means large, which does not match the meaning of unit of object. The best match to the meaning unit or object is choice (C).

17. **A** In this sentence *successful* refers to the end of the American Revolution. Choice (B) can be eliminated because the passage states after the Revolution ended peace and American freedom were attained. The passage does not say democracy was established at this time. Choice (C) can be eliminated because successful is not referring to the creation of the subsequent American government. Choice (D) can be eliminated because there is no mention of foreign diplomacy in the passage. Since choice (A) is the only choice that refers to the end of the war, and therefore it is the best answer.

18. **B** Since this questions asks about how the modern-day Congress differs from the Congress of Confederation, focus on the last two passages which discuss those two entities and POE as you can. The passage states that the current Congress *represents a few more states than its predecessors*, so eliminate choice (A). The Constitution *laid the ground work for a stronger central government* and that under that document *the Congress of the Confederation became the Congress of the United States*,

so eliminate choice (C). Since the passage states that the Congress of the United States *is the same Congress that we elect today*, choice (D) can be eliminated as well. While it is true that the modern-day Congress was established by a document, the Constitution, it is also true that the Congress off the Confederation was established by a document as well: The Articles of the Confederation. Since both Congresses were established by documents, they do not differ on this point. The correct answer is (B).

19. **C** This is a very open-ended question, so rely on POE. According to the graphic the Congress of the United States began on March 4, 1789, while George Washington was inaugurated president of the United States on April 30, 1789. Therefore, the Congress of the United States already existed before the beginning of Washington's presidency, so eliminate choice (A). The Congress of the United States does not have an end date listed in the graphic, so eliminate answer choice (B). The American Revolution began on April 19, 1775, and Washington was inaugurated on April 30, 1789, which is more than fourteen years. The war ended with the signing of the Treaty of Paris on September 3, 1783, which is slightly less than six years before Washington's inauguration. These findings both support choice (C). Because the Continental Congress was established in September of 1784, any power they had would have begun at that point and not in October with the Petition to the King. That eliminates choice (D), making (C) the best answer.

20. **A** This question is focused on the passage in its entirety and the reason it was written. Because this is an open-ended question, use POE to eliminate incorrect answer choices. Although the author does explain what the FCC's stance is when it comes to net neutrality, choice (D) is too limited as that is not the primary purpose of the passage and so it should be eliminated. The author does not make an argument in this passage, merely provides factual information to the reader in an unbiased manner, so eliminate choice (C). Likewise, the author does not try to convince the reader of anything, including the likelihood of net neutrality occurring, so eliminate choice (B) as well. That leaves answer choice (A), which states the author is trying to provide a better understanding of what regulation is and the challenges it faces in this instance. That is supported by the neutral tone and subject matter of the passage, so it is the best answer.

21. **C** The sentence *Take the internet* connects the first and second paragraph, functioning as a link between the two. The first paragraph discusses the slow response of the government in regards to regulation. The second paragraph discusses how this has occurred with the internet specifically. Choice (A) is incorrect because it contains extreme language and is not supported by the passage; at no point does the passage state that the internet is the *most difficult* technology for the government to regulate. Choice (B) is incorrect as it contains the deceptive language *television, radio, and cable*, which are mentioned later in the passage and are not relevant to this question. The passage does not discuss the influence of the internet on the *average American day*, so choice (D) should be eliminated as well. Choice (C) states the phrase is being used as an example of something that government regulation has not caught up with, which establishes a link between the first two paragraphs. Therefore choice (C) is the best answer.

22.   **A**   In this sentence the author provides the definition of what a public utility is and clarifies by including the phrase *such as natural gas, electricity, water, and sewage;* consequently, these items are examples of public utilities. Choice (B) contains the deceptive language *overcharged*, which is not discussed until later in the paragraph and is not why the author mentions the two examples in this sentence. Choice (C) is not supported by the passage, as the author never states if these utilities were once unregulated. The words *such as* implies examples, but does not indicate that all utilities are limited to these examples, so eliminate choice (D). Only choice (A) correctly identifies the two examples in the question as clarification for the reader, and is therefore the best answer.

23.   **B**   In the previous sentence, internet providers are characterized as *existing for capital gain.* In the following sentence, government regulation would *insure fair provision.* So currently, the unregulated internet may not be provided in a fair way. In the sentence *exploit* most nearly means take advantage of. Since choices (A), (C), and (D) do not match the meaning take advantage of, they can be eliminated. The only answer choice that means to take advantage of is choice (B).

24.   **D**   In the provided quote, the FCC states that it wants to insure that better service is not provided to those who can pay more (*paid prioritization*) and that internet providers do not block lawful content. Choice (A) is deceptive since the quote does reference people being able to *go where they want, when they want.* However, the author is applying that freedom to the internet, not literal movement of the public. The same is true of choice (B), as the quote contains a reference to *innovation.* Although that is mentioned at the end of the quote, it is not what the FCC is mainly concerned with, so eliminate choice (B). Choice (C) also contains deceptive language since the quote contains the word *mobile*, which is referring to broadband as opposed to people. Only choice (D) contains the main concerns of the FCC, and is therefore the best answer.

25.   **D**   For open-ended questions, use POE to eliminate incorrect answers. Choice (A) states that the need to regulate criminal activity on the internet has been a recent consideration. However, earlier in the passage the author states that restrictions have been limited to criminal activity up to this point, so choice (A) is incorrect. Choice (B) is deceptive as the passage does state that it will be difficult to enforce regulation, but not that the FCC will have trouble convincing the government to do so. Choice (C) can be eliminated as the FCC regulates communications, not other public utilities. The best answer is choice (D), which is supported when the passage states that the tricky part of internet regulation is *how to enforce that regulation.*

26.   **B**   The previous question asked about the FCC. Choice (A) references a line that is about the U.S. government in general, and not the FCC specifically so it is not the best support for the previous answer. Choice (B) describes why the internet is so difficult for the government to regulate, which supports the previous answer that the internet is difficult to regulate. Choice (C) references public utilities that are regulated, and is not relevant to the regulation of the internet. Choice (D) refers to the fact that the internet has only recently been under consideration as a utility by the government, which does not offer any insight into the difficulty into regulating it. Therefore, the most supportive answer choice is (B).

27. **C**   On EXCEPT questions, the best approach is to start with POE based on what you have already read. The passage referred to two different types of regulation—criminal and commercial. In the paragraph discussing criminal regulation, the author mentions *gambling*, so choice (D) will not be correct. In the paragraphs discussing the need for commercial regulation, the concerns are over internet providers providing slower internet and blocking content for those who pay less. This eliminates choices (A) and (B). The only thing that is not mentioned in the passage that should be regulated is choice (C), file protection. Therefore, choice (C) is the best answer.

28. **D**   In the sentence, the author is stating that regulating internet provision is not very easy to do. So in this context *tricky* means not easy or hard. Because choices (A), (B), and (C) do not match those meanings at all, they will not be the correct answer. The only possible answer for this questions is (D), difficult.

29. **D**   The sentence is stating that based on features of animal, the researchers were able to draw conclusions about what type of dinosaur it was. Therefore, surmise means to draw conclusions. Choices (A) and (B) are not words that mean to draw conclusion, so they are incorrect. When comparing choices (C) and (D), (C) is clearly a more definite word. To know something is to be certain about it. Since the researchers are only making educated guesses based on their findings, the best answer choice is (D) conjecture.

30. **B**   In the fifth paragraph the passages states that Case and Martin believed the finding could be classified as a theropod based on the *shape of the teeth and features of the feet*. Since teeth and feet count as oral and skeletal characteristics, the best supported choice is (B). Although the location, choice (A), and the time period, choice (C), are both mentioned in regards to this finding, they are including as pieces of additional information rather than support for the type of dinosaur. Answer choice (D) refers to a pelvis bone, which pertains to the discovery discussed later in the passage. The best answer here is choice (B).

31. **A**   The answer to the average question is (B) skeletal and oral aspects of the remains. Choice (A) is from the beginning of the fourth paragraph and references the physical features of the skeletal remains, which offers strong support for the answer to the previous question. Choice (B) is a part of the passage on the finding of the pelvis in the second discovery discussed in the passage, not the first discovery so this choice can be eliminated. Choice (C) discusses the environment that the creature would have inhabited, but nothing about what characteristics likely identify the dinosaur. Choice (D) does discuss the type of dinosaur the researchers believe they found, but does not offer any evidence of why that conclusion was made. The best answer here is choice (A).

32. **C**   The author mentions the film *Jurassic Park* at the end of a sentence discussing dinosaurs that the newly discovered remains is likely related to. Thus the author is offering the example of *Jurassic Park* to try to illustrate for the reader a clearer picture of the newly discovered dinosaur. Choice (A) is not supported by the passage as the author does not state whether he liked or disliked the film. The author does not imply that *Jurassic Park* is anything but a film, so choice (B) is also incorrect. No time period is mentioned in relation to the film *Jurassic Park*, so (D) does not make sense as an

answer. The best supporting choice is (C), in that the author is offering an example to help relate the discovery to something more familiar to the reader.

33. **D** The passage does not provide a great deal of information about the specific researchers, so this is a good POE opportunity. Based on the job descriptions of the three researchers, all have differing specialties. Also, only the team lead by Case and Martin discovered the remains of a carnivorous dinosaur, the team lead by Hammer discovered a plant-eating dinosaur. So choice (A) is not correct. The passage does not mention grants or funding, so choice (B) should also be eliminated. Although the passage clearly states that both discoveries were located in Antarctica, there is nothing in the passage that supports the claim that the researchers held the belief it was the "best" place for their research. Eliminate choice (C). Each of the three researchers had an educational institution included in the job description provided, so choice (D) is best supported.

34. **B** This paragraph gives a description of where the remains were found, which was on the sea floor. Since this was a land-dwelling dinosaur, the author offers an explanation from the research team as to how the remains could have ended up in that location. The purpose of this explanation is best indicated by choice (B). Choice (A) is not supported by the passage since marine lizards are not referred to as the primary predator of theropods. Choice (C) does not make sense as there is no danger mentioned to the researchers themselves in this paragraph. The passage does not go on to discuss the discovery of a marine lizard, so (D) is also incorrect. The best answer is choice (B).

35. **A** This is a very open-ended argument, so approach it with POE. The passage does discuss Antarctica, but only to state that it is the location where both discoveries occurred. There is no information provided to indicate that Antarctica is popular for any specific reason, and nowhere is the desolate landscape of Antarctica mentioned. Eliminate choice (C). The author mentions birds in relation to dinosaurs, stating that theropods walked on two legs like birds and that *recent research has shown that birds are direct descendants of theropods*. Choice (D) is deceptive as it includes language very similar to this but is technically saying the opposite, that dinosaurs are descendants of birds rather than the other way around. Eliminate choice (D).

36. **C** This sentence is discussing how Mt. Kirkpatrick was a riverbed until tectonic activity resulted in it become more *skyward*. In this context *elevated* is used to mean "pushed" or "sent" toward the sky. Because choices (A) and (B) do not match theses meanings at all, they can be eliminated. Between choices (C) and (D), choice (C) is a more literal match to "pushed" or "sent" toward the sky. The best choice is (C).

37. **C** Although theropods shared more characteristics with mammals than reptiles, this does not prove that theropods (including the newly discovered species) are more closely related to mammals. Choice (A) is incorrect. The passage states that birds are the direct descendants of theropods, eliminating choice (B). There is no evidence in either the passage or graphic for choice (D). However the graphic does state that theropods (including tyrannosaurs) maintained a constant body temperature. Choice (C) is correct.

38.   **C**   According the author of the first passage, vaccines are beneficial and the risks are minimal. While she clearly argues in favor of vaccines and believes that children should be vaccinated, she does not address the best way to convince those who are anti-vaccine of this fact. This makes choice (A) unsupported and therefore incorrect. Although the author clearly believes that the use of vaccines would help to decrease instances of childhood diseases and deaths resulting from those diseases, the author does not address "all childhood death." This makes choice (B) extreme and therefore incorrect. The author does state at the end of the passage that the author has a family and is in favor of mandatory vaccination, which would indicate that the author is likely to vaccinate her own children as stated in choice (C). The passage provides no information regarding the author's vaccine history, so choice (D) is not correct. The best answer is choice (C).

39.   **B**   The correct answer to the previous question is choice (C) she herself is likely to vaccinate her own children. The author is clearly in favor of vaccinations, so the line reference that will best support this choice is one that directly references her own children. The only way to show this is the last line, which states that the author is *an American with children of [her] own*. She then goes on to say that she is in favor of mandatory vaccination, so it cannot be that she is against vaccinations for her own children. This makes answer choice (B) the best answer. While all other answer choices are pro-vaccine, they do not specifically support how the author feels about vaccines for her own children.

40.   **D**   The reactions that are being listed in this sentence, *anaphylaxis, illness, or even death,* are harmful ones. Since vaccines are meant to protect people from harmful illnesses, these *adverse reactions* are the not what doctors are hoping to accomplish through vaccinations. The best meaning for the word *adverse* in this context is unwanted, unintended, or harmful. As choices (A), (B), and (C) do not match either of these meanings, the best answer is choice (D). Undesirable matches unwanted or unintended, making that word the best answer.

41.   **A**   The third paragraph in the first passage discusses the fact there can be harmful drawbacks to vaccines. However, the author makes it clear that these drawbacks are not serious or widespread enough to deter people from vaccinating their children. The answer that best matches this stance is choice (A). Choice (D) is supported by information in the fourth paragraph, not the third paragraph, so it can be eliminated. Both choices (B) and (C) are deceptive. Choice (B) discusses the wide range of the number of people harmed, but not only is that mentioned in a different paragraph it is also not indicated that physicians are attempting to avoid accountability. Eliminate choice (B). Although the vaccination schedule brought up in choice (C) is also mentioned, it too is referenced in another part of the passage and it is not stated that physicians are strict about it. This leaves choice (A) as the only possible correct answer.

42.   **B**   In passage 2 Socrates is mentioned when the author includes a quote from him. The author uses this quote to introduce the idea that people may not always know as much as they think they do, which is a central theme of the author's argument. Since the FDA is never mentioned in the passage, choice (D) cannot be correct. It is also never stated that Socrates influenced scientific and medical research in any way, so choice (C) can also be eliminated. The author does not mention

Socrates because he is a well-known scholar but because the quote is appropriate for the point she is making. So choice (A) is also not the best answer. Since the author is using the quote to introduce the reasoning behind her argument, the best supported choice is (B).

43.　**A**　The author mentions the quote at the beginning of the passage because she believes it is very relevant when it comes to vaccines and children's health. So when she says *there is never a time that this fact is as salient as when it comes to the health of the most vulnerable in our society*, what she means by *salient* is relevant. So the correct answer will match the meaning of relevant. This best matches answer choice (A).

44.　**C**　Formaldehyde is mentioned in the third paragraph, in which the author of passage 2 lists potentially harmful ingredients that are included in various vaccines. It is used as an example of one of these ingredients, and is described as having very harmful short-term effects and unknown long-term effects. Since the author is including formaldehyde as a harmful ingredient in the short term and possibly the long term, choice (B) cannot be correct. The author does not cite any specific instances when a vaccine containing formaldehyde resulted in the death of a patient, so eliminate choice (D). The author does not state that they think doctors actively manipulate, only that they aren't as knowledgeable as they may seem when it comes to vaccines, so choice (A) is also incorrect. The answer choice that best matches the information provided is choice (C), that formaldehyde has known effects, the short-term ones, and unknown effects, the possible long-term ones.

45.　**B**　This question is very open-ended, so the best approach to use POE. In the last paragraph the author states that while she believes vaccines can help, she thinks it is possible they may cause an unknown amount of harm. There is no scientific evidence offered, eliminate choice (C). No doctors are mentioned in the final paragraph, so choice (D) cannot be correct. Although the author does acknowledge that vaccines can be helpful, she goes on to say that they may cause known harm. So while she makes a concession, she does not undermine her own argument in the end. This eliminates choice (A), and best supports choice (B).

46.　**C**　The first passage focuses on the benefits of vaccines. Choice (B) and choice (C) do not match this information for passage one, so they are both incorrect. The second passage focuses on the lack of knowledge regarding the possible harm that can come from vaccines. However, the passage does not provide any specific instances of vaccinations having caused harm, so choice (A) is incorrect for the central idea of passage two. This leaves choice (C) as the best answer for the central idea for both passages.

47.　**D**　In the first passage, the author quotes the American Academy of Pediatrics multiple times: *most child vaccines are 90%-99% effective in preventing disease* and *one per several hundred thousand to one per million vaccinations*. In the second passage the author quotes Socrates at the beginning: *I know that I know nothing*. The correct answer is (D), both passages contain a quotation.

Chapter 6
Reading Test
Drill 2

Reading Test

60 MINUTES, 47 QUESTIONS

Turn to Section 1 of your answer sheet to answer the questions in this section.

DIRECTIONS

Each passage or pair of passages below is followed by a number of questions. After reading each passage or pair, choose the best answer to each question based on what is stated or implied in the passage or passages and in any accompanying graphics (such as a table or graph).

Questions 1–9 are based on the following passage.

The following is an excerpt from *The Social Contract,* a book written by Jean-Jacques Rousseau in 1762. Rousseau was a Genevan writer, philosopher, and composer whose philosophical writings profoundly influenced modern political thinking.

Let us take it that men have reached the point at which the obstacles to their survival in the state of nature overpower each individual's resources for
Line maintaining himself in that state. So this primitive
5 condition can't go on; the human race will perish unless it changes its manner of existence.

Now, men can't create new forces; they can only bring together ones that already exist and steer them. So their only way to preserve themselves is to unite
10 a number of forces so that they are jointly powerful enough to deal with the obstacles. They have to bring these forces into play in such a way that they act together in a single thrust.

For forces to *add up* in this way, many people have
15 to work together. But for each, man's force and liberty are what he chiefly needs for his survival; so how can he put them into this collective effort without harming his own interest and neglecting the care he owes to himself? This difficulty, in the version of it that arises
20 for my present subject, can be put like this:

Find a form of association that will bring the whole common force to bear on defending and protecting each associate's person and goods, doing this in such a way that each of them, while united himself with all,
25 still obeys only himself and remains as free as before.

There's the basic problem that is solved by the social contract. The clauses of this contract settled by the nature of the act that the slightest change would make them all null and void; so that although they may never
30 have been explicitly stated, they are everywhere the same and everywhere tacitly accepted and recognized, until the social compact is violated and each individual regains his original rights and resumes his natural liberty, while losing the liberty-by-agreement which
35 had been his reason for renouncing them.

Properly understood, these clauses come down to one—the total alienation of each associate, together with all his rights, to the whole community. This may seem drastic, but three features of it make it
40 reasonable.

I. Because each individual gives himself *entirely*, what is happening here for any one individual is the same as what is happening for each of the others, and, because this is so, no one has any interest in making
45 things tougher for everyone but himself.

II. Because the alienation is made without reserve, i.e. without anything being held back, the union is as complete as it can be, and no associate has anything more to demand. To see why the association *has to* be
50 done in this way, consider what the situation would be if the individuals retained certain rights. In the absence of any superior to decide issues about this, each individual would be his own judge across the board; this would continue the state of nature, and the
55 association would necessarily become inoperative or tyrannical.

III. Each man in giving himself to everyone gives himself to no one; and the right over himself that others get is matched by the right that he gets over
60 each of them. So he gains as much as he loses, and *also* gains extra force for the preservation of what he has.

Filtering out the inessentials, we'll find that the social compact comes down to this: Each of us puts his person and all his power in common under the
65 supreme direction of the general will, and, in our corporate capacity, we receive each member as an indivisible part of the whole.

1

As used in line 13, "thrust" most nearly means

A) shove.

B) direction.

C) gist.

D) assault.

2

The passage most strongly suggests that which of the following is true of the author?

A) He believes that when people unite together they are stronger than when they remain separate.

B) He thinks that people should not be as selfish as their nature inherently makes them.

C) He trusts that once a group comes together in shared understanding, they will never break their word.

D) He asserts that once society develops to the point of capitalism and corporations, we will have more to bind us together.

3

Which choice provides the best evidence for the answer to the previous question?

A) Lines 63-67, ("Each of . . . whole")

B) Lines 15-19, ("But for . . . himself?")

C) Lines 57-61, ("Each man . . . he has")

D) Lines 7-8, ("Now, men . . . them")

4

As used in line 31, "tacitly" most nearly means

A) delicately.

B) skillfully.

C) obviously.

D) implicitly.

5

Over the course of the passage, the main focus of the narrative shifts from

A) the natural state of humanity to the socially evolved relationships humanity can create.

B) the capacity for violence that humanity has to the capacity for mercy that humanity has.

C) the desire to express one's independence versus the desire to fit in.

D) the negative aspects of the social contract to the positive aspects of the social contract.

6

The "forces" the author refers to throughout the passage refer to

A) armies of men.

B) solely the physical power one person has over another.

C) the ability of the group to coerce members into joining.

D) the physical and mental capacities that we are all naturally endowed with.

7

The passage most strongly suggests that what be done in order for people to unite together?

A) They must be willing to give up all liberties.

B) They must enter into an agreement in which individual rights are commited for the sake of communal right.

C) They must bring their forces to bear upon one another, so that the strongest force can prevail and unite the community together.

D) They must put their survival and the survivial of their families above all else.

8

What claim about force and liberty is best supported by the passage?

A) Force and liberty are the most valued assets in a system of commercial exchange.

B) By giving up force and liberty, a person ultimately sacrifices his or her natural claims to independence, and become a slave to the will of the people.

C) If someone freely gives his or her force and liberty in order attain a shared force and liberty, then nothing is being given up.

D) Force and liberty are of little importance, as they are found primarily in nature and have little to do with civilized, structured society.

9

The central idea of the passage is that

A) it is better to have known what it is to be free and then be enslaved than to have never known freedom at all.

B) it is in man's best interest to conform to society, or else he risks being stripped of his liberty.

C) it is not enough to merely live in harmony with one another, a legal contract must be entered into to insure that way of life will endure.

D) by relinquishing individual rights to a communal power, the rights of all are enhanced and even more greatly secured.

THIS PAGE IS LEFT INTENTIONALLY BLANK.

Questions 10–18 are based on the following passage.

The following passage discusses the cultural significance of the number 13 both historically and in the present day.

Every culture comes with its own superstitions and taboos. Certain things that seem so innocuous to us in the modern day that they hardly warrant emotion were
Line viewed with irrational fear. And sometimes, this fear
5 carried on even into the modern day. Such is the case with Friday, the number 13, and Friday the 13th.

Historically, in many cultures Friday has been treated as an unlucky day. This is especially true of Western, Christian cultures. The original references
10 to Friday as an unlucky day are based on two biblical occurrences believed to have taken place on a Friday: the day that Adam and Eve ate from the tree of knowledge, and the crucifixion of Jesus. This superstition was believed most firmly by Christian
15 maritime cultures, who associated bad luck in sailing with Friday. It was strongly believed that any ship that departed from harbor on a Friday would have ill-luck during the voyage, and commercial sailing schedules were set around this belief.
20 The fear of the number 13 is much more common across the globe, and much more standard than is the fear of Friday. It is what is called a specific phobia, because sufferers are afraid of 13 specifically, rather than a larger range of fears. This phobia is called
25 *triskaidekaphobia*. This fear also has biblical roots for the western, Christian cultures that fear it (which, interestingly enough, does not include Italian culture). There were 13 people present at the Last Supper, which occurred the day before Jesus' death, and to
30 this day many believe that sitting down to a table of 13 people will bring death. Also, the number 13 was highly inconvenient for church officials in the Middle Ages when it came to the number of moon cycles in a year. The Greco-Roman calendar was based primarily
35 on a twelve-moon year, as a typical century has 63 years with twelve moons and 37 with 13 moons. As all official religious events were scheduled on a twelve-moon year, the inclusion of a 13th moon proved very problematic for the monks. It was they who were in
40 charge of keeping the calendar, and the discrepancy caused many issues throughout the year for them. Hence, the number was viewed as a highly unlucky one for the more educated members of Christian societies. But obviously the fear spread and continues to this

45 day. It is not uncommon for buildings to omit the 13th floor of buildings or rooms numbered 13 by referring to them as 12A, M (for the 13th letter of the alphabet), or skipping that number in the floor numbering pattern altogether. The number is also avoided as an
50 interstate highway number.

But it is the combination of Friday and the number 13 that constitutes one of the most well-known superstitions still in existence today. The superstition of Friday the 13th has also been given a name due to
55 the widespread belief in it: *paraskevidekatriaphobia*. And it truly is a combination of the two discrete fears that make this fear what it is. As anthropologist Phillips Stevens, Jr. put it "There were 13 people at the table and the 13th was Jesus. The last supper was on
60 a Thursday, and the next day was Friday, the day of crucifixion. When 13 and Friday come together, it is a double whammy."

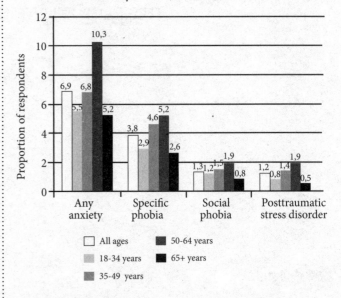

10

As used in line 3, "warrant" most nearly means
A) insure.
B) arrest.
C) licenses.
D) deserve.

11

Which of the following supports the belief that the number 13 is unlucky?

A) Judas was the last person to attend the Last Supper, becoming the 13th guest at dinner.

B) The fact that there were more often 13 moons in a year made the twelve year calendar an unfortunate choice.

C) The number 13 was an inconvenient astronomical occurrence for the religious authority.

D) Adam and Eve are believed to have partaken of the fruit of knowledge on a Friday.

12

Which choice provides the best evidence for the answer to the previous question?

A) Lines 9-13 ("The original . . . Jesus")

B) Lines 34-36 ("The Greco-Roman . . . moons")

C) Lines 28-31 ("There were . . . death")

D) Lines 31-34 ("Also . . . in a year")

13

It can be reasonably inferred from the information in the passage that

A) to this day ships will not set sail on a Friday if it is at all avoidable.

B) the majority of superstitions are based on biblical references.

C) the fear of the number 13 is more common than is the fear of Friday.

D) the Greco-Roman calendar was altered centuries ago to accommodate the differing number of moons that occur each year.

14

The central idea of the passage is

A) a common fear is based on two separate fears that trace their origin to the same root cause.

B) it is more common to fear the number 13 than it is to fear Friday.

C) without the influence of religious authority during the Middle Ages, it is doubtful whether or not the fear of Friday the 13th would ever have existed.

D) of all cultures, maritime cultures tend to be the most religious and most superstitious.

15

As used in line 52, "constitutes" most nearly means

A) establishes.

B) starts.

C) charters.

D) conditions.

16

In the context of the passage, the author's use of the phrase "which, interestingly enough, does not include Italian culture" is primarily meant to convey

A) confusion over what number is considered to be unlucky by the Italians.

B) curiosity in a seemingly odd exception to the cultures that share a belief in the unlucky nature of 13.

C) distrust in Italy due to its lack of conformity to other cultures' beliefs.

D) interest in why the seed of the Roman Empire would not be aware of the biblical origins of a belief.

17

The author most likely includes the names of the phobias associated with certain fears in the passage in order to

A) indicate that they are highly complex conditions which require names in order to properly reference them.

B) demonstrate the prevalent nature of the fears.

C) impress upon the reader the importance of knowing the correct names and definitions when discussing various topics in order to avoid confusion.

D) share with the reader little-known facts in order to maintain their interest in an otherwise dry subject matter.

18

Which of the following is supported by the passage and the graph?

A) *Triskaidekaphobia* is most common among those 50 to 64 years of age.

B) Because it is the combination of two fears, the fear of Friday the 13th plagues occurs at twice the rate as the fear of the number 13 or the fear of Friday.

C) Specific phobias are unique to Western, predominantly Christian cultures.

D) Those 65 years and old are least likely to be plagued by specific phobias, because they are less likely to subscribe to Western values.

THIS PAGE IS LEFT INTENTIONALLY BLANK.

Questions 19–28 are based on the following passages.

Both Passage 1 and Passage 2 discuss a mysterious event in American history.

Passage 1

History is full of puzzles that strike a chord in the human imagination, regardless of how unsolvable they may be. No event illustrates the lure of the unknowable
Line more than the disappearance of the *Mary Celeste*.
5   The *Mary Celeste* was an American merchant brigantine. On November 7, 1872, it set sail from New York harbor in route to Genoa to deliver 1,701 barrels of crude alcohol. The ship was captained by Benjamin Briggs and carried a crew of seven men, as well
10   Brigg's wife and young daughter. It was discovered on December 4 completely abandoned.

Although it appeared that the sails and rigging of the ship had received minimal damage and that two hatch doors had been broken, it was in otherwise
15   completely sailable condition. The cargo was mostly intact, there was a six-month supply of food and water, and there were no visible signs of panic, violence, or fire. The ship's sole lifeboat was missing along with navigational equipment and many of the ship's papers,
20   but the passenger's valuables were still present. The sea log was present, with the last entry having been made ten days previously. But not a single soul was found on board, nor was one ever seen or heard from again.

What would make an entire crew, and a captain
25   with his wife and child aboard, abandon a sailable ship with no evident reason? Did the crew mutiny and then abandon the ship? Did pirates attack and leave the cargo? Many reasons have been put forth but none has ever been widely accepted, and it would be very
30   difficult for any to be proven correctly.

Passage 2

The enigmatic history of the *Mary Celeste* has long intrigued historians and maritime experts since 1872. Many theories have been postulated regarding its abandonment, ranging from the levelheaded to the
35   ludicrous. In terms of the latter, it has been suggested that the ship was abandoned for such reasons as underwater sonic earthquakes, giant squid attacks, and even drunken mutiny (did the crew mutiny itself?).

The most likely reason seems clear now, but would
40   have easily slipped by the hasty investigation that took place after the *Mary Celeste's* discovery. When

discovered, it was found that nine of the 1,701 alcohol cargo barrels were constructed of red oak, while the rest were constructed of white oak. All nine of the
45   red oak barrels were emptied—the only barrels to be found so. Although it is possible that the alcohol was drunk by the crew, it is doubtful such a large amount of unrefined alcohol could be so quickly. And even if the crew did drink the alcohol, would they then kill
50   the captain and his family only to abandon the ship entirely? There is a more likely explanation for both the disappearance of the alcohol and all aboard. Because red oak is more porous than white oak, it would have been very easy for alcoholic fumes to escape from the
55   barrels and buildup down in the hold. If a great enough buildup occurred, then the hatch doors would be forced ajar. If this occurred, the most likely reaction of the captain and crew would be to abandon ship for fear of the explosive capability of such a buildup of gas.

60   In such a case, it would be common practice to load into the lifeboat, tether it to the ship, and float a safe distance away until the risk of explosion appeared to abate. Due to the complete disappearance of the crew, with little taken with them, it is probably that the
65   tether keeping the ship and lifeboat connected was not made strongly enough, resulting in the loss of the ten souls aboard.

19

Which of the following is mentioned by both of the authors?

A) The number of cargo barrels aboard

B) The name of the captain of the *Mary Celeste*

C) The date the *Mary Celeste* set sail

D) Natural phenomenon behind the disappearance

20

Passage 1 most strongly suggests which of the following about the *Mary Celeste*?

A) There was no identifiable reason that the crew could not have completed the voyage with the boat as it was discovered.

B) The *Mary Celeste* serves as strong evidence as to why women and children should not be taken as passengers on possible dangerous expeditions.

C) The majority of reasons suggested for the dereliction of the *Mary Celeste* should be dismissed as meritless.

D) It would not be difficult to discover the true reason behind the disappearance of those aboard the *Mary Celeste* if there was motivation to do so.

21

Which choice provides the best evidence for the answer in the previous question?

A) Lines 33-35 ("Many theories . . . ludicrous")

B) Lines 12-15 ("Although it . . . condition")

C) Lines 8-10 ("The ship . . . daughter")

D) Lines 28-30 ("Many reasons . . . correctly")

22

The main rhetorical effect of the series of the three questions in the last paragraph of Passage 1 is to

A) stress the mysterious nature of the desertion of the *Mary Celeste*.

B) demonstrate the ignorance of maritime historians, both in the 1800s and the modern day.

C) point out that you never know what is behind the actions of a certain individual or group.

D) increase the intensity of the need to determine the true story of the *Mary Celeste*.

23

As used in line 31, "enigmatic" most nearly means

A) straightforward.

B) interesting.

C) disappointing.

D) perplexing.

24

The author of Passage 2 references "giant squid" (line 37) in order to

A) contradict an opinion offered in the previous passage.

B) provide an instance of a natural occurrence.

C) give an example of an assertion made earlier in the paragraph.

D) offer a detailed description of an alternative theory.

25

In the context of the Passage 2, the author's use of the phrase "did the crew mutiny itself" (line 38) is primarily meant to convey

A) confusion over how everyone on board the *Mary Celeste* disappeared.

B) mockery of those who are not intelligent enough to have solved the mystery of the *Mary Celeste*.

C) disbelief in a proposed solution to the puzzle of a derelict ship.

D) lost hope in the certainty of the inevitable death of the crew that was lost at sea.

26

As used in line 57, "ajar" most nearly means

A) off.

B) open.

C) shut.

D) gouged.

27

Which of the following choices best supports Passage 2 author's reasoning that the passengers on board the *Mary Celeste* left temporarily and had intended to return?

A) Lines 20-22 ("The sea . . . previously")

B) Lines 24-26 ("What would . . . reason?")

C) Lines 22-23 ("But not . . . again")

D) Lines 18-20 ("The ship's . . . present")

28

The central ideas of the two passages differ in that Passage 1

A) discusses a historical description of a mystery, while Passage 2 discusses the various ways a ship may be abandoned.

B) discusses the individual souls who were lost at sea, while Passage 2 discusses the way in which alcohol can emit noxious fumes.

C) discusses the facts of an unsolved maritime disappearance, while Passage 2 discusses a probable reason for the abandonment of specific ship.

D) discusses the cargo-related cause of the loss of a crew and captain, while Passage 2 discusses the background of an ill-fated ship.

THIS PAGE IS LEFT INTENTIONALLY BLANK.

Questions 29–37 are based on the following passage.

The following passage discusses three diseases that have the unique characteristic of leaving signs of their pathology on the human skeleton.

When studying ancient human remains, it is often difficult to tell how the people those remains were met their end. Unless there are clear signs of how death
Line may have occurred, it can be impossible. When people
5 die from natural causes, rarely is there evidence of the affliction or disease left on the skeletal remains. Luckily for paleopathologists, this is not always the case.

Paleopathology is the study of ancient diseases. Certain diseases that were common in the ancient
10 world, and still are today, leave clear signs of their pathology on the skeleton itself. The three primary diseases for which this phenomenon is known to occur most often are leprosy, tuberculosis, and syphilis.

Leprosy is a chronic infectious disease that is
15 caused by the parasite *Mycobacterium leprae*, and dates back to 4000 B.C. Once leprosy has been contracted, it begins to breakdown the skin and nerve cells, resulting in a lack of sensation and greater occurrence of injury. Injury commonly results in the loss of
20 fingers and toes, due to the lack of pain reception and high utility of those body parts. The disease will then attack the skeleton itself, infecting bone marrow. This weakens the skeleton, leading to a common pattern of deformation.
25 Leprosy is not highly contagious. It is spread through long-term contact with individuals who have it either through long-term contact with infected skin, or through infected skin cells or ejected mucous being released into the environment. Because the parasite
30 has a low rate of contagion and takes years of close contact to spread, it is common to find groupings of skeletal remains with signs of leprosy in isolated, small populations rather than large, dispersed ones.

Tuberculosis, another disease that leaves clear
35 marks on the skeleton, is much older, contagious, and deadly than leprosy. Dating as far back at 10,200 B.C., tuberculosis was most likely first contracted from ingesting infected animal products. Once a human is infected, that person can easily spread the disease by
40 releasing infected mucous into the air when coughing. The symptoms of tuberculosis are chronic cough accompanied with bloody sputum, fever, night sweats, and weight loss.

Tuberculosis has a long period of maturation, up
45 to two decades, during which the body goes through cycles of weakening and recovery. From its onset, the bacteria that causes tuberculosis penetrates into the growth areas of spongy bone tissue, the cancellous tissue, near the knee and hip joints and the spine.
50 During a weakening period, the bacteria will begin to slowly destroy the bone in those areas, and during recovery periods the bone will heal itself. These alternating cycles lead to calcified lesions on those areas of the skeleton, clearly indicating the presence
55 of the disease to paleopathologists. Tuberculosis can also be established through DNA testing, a unique attribute.

Compared to the previous two diseases, syphilis is far and away the most contagious and deadly,
60 and the most clearly marked on skeletal remains of the untreated. Syphilis progresses over four stages: primary, secondary, latent, and tertiary. The first three stages present with relatively minimal and simple symptoms; in primary there is the presentation of a
65 single chancre (a ulceration with no sensation), in secondary there is a rash that presents on the hands and feet, and in latent there are is no presentation of symptoms. But the tertiary stage, which occurs anywhere from three to fifteen years after infection,
70 presents with symptoms that include gummas (soft, tissue like balls of inflammation on the body), nervous system decay, seizure, dementia, and aneurysm.

Despite the seemingly innocuous symptoms of the first stages, indications of syphilis on the skeleton
75 begin immediately after infection. During the primary and secondary stage, the bone marrow of the infected swells, producing lesions on the bone. This is typically seen on the skull and tibiae. In the later stages, the bone literally begins to decay, resulting in pore-shaped
80 lesions that have been described as looking like "worm-holes" by paleopathologists.

Paleopathology, though limited in its application to very specific diseases, plays an important role in both deciphering the past and helping to prepare for
85 the future. The three diseases listed above are still very much a concern for both the developed and developing worlds today. With a greater understanding the history, rates, and pattern of infection of these diseases, we will be better enabled to combat them more effectively now
90 and in the future.

Instances of Leprosy 2010

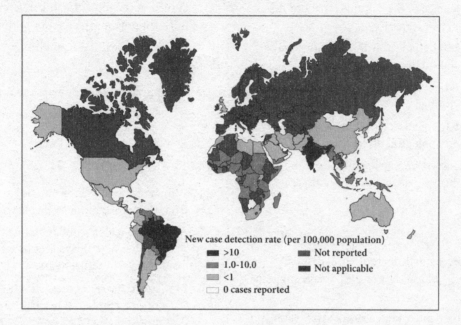

New case detection rate (per 100,000 population)
- >10
- 1.0-10.0
- <1
- 0 cases reported
- Not reported
- Not applicable

29

The tone of the passage is best described as

A) pedantic.

B) judgmental.

C) descriptive.

D) conciliatory.

30

Based on the information in the first paragraph it can be reasonably inferred that

A) it is easy to identify the cause of death for ancient human remains when the cause of death was not natural.

B) paleopathology is considered a lucky profession by many in the archaeology field.

C) ancient populations often died of undiagnosed cancers that left no marks on the skeleton.

D) a cause of death cannot be determined for some skeletal remains.

31

As used in line 18, "sensation" most nearly means

A) stir.

B) fuss.

C) perception.

D) wonder.

32

As used in line 16, "contracted" most nearly means

A) diminished.

B) restricted.

C) commissioned.

D) caught.

33

In the sixth paragraph, the author draws a distinction between

A) tuberculosis in animals and humans.

B) tuberculosis and leprosy.

C) tuberculosis and syphilis.

D) knee and hip joints and the spine.

34

The author's reference to the "unique attribute" in lines 56-57 primarily serves to

A) indicate that tuberculosis is the most distinctive paleopathological disease.

B) imply that other paleopathological diseases cannot be verified through DNA testing.

C) explain why tuberculosis is the most commonly found paleopathological disease.

D) counter the assertion that syphilis is the most easily identifiable paleopathological disease.

35

In discussing the last paleopathological disease reviewed, syphilis, the author of the passage suggests that

A) it is easier to identify indicators of syphilis on ancient human remains than the indicators of other paleopathological diseases.

B) if syphilis is treated and cured by the latent period, both the skeleton and body experience little to no symptoms of its presences.

C) syphilis takes a longer time to progress than tuberculosis does, despite being more deadly.

D) the three major stages of tuberculosis are the primary, secondary, and tertiary.

36

Which of the following line references provides the most support for the answer to the previous question?

A) Lines 62-64 ("The first three . . . symptoms")

B) Lines 73-75 ("Despite the . . . infection")

C) Lines 58-61 ("Compared to . . . untreated")

D) Lines 68-72 ("But the . . . aneurysm")

37

Which of the following can be reasonably inferred from the information in the passage and the graphic?

A) Due to its low contagion rate, it is unlikely the number of leprosy cases in the United States will increase in future years.

B) Due to its low contagion rate, it is likely that the current number of leprosy cases that exist in the United States will decrease in future years.

C) Due to its high contagion rate, it is likely that the occurrence of leprosy in India will remain greater than 10 cases per 100,000 people.

D) Due to its high contagion rate, occurrences of leprosy are likely to increase across central and western Africa.

THIS PAGE IS LEFT INTENTIONALLY BLANK.

Questions 38–47 are based on the following passage.

The following passage is excerpted from the article "How to grow mussels," originally published by the National Science Foundation on September 25, 2014.

Blue mussels, *mytilus edulis*, live on northern Atlantic shores in the area between high and low tides.

"Mussels are one of the most significant filter-
Line feeders in the marine environment," said Brian Beal, a
5 marine ecologist at the University of Maine at Machias. "They are responsible not only for efficiently producing high-quality protein but for cleaning the waters around them through their feeding activities."

Because many creatures—especially humans—
10 enjoy eating blue mussels, farmers grow mussels using aquaculture, or aquatic farming. More than 650,000 pounds of blue mussels were cultured and harvested in Maine in 2012, according to the state's Department of Marine Resources.

15 Young mussels may be cultivated in the wild, or they may grow on ropes that are submerged in culture tanks, where they are protected from storms and predators. Once the mussels reach a certain size, they are moved into ocean pens to mature.

20 But practitioners often struggle in their efforts to increase the number, size and overall health of their mussels. Like many farmers, they turn to science and engineering to improve their harvest.

Beal, along with a team of National Science
25 Foundation (NSF)-funded researchers at the University of Maine at Machias and the Downeast Institute, is investigating the growing conditions and practices that will reliably yield healthy and plentiful blue mussels.

"Our goal is to develop methods in the hatchery
30 to create consistent quantities of seed-size mussel juveniles," Beal said. "At present, mussel farmers rely on wild settlement, which can be very spotty from year to year and from place to place." Maine's annual harvest of cultured blue mussels commonly varies by
35 hundreds of thousands of pounds.

Young mussels go through several stages of development. After swimming for their first few weeks of life, mussel larvae adhere to an underwater surface such as a rope. They attach themselves using byssus
40 threads, which are flexible strands of protein.

"A narrow range of seawater temperatures combined with relatively high salinities results in healthy, active juveniles," Beal said, "and different

phytoplankton diets fed to the swimming larvae affect
45 their ability to settle effectively onto substrates such as rope."

Beal's team plans to use what they learn about blue mussel development to optimize how many and how well larvae secure themselves to rope used in
50 aquaculture. They are now conducting field studies to examine the effects of stocking densities on mussel growth and survival.

The researchers also are investigating exactly when to transition the young mussels into ocean pens, and
55 where in the pens they grow best.

With better understanding of their cultivation, the researchers and their partner New DHC, an aquaculture company, hope to improve commercial prospects for sustainably grown blue mussels.

60 "A consistent seed supply also will allow aquaculturists to create business plans that project their annual production more realistically," Beal explained.

The collaboration is supported by the NSF
65 Partnerships for Innovation program, which stimulates regional innovation based on science and engineering discoveries.

In speaking of Beal, NSF program director Sally Nerlove said, "His life's work is of tremendous potential
70 importance to the economy and the ethos of region, and, at the same time, his accomplishments track the evolution of the NSF Partnerships for Innovation program."

38

The quotes included in the second paragraph primarily serve to

A) establish the main motivation behind the commercial farming of blue mussels.

B) demonstrate the important role a species plays that the reader may not be aware of

C) encourage the reader to decrease their personal consumption of blue mussels.

D) indicate the expertise of a scientist quoted later in the passage.

39

According to the fourth paragraph, growing mussels in culture tanks helps to

A) enhance their size.

B) increase their maturity.

C) prepare them for the wild.

D) protect them from harm.

40

As used in line 19, "mature" most nearly means

A) marinate.

B) mellow.

C) develop.

D) stabilize.

41

What claim about blue mussels is best supported by the passage?

A) Were it not for their commercial importance, researchers would not be interested in sustainable growth for mussels.

B) Blue mussels grow best in ocean pens rather than the open water.

C) Mussels have multiple natural predators.

D) Immediately after birth, mussels must attach to a physical object to increase their chances of survival.

42

Which choice provides the best evidence for the answer to the previous question?

A) Lines 56-59 ("With better . . . mussels")

B) Lines 9-11 ("Because many . . . farming")

C) Lines 53-55 ("The researchers . . . best")

D) Lines 39-40 ("They attach . . . protein")

43

The passage most strongly suggests that researchers from the University of Maine at Machias and the Downeast Institute share which assumption?

A) Mussels prefer to attach to rope as opposed to other materials after maturing past the larvae stage of development.

B) Blue mussels are the most important species for maintaining a clean ocean environment.

C) Because farmers are unwilling to wait for mussels to fully develop they often sacrifice a great deal of their potential crop as seed supply.

D) That wild settlement is not the most reliable method to farming blue mussels.

44

What is the primary purpose of the ninth paragraph?

A) Illustrate the way in which blue mussel development differs from other ocean life such as phytoplankton.

B) Review previously known information that has been utilized by the mussel farming industry for decades.

C) Provide an example of the insight the researchers have gained on aspects of mussel development.

D) Offer a comprehensive review of the developmental needs of mussels determined by the research team.

45

The stance that Brian Beal takes in the passage could best be described as

A) an environmentalist fighting for a species' survival.

B) a capitalist searching for the most efficient answer to a problem

C) an academic writing a book on a scientific matter for public consumption.

D) a scholar investigating a series of hypotheses.

46

As used in line 54, "transition" most nearly means

A) shift.

B) evolve.

C) modify.

D) alter.

47

The central idea of the passage is that

A) a more efficient aqua-farming approach for raising blue mussels would greatly benefit the mussel species, commercial farming productivity, and the marine environment.

B) if something is not done soon, it is likely that blue mussels will soon be extinct due to overconsumption by humans.

C) the larger a mussel is, the better it is at filter-feeding the environment around it.

D) the optimal conversion point between larvae development, where mussels attach to rope, to ocean pens is one question researchers are focused on.

Redesigned PSAT

1. Student Information

Your Name: _____
(Print)   Last   First   M.I.

Email Address: _____ Date: _____ / _____ / _____
(Print)   MM   DD   YYYY

Home Address: _____ Apartment No. _____
(Print)   Number and Street

_____
City   State   Zip Code

High School: _____ Class of: _____

2. Your Name

First 4 letters of last name				FIRST INIT	MID INIT
Ⓐ	Ⓐ	Ⓐ	Ⓐ	Ⓐ	Ⓐ
Ⓑ	Ⓑ	Ⓑ	Ⓑ	Ⓑ	Ⓑ
Ⓒ	Ⓒ	Ⓒ	Ⓒ	Ⓒ	Ⓒ
Ⓓ	Ⓓ	Ⓓ	Ⓓ	Ⓓ	Ⓓ
Ⓔ	Ⓔ	Ⓔ	Ⓔ	Ⓔ	Ⓔ
Ⓕ	Ⓕ	Ⓕ	Ⓕ	Ⓕ	Ⓕ
Ⓖ	Ⓖ	Ⓖ	Ⓖ	Ⓖ	Ⓖ
Ⓗ	Ⓗ	Ⓗ	Ⓗ	Ⓗ	Ⓗ
Ⓘ	Ⓘ	Ⓘ	Ⓘ	Ⓘ	Ⓘ
Ⓙ	Ⓙ	Ⓙ	Ⓙ	Ⓙ	Ⓙ
Ⓚ	Ⓚ	Ⓚ	Ⓚ	Ⓚ	Ⓚ
Ⓛ	Ⓛ	Ⓛ	Ⓛ	Ⓛ	Ⓛ
Ⓜ	Ⓜ	Ⓜ	Ⓜ	Ⓜ	Ⓜ
Ⓝ	Ⓝ	Ⓝ	Ⓝ	Ⓝ	Ⓝ
Ⓞ	Ⓞ	Ⓞ	Ⓞ	Ⓞ	Ⓞ
Ⓟ	Ⓟ	Ⓟ	Ⓟ	Ⓟ	Ⓟ
Ⓠ	Ⓠ	Ⓠ	Ⓠ	Ⓠ	Ⓠ
Ⓡ	Ⓡ	Ⓡ	Ⓡ	Ⓡ	Ⓡ
Ⓢ	Ⓢ	Ⓢ	Ⓢ	Ⓢ	Ⓢ
Ⓣ	Ⓣ	Ⓣ	Ⓣ	Ⓣ	Ⓣ
Ⓤ	Ⓤ	Ⓤ	Ⓤ	Ⓤ	Ⓤ
Ⓥ	Ⓥ	Ⓥ	Ⓥ	Ⓥ	Ⓥ
Ⓦ	Ⓦ	Ⓦ	Ⓦ	Ⓦ	Ⓦ
Ⓧ	Ⓧ	Ⓧ	Ⓧ	Ⓧ	Ⓧ
Ⓨ	Ⓨ	Ⓨ	Ⓨ	Ⓨ	Ⓨ
Ⓩ	Ⓩ	Ⓩ	Ⓩ	Ⓩ	Ⓩ

3. Phone Number

Area Code			Phone number						
⓪	⓪	⓪	⓪	⓪	⓪	⓪	⓪	⓪	⓪
①	①	①	①	①	①	①	①	①	①
②	②	②	②	②	②	②	②	②	②
③	③	③	③	③	③	③	③	③	③
④	④	④	④	④	④	④	④	④	④
⑤	⑤	⑤	⑤	⑤	⑤	⑤	⑤	⑤	⑤
⑥	⑥	⑥	⑥	⑥	⑥	⑥	⑥	⑥	⑥
⑦	⑦	⑦	⑦	⑦	⑦	⑦	⑦	⑦	⑦
⑧	⑧	⑧	⑧	⑧	⑧	⑧	⑧	⑧	⑧
⑨	⑨	⑨	⑨	⑨	⑨	⑨	⑨	⑨	⑨

Reading

SECTION 1

1. Ⓐ Ⓑ Ⓒ Ⓓ
2. Ⓐ Ⓑ Ⓒ Ⓓ
3. Ⓐ Ⓑ Ⓒ Ⓓ
4. Ⓐ Ⓑ Ⓒ Ⓓ
5. Ⓐ Ⓑ Ⓒ Ⓓ
6. Ⓐ Ⓑ Ⓒ Ⓓ
7. Ⓐ Ⓑ Ⓒ Ⓓ
8. Ⓐ Ⓑ Ⓒ Ⓓ
9. Ⓐ Ⓑ Ⓒ Ⓓ
10. Ⓐ Ⓑ Ⓒ Ⓓ

11. Ⓐ Ⓑ Ⓒ Ⓓ
12. Ⓐ Ⓑ Ⓒ Ⓓ
13. Ⓐ Ⓑ Ⓒ Ⓓ
14. Ⓐ Ⓑ Ⓒ Ⓓ
15. Ⓐ Ⓑ Ⓒ Ⓓ
16. Ⓐ Ⓑ Ⓒ Ⓓ
17. Ⓐ Ⓑ Ⓒ Ⓓ
18. Ⓐ Ⓑ Ⓒ Ⓓ
19. Ⓐ Ⓑ Ⓒ Ⓓ
20. Ⓐ Ⓑ Ⓒ Ⓓ

21. Ⓐ Ⓑ Ⓒ Ⓓ
22. Ⓐ Ⓑ Ⓒ Ⓓ
23. Ⓐ Ⓑ Ⓒ Ⓓ
24. Ⓐ Ⓑ Ⓒ Ⓓ
25. Ⓐ Ⓑ Ⓒ Ⓓ
26. Ⓐ Ⓑ Ⓒ Ⓓ
27. Ⓐ Ⓑ Ⓒ Ⓓ
28. Ⓐ Ⓑ Ⓒ Ⓓ
29. Ⓐ Ⓑ Ⓒ Ⓓ
30. Ⓐ Ⓑ Ⓒ Ⓓ

31. Ⓐ Ⓑ Ⓒ Ⓓ
32. Ⓐ Ⓑ Ⓒ Ⓓ
33. Ⓐ Ⓑ Ⓒ Ⓓ
34. Ⓐ Ⓑ Ⓒ Ⓓ
35. Ⓐ Ⓑ Ⓒ Ⓓ
36. Ⓐ Ⓑ Ⓒ Ⓓ
37. Ⓐ Ⓑ Ⓒ Ⓓ
38. Ⓐ Ⓑ Ⓒ Ⓓ
39. Ⓐ Ⓑ Ⓒ Ⓓ
40. Ⓐ Ⓑ Ⓒ Ⓓ

41. Ⓐ Ⓑ Ⓒ Ⓓ
42. Ⓐ Ⓑ Ⓒ Ⓓ
43. Ⓐ Ⓑ Ⓒ Ⓓ
44. Ⓐ Ⓑ Ⓒ Ⓓ
45. Ⓐ Ⓑ Ⓒ Ⓓ
46. Ⓐ Ⓑ Ⓒ Ⓓ
47. Ⓐ Ⓑ Ⓒ Ⓓ

Chapter 7
Reading Test
Drill 2: Answers
and Explanations

ANSWERS AND EXPLANATIONS

Section 1—Reading Test

1. **B** The second paragraph of the passage describes the need for men to *bring together* forces and *steer them...in such a way that they act together in a single thrust.* All forces should work together as a single force or unit, so in context the word *thrust* means something similar to "movement." Choices (A), (C), and (D) do not mean "movement," which leaves choice (B). *Direction* is the most similar word to "movement" and is, therefore, the best answer.

2. **A** Choice (A) captures the main idea of the passage and is reiterated in lines 57-61 *(Each man...he has.)*—that uniting together will result in a stronger whole. The author does state that *man's force and liberty are what he chiefly needs for his survival* and raises the question of *how can he put them into this collective effort without harming his own interest and neglecting the care he owes to himself.* However, the author never says that this is selfish or that *selfishness* is an *inherent quality* in man, so eliminate choice (B). Eliminate choice (C) because there is nothing in the passage to support that the group will never break its word. Choice (D) is incorrect because it introduces terms that are never discussed in the passage.

3. **C** The answer to the previous question is best support by choice (C) since these lines summarize the author's belief that when people unite together, they are stronger than when they remain separate. Choice (A) is incorrect because this sentence only discusses coming together but doesn't draw any conclusions about being stronger as the result of coming together. Choices (B) and (D) fail to discuss the strength benefit gained by coming together, so both answers should also be eliminated.

4. **D** Earlier in this sentence, the author writes that *although they may never have been explicitly stated*, the clauses of this contract were *tacitly accepted and recognized.* If the clauses were not clearly or directly stated, then they must have been accepted in an understood or implied manner, without being spoken. In context, the word *tacitly* means "understood" or "unspoken." Choices (A), (B), and (C) do not mean "understood" or "unspoken," which leaves choice (D). *Implicitly* is the most similar word to "understood" and "unspoken" and is, therefore, the best answer.

5. **A** In the first sentence of the passage, the author states that the human race has reached a point from where it *can't go on*, which is the natural state of humanity. The author goes on to propose a way to improve the natural state of humanity: uniting together, which is a socially evolved relationship. Therefore, choice (A) is the correct answer. Choice (B) is incorrect because *violence* and *mercy* are topics never discussed in the passage. Choice (C) is incorrect because the author never mentions any *desire to fit in*. Finally, choice (D) is incorrect because the narrative isn't about comparing the positive and negative aspects of the social contract; it's about why a social contract is imperative.

6. **D** The "forces" the author refers to are not actual *armies of men*, so eliminate choice (A). The author never mentions asserting physical power of someone nor does the author mention a group pressuring individuals to join it, so choices (B) and (C) are incorrect. By POE, choice (D) is left and is, therefore, the best answer.

7. **B** The author says in lines 41-45 *(Because each individual…everyone but himself.)* that individuals do give up their rights; however, there is more to uniting together than just giving up their rights (eliminate choice (A)). Whatever an individual gives to a group he gets back *(So he gains as much as he loses.)*, so the individual understands that he is sacrificing his rights for the good of the group. Therefore, choice (B) is the best answer. The author is encouraging people to work together, not fight against one another, so eliminate choice (C). Choice (D) contradicts the main idea of the passage since the author explicitly states in the three features (lines 41-62) that working together will result in not only better results for the whole community but also for each individual.

8. **C** Choices (A) and (B) are incorrect because the author never discusses *commercial exchange* or *becoming a slave.* The entire passage is about the author's desire to create a stronger civilized society by individuals willingly giving up their forces and liberties to the group, so choice (D) should be eliminated, making choice (C) the correct answer.

9. **D** The answer to this question should be in line with the answers to questions 2, 3, 5, 7, and 8. The central idea of the passage is that an individual will *gain as much as he loses* as when he does so the group is *jointly powerful enough to deal with the obstacles.* Therefore, the best answer is choice (D). Choices (A) and (C) are incorrect because the author never discusses *enslavement* or a *legal* contract. Choice (B) is counter to what the author says. Individuals are not being stripped of their liberties, rather individuals voluntarily gives up their liberties to form a stronger group.

10. **D** The sentence in question describes how *certain things* seem harmless *to us in the modern day* and that an emotional response to them is hardly even necessary, yet to many cultures these same things have traditionally caused *irrational fear.* Since emotion is hardly required, the word *warrant*, in context, means something similar to "requires." Choices (A), (B), and (C) do not mean "requires," which leaves choice (D). *Deserves* is the most similar word to "requires" and is, therefore, the best answer.

11. **C** Choice (A) should be eliminated because *Judas* is never mentioned in this passage (don't bring outside knowledge into the test. The answer will be supported by the provided text.). Choice (B) can be disproven by the passage: *As all official religious events were scheduled on a twelve moon year, the inclusion of a 13th moon proved very problematic for the monks.* However, this sentence as well as a previous sentence *(Also, the number 13 was highly inconvenient…when it came to the number of moon cycles in a year.)* offer reasons that the number 13 is unlucky and do support choice (C). Although choice (D) is mentioned in the text, it does not answer the question being asked—why is the number 13 unlucky, not a certain day of the week—and should be eliminated. Therefore, choice (C) is the correct answer.

12. **D** Choice (C) provides the best support for the previous answer. Choice (A) is incorrect because those lines support why the day Friday is consider unlucky, not the number 13. Choice (B) does not offer specific support for why the number 13 is unlucky, rather those lines provide information about the moon cycles. Since the previous answer was about 13 being an inconvenient astronomical occurrence, choice (D) should be eliminated because those lines are referring to Biblical, not astronomical, reasons, why 13 is an unlucky number. Choice (C) does provide the necessary support for the previous answer and is the correct answer.

13. **C** The only answer that can be supported by information from the text is choice (C). Choice (A) makes an assumption beyond the scope of the passage—paragraph 2 only states that in commercial sailing schedules *were set* around departing on Friday. There is no mention about "to this day." Choices (B) and (C) are incorrect since there is no reference to either one in the passage. Choice (C) is supported by the first sentence of paragraph 3 (*The fear of the number 13…than is the fear of Friday.*) and is the correct answer.

14. **A** The quote in the last paragraph by anthropologist Phillips Stevens, Jr. provides a nice summary of the passage since it discusses the fear of Friday the 13th by explaining the two fears that form it and discussing their origins, both of which stem from a religious event. Therefore, choice (A) is the best answer. Choice (B) is supported by the passage; however, it is only a detail and not the central idea expressed by the passage. Choices (C) and (D) do not summarize the central idea of the passage, nor can they be supported by text from the passage.

15. **A** The sentence in question describes how the combination of two superstitions (Friday and the number 13) has "set up" or "created" *one of the most well-known superstitions still in existence today*. In context, the word *constitutes* means something similar to "sets up." Choices (B), (C), and (D) do not mean "sets up," which leaves choice (A). *Establishes* is the most similar word to "sets up" and is, therefore, the best answer.

16. **B** Eliminate choice (A) because the author is not discussing what number is considered to be unlucky by Italians. Choice (C) is incorrect because is there no evidence about the author's personal opinion to suggest that her or she distrusts Italy. Finally, eliminate choice (D) because the author does not state that Italy is not aware of the biblical origins of this fear, just that they do not share this belief with other western, Christian cultures. The author uses the word *interestingly*, so he or she finds it curious that Italy, the "odd exception," does not agree with what is otherwise a widely shared belief. Therefore, the best answer is choice (B).

17. **B** In the third paragraph, the author states the fear of the number 13 is so common that "it has been given a name: *triskaidekaphobia*." The author states in the final paragraph that "The superstition of Friday the 13th has also been given a name due to the widespread belief in it: *paraskevidekatriaphobia*." Since the fears are so prevalent, there has been a need to have a specific name for these two fears. Therefore, choice (B) is the correct answer. There is no mention of these fears being *highly*

complex conditions (eliminate choice (A)) or that the author is providing the names of the phobias because he or she is concerned about the importance of others knowing the names (eliminate choice (C)). The author is not providing the scientific names to share little-known facts—the fears are very common and widespread—so eliminate choice (D). The best answer is choice (B).

18.   **A**   Check to see which of the answer choices are supported by information both in the passage and in the graph. While the fear of Friday the 13th is the combination of two fears, there is no evidence in the passage or in the graph to suggest it occurs at twice the rate of those singular fears. Choice (B) can be eliminated. While specific fears do occur in Western cultures, there is no evidence that these fears are unique to them, so choice (C) can be eliminated. According to the graph those 65 and older are least likely to have specific phobias, but there's no evidence that this has anything to do with their relationship to Western values. Therefore, choice (D) is incorrect. The passage states that *triskaidekaphobia* is a specific phobia, and specific phobias occur most often among those 50 to 64 years of age. (A) is correct.

19.   **A**   The correct answer must be mentioned in both passages. Use POE to check each answer. Only Passage 1 mentions the name of the captain of the *Mary Celeste* (eliminate choice (B)) and the date that the ship set sail (eliminate choice (C)). Only Passage 2 discusses the possible natural phenomenon behind the disappearance (the porousness of the cargo barrels), so choice (D) is incorrect. The author of Passage 1 states that the *Mary Celeste* was carrying *1,701 barrels of crude alcohol*. The author of Passage 2 states that *nine of the 1,701 alcohol cargo barrels were constructed of red oak*. Thus, choice (A) is correct.

20.   **A**   The author of Passage 1 states that other than some minimal damage, the ship was in *completely sailable condition* when it was found. Furthermore, *the cargo was mostly intact, there was a six-month supply of food and water, and there were no visible signs of panic, violence, or fire*. Therefore, the passage suggests that no identifiable reason can be given, based on what was found, for why the voyage could not have been completed (choice (A)). Passage 1 makes no reference as to whether or not women and children should be taken as passengers on expeditions (eliminate choice (B)). The passage is not suggesting that the reasons for abandoning the ship are meritless—just that no reason has ever been widely accepted and that any reason would be very difficult to prove (eliminate choice (C)). The passage also does not suggest that there is a lack of motivation to discover the true reason for the disappearance of the ship, so choice (D) is incorrect, making choice (A) the best answer.

21.   **B**   Only choice (B) provides the best evidence for the previous question since it contains information that the ship was found in *completely sailable condition*. Therefore, those who discovered the abandoned ship could find no identifiable reason that the crew could not have completed the voyage. Choice (A), (C), and (D) do not provide support for the answer to the previous question and should be eliminated.

22.   **A**   The author concludes the three questions with the comment *many reasons have been put forth but none has ever been widely accepted*. Thus, the author is emphasizing the mysterious nature of the ship's abandonment, which makes choice (A) the best answer. There is no reason to believe that the author thinks the historians are ignorant since the author's tone is neutral and there is no evidence in Passage 1 to support this choice (eliminate choice (B)). The author is not using the series of questions to make a general claim about the motivations of individuals or groups of people, rather the author wants to stress the uncertainty surrounding the disappearance of the ship's passengers and crew by listing possible scenarios. Choice (D) is incorrect because the author states in the last sentence of the passage that any of the reasons would be difficult to prove, so the author is not advocating that the *true* story needs to be determined since it's unlikely that it could be.

23.   **D**   The sentence in question states that the history of the *Mary Celeste* has *intrigued* historians and experts since 1872. Following this sentence, the author states that *many theories have been postulated regarding its abandonment*. The word *enigmatic* is describing history, and the history of the ship has *intrigued* these people. Since many theories have developed, the historians and experts are "puzzled" by the ships abandonment. Therefore, the word *enigmatic*, in context, means something similar to "puzzling." Choices (A) and (C) do not mean "puzzling" and should be eliminated. Though choice (B) is tempting (the historians are interested in the ship's history), choice (D) provides a closer match to "puzzling." These people find the history of the ship's abandonment more than just interesting; they find the history intriguing and have developed many theories to account for the abandonment. Thus, since *perplexing* is the most similar word to "puzzling" and captures the author intended meaning, choice (D) is the best answer.

24.   **C**   At the beginning of this sentence, the author of Passage 2 uses the phrase *in terms of the latter* to refer to the *ludicrous* theories that have been postulated regarding the ship's abandonment. One such ridiculous reason is that there were *giant squid attacks*. Therefore, the author uses the *giant squid* reference in order to provide an example of the *ludicrous* theories some have developed, making choice (C) the best answer. Eliminate choice (A) because the phrase is supporting, not contradicting, previous information in the passage. The author doesn't suggest that a giant squid attack a ship is a natural occurrence; the author presents that and the other theories as rather unlikely occurrences (eliminate choice (B)). Choice (D) is incorrect because the phrase referenced does not offer a detailed description.

25.   **C**   All the theories mentioned in the last sentence of this paragraph are theories the author believes to be absurd, so the author does not use the phrase "*did the crew mutiny itself*" to convey confusion or lost hope (eliminate choices (A) and (D)). The author may be mocking; however, the author is not mocking people who can't solve the mystery, so choice (B) is also incorrect. Since the author feels it is unlikely that any of these *ludicrous* theories are the reason for the ship's abandonment, the author used the phrase in parentheses to express his or her disbelief in this theory as a viable solution. Therefore, choice (C) is correct.

26. **B**   Prior to the sentence in question, the author states that alcoholic fumes could have easily escaped from barrels, and those fumes could have built up down in the hole. The author then states that if the pressure from the build up became great enough, the hatch doors would be forced to do something. If the pressure is building behind the hatch doors, the word *ajar*, in context, means something similar to "wide open." Choices (A), (C), and (D) do not mean "wide open," which leaves choice (B). *Open* does mean "wide open" and is, therefore, the best answer (choice (B)).

27. **D**   The author of Passage 2 states that in a case in which there was a fear of explosion on a ship, *it would be common to load into the lifeboat, tether it to the ship, and float a safe distance away until the risk of explosions appeared to abate.* The author of Passage 1 indicated that only the ship's lifeboat, navigational equipment, and many of the ship's papers were missing, yet the valuables of the passengers were still present. This provides strong support that the passengers on board the *Mary Celeste* intended to return to the ship. Therefore, choice (D) is the best answer. Choice (A) does not provide a reason as compelling as choice (D), so eliminate it. Choice (B) is asking a question and not providing support for Passage 2 author's reasoning, so eliminate it. Choice (C) does not address the fact that the passengers intended to return and cannot support the author's reasoning.

28. **C**   Use POE and focus on one passage at a time. Start with Passage 1. The central idea of Passage 1 is to describe the unsolved mystery of the *Mary Celeste*. Eliminate choice (B) since the central idea of Passage 1 is not to discuss the individuals lost at sea, and eliminate choice (D) because Passage 2, not Passage 1, discusses the cargo-related cause of the ship's abandonment. The central idea of Passage 2 is to describe a likely scenario, related to the cargo onboard, that could account for the ship's abandonment. Compare choices (A) and (C) since those are the two choices remaining. Choice (A) is incorrect because the central idea of Passage 2 is not to discuss various ways the ship may have been abandoned but rather to discuss one specific way. Choice (C) accurately expresses the central idea of Passage 2. Therefore, choice (C) is the answer that best explains the differences between the two passages.

29. **C**   The passage discusses the function and purpose of the field of paleopathology and reviews factual information of three diseases related to that field. The author is positive regarding the field of paleoanthropology at the end of the passage and is neutrally toned during the rest of it. Anything that goes against the idea of the author being positive or neutral can be eliminated, such as choice (B) *judgmental*. Although the author does present a great deal of information she does so in a very accessible way, rather than an overly educated or ostentatious way, so eliminate choice (A) *pedantic*. Choice (D) does not make sense with this passage; for the author to be *conciliatory* she would have to be appeasing or apologizing for something, and there is no indication of that in the passage. The best answer is choice (C) *descriptive*. The author gives us a great deal of descriptive detail on a field and what it studies.

30.   **D**   The first paragraph is introducing the topic of the passage, paleopathology. It states that without clear indications of disease on ancient human remains, it is difficult to determine the cause of death with certainty. Choice (A) is off-topic; the author is only refers to determining cause of death based on natural causes. Choice (B) references *luckily* from the passage, stating that paleopathologists are themselves lucky. This is deceptive, as the passage says *luckily for paleopathologists*, not that they are in fact lucky, so eliminate choice (B). Choice (C) is not supported by the text of the passage since at no point does the author mention any diseases other than paleopathological ones. Choice (D) correctly states that the cause of death can't be determined in the case of some remains, which is supported by the paragraph's emphasis that *unless there are clear signs of how death…occurred*, a cause of death may be impossible to determine. Therefore, choice (D) is the best answer.

31.   **C**   The sentence is discussing the symptoms of leprosy and the breakdown of *the skin and nerve cells*. The following sentence states that injuries occur because of the *lack of pain reception*. So the loss that is occurring here is the ability to feel or sense pain. Therefore, *sensation* must mean feeling or pain reception. Choices (A), (B), and (D) all refer to a different use of the word sensation than feeling, so they can be eliminated. This leaves choice (C), which best matches the meaning of feeling.

32.   **D**   The sentence reads *tuberculosis was most likely first contracted from ingesting infected animal products*. The following sentence goes on the say *once a human is infected….* Therefore, *contracted* most closely matches the meaning of *infected* in the following sentence. Choices (A), (B), and (C) do match the meaning of *infected*, so they cannot be the correct meaning of the word *contracted* in this context. The best match is choice (D) *caught*, which can be used synonymously with the word infected when regarding infections and diseases.

33.   **B**   The sixth paragraph introduces the disease tuberculosis and provides background information on the disease. In order to answer this question, compare the answer choices against the information provided in the paragraph and use POE for answer choices that do not match. Choice (A) refers to tuberculosis in animals and humans. Although both animals and humans are mentioned, we are only told about the spread of the disease between the two and not the distinction between the disease in them. Eliminate choice (A). Choice (B) refers to tuberculosis and leprosy. In the first sentence of the paragraph, the author mentions both by comparing tuberculosis to leprosy and noting how they differ. Therefore, choice (B) is strongly supported by the paragraph. Choice (C) is incorrect as it references syphilis, which has not yet been discussed in detail yet and is not mentioned in this paragraph at all. Knee and hip joints and the spine are not mentioned in this paragraph but the following one. In that paragraph they are treated as a connected list of skeletal areas affected by tuberculosis and are not contrasted to one another. The best answer for this question is choice (B).

34.   **B**   In this context, the word *unique* is used to mean that something is specific to tuberculosis. That something is the fact that DNA testing can be used to determine the presence of tuberculosis in human remains. Since this is specific to tuberculosis, it can be inferred that DNA testing cannot be used in the same manner for other paleopathological diseases. Answer choice (A) is extreme and unsupported by the passage; tuberculosis itself is not unique, just the fact that it can be tested for through DNA. Eliminate choice (A). Choice (B) is supported by the text of the passage as that is

what the phrase implies. The passage does not say what the most commonly found paleopathological disease is, so get rid of choice (C). This statement is about tuberculosis, not about syphilis, so get rid of choice (D) as well. The best answer is choice (B).

35.   **A**   There is a great deal of information regarding syphilis, so the best approach to this question is POE. Choice (A) states that it is easier to identify syphilis from indications on human remains than other paleopathological diseases, which is supported by the opening sentence of the seventh paragraph. Choice (B) refers to curing syphilis, which is not mentioned in the passage. It also states no symptoms appear on the skeleton if syphilis is treated and cured by the latent period, but the passage says that skeletal changes occur immediately after infection. So get rid of choice (B). Choice (C) references how long it takes syphilis to progress compared to tuberculosis. Since we are given a large time range for the progress of both diseases in the passage, it cannot be determined which one is faster than the other as the timing can vary for both. Since choice (C) is not supported by the passage, eliminate it. Choice (D) refers to only three stages of syphilis when the passage states that there are four: *primary, secondary, latent, and tertiary.* So choice (D) cannot be correct. The best answer is choice (A).

35.   **C**   Since the correct answer to the previous question is that syphilis is more easily identifiable from human remains than other diseases, the answer will be a line that contains that information in it. The only line that does this is choice (C), the first sentence of the seventh paragraph. According to that sentence, syphilis is the *most contagious and deadly, and the most clearly marked on skeletal remains.* Choice (A) discusses the symptoms of the first three stages, not the indicators on the skeleton. Choice (B) refers to the timing of the indications on the skeleton, not how clearly they appear as compared to other diseases. Choice (D) refers only to the non-skeletal symptoms of the tertiary stage of syphilis, so it is irrelevant. The best answer here is choice (C).

36.   **A**   Read the question carefully! The questions asks what can be inferred based on information in both the passage and the graphic. Since the graphic presents data on leprosy only, eliminate answer choices based on what doesn't match the information in the passage. The passage states that *leprosy is not highly contagious.* Based on that fact, choices (C) and (D) can be eliminated since they both incorrectly state that leprosy has a high contagion rate. Now compare choices (A) and (B). Both are focused on the United States, which currently does not experience any rate of leprosy. Since it would be impossible to decrease from a rate of 0, choice (B) does not make sense. The best answer is choice (A).

37.   **C**   In order to answer this question, begin by reading the answer choices and eliminating anything that can be supported by the passage. Choice (A) refers to tuberculosis and leprosy both being spread through infected particles released in the air. In the fourth paragraph, the passage states that leprosy can be spread through *ejected mucous being released into the environment.* In the fifth paragraph, the passage states that tuberculosis can be spread through *releasing infected mucous into the air while when coughing.* Since choice (A) is supported by the passage, it cannot be the answer. The only disease in the passage that is said to have stages is syphilis, not leprosy or tuberculosis. This supports choice (B); therefore, it cannot be the answer either. The passage states that a

symptom of leprosy is the breakdown of the skin and that symptoms of the primary and secondary stages of syphilis are ulcerations and rash. These symptoms support choice (D), so it can be eliminated as well. All three diseases affect the bone in some way, which is why they are considered paleopathological diseases. This fact makes (C) look like a well-supported answer that can be eliminated, but read very carefully. Choice (C) refers to bone marrow specifically, not just bone. Leprosy and syphilis both affect bone marrow, but tuberculosis affects the *spongy bone….cancellous tissue*. Because it is not the marrow that is affected in all three diseases, choice (C) is best answer.

38. **B** The quote in the second paragraph provides background information on the blue mussel, especially the beneficial role they play in the environment. Therefore, the answer will likely be connected to the positive role of mussels. Since this quote only discusses mussels, and not the people studying them, it does not indicate anything about a scientist. Eliminate choice (D). This quote is only informative and does not contain any reference to human behavior, let alone a change to that behavior, so choice (C) cannot be the correct answer. Later in the passage it discusses the farming of blue mussels due to their popularity as a food item, so choice (A) is also incorrect. Commercial farming raises mussels to sell, not to help the environment. Choice (B) refers to the important role played by mussels and accounts for the purpose of giving the reader this background information as the reader may not be aware of it. Choice (B) is the best answer.

39. **D** The only information provided on the culture tanks is that when grown in them mussels are *protected from storms and predators*. Choices (A), (B), and (C) all contain deceptive language from the passage. In the same paragraph it states that mussels can also be grown in the wild OR culture tanks, so get rid of Choice (C). Maturity is also mentioned in the same paragraph, but in relation to ocean pens rather than culture tanks. So get rid of choice (B) as well. The following paragraph discusses the size of mussels, but does not say that is why they are grown in culture tanks, so eliminate choice (A). The only choice that fits with protecting the mussels is choice (D).

40. **C** This paragraph is discussing the process of cultivating, or growing, young mussels. The sentence says that mussels are *moved into ocean pens to mature* after they have *reached a certain size*. This sentence is about the growth of mussels, so the word *mature* means growth in this context. As choices (A), (B), and (D) do not match this meaning of the word mature, the only possible answer is choice (C).

41. **C** This is a very open-ended question, so take each answer choice one at a time. Choice (A) contains extreme language, stating that researchers would not be interested in mussels if it weren't for their commercial importance. However, at the beginning of the passage the environmental importance of the mussels is discussed in a quote made by a researcher. Since there is evidence of another interest in mussels and no evidence that commercial farming is the most important aspect of mussels, eliminate choice (A). Choice (B) also contains extreme language, discussing how *mussels grow best*. The passage is discussing the research being conducted on growing mussels, and there is no evidence that a "best" method has been discovered. Choice (B) is not correct. In the third paragraph the author says that *many creatures—especially humans—enjoy eating blue mussels*, which clearly supports answer choice (C). In the eighth paragraph the passage describes mussels as *swimming for*

their first few weeks of life, which would indicate that they do not immediately adhere to an object after birth as in choice (D). The correct answer is choice (C).

42. **B** The correct answer to the previous question is that mussels have multiple natural predators. In the third paragraph the author says that *many creatures—especially humans--enjoy eating blue mussels*, which clearly supports that answer. Choice (B) correctly identifies this line as the best support for the answer to the previous question. The remaining answer choices do not offer line references that support the answer to the previous question. Choice (A) discusses the improvement of commercial prospects for mussels, choice (C) discusses the use of pens for best growing practices, and choice (D) discusses how mussels attach to objects. Therefore, the best answer is choice (B).

43. **D** The passage states that Beal and a team from the two institutions listed in the question are *investigating the growing conditions and practices that will reliably yield healthy and plentiful blue mussels*. The passage then goes on to quote Beal as referring to *our goal*, which is to develop methods to enhance consistent quantities of mussels. He states that currently *mussel farmers rely on wild settlement, which can be very spotty from year to year and from place to place*. The assumption indicated here is that wild settlement is not the most consistent method for raising mussels, and the use of the phrase "our goal" indicates this belief is true for the whole group. The best answer that matches this information is choice (D), that wild settlement is not the most reliable method for farming mussels. Choice (C) is not supported by the passage as the behavior of the farmers is not discussed, only the current farming practices. Choice (B) refers to the environmental aspect of mussels, which was discussed only by Beal earlier in the passage. Choice (A) refers to the mussels' preference for rope as an adherence object, which is never stated. Choice (D) is the best answer.

44. **C** Paragraph nine reviews the variables that lead to healthy mussel growth and behavior identified by Beal and his team. The following paragraph then discusses that *Beal's team plans to use what they learn about blue mussel development to optimize how many and how well larvae secure themselves to rope used in aquaculture*. The information presented in paragraph nine constitutes at least some of what Beal's team has learned. Choice (A) is deceptive as the paragraph does not compare mussels to phytoplankton; it states that mussels eat phytoplankton. Choice (B) does not make sense as the farming industry is not discussed in these paragraphs. Choice (D) is extreme due to the word *comprehensive*: this is a short list of findings the research team has discovered. By comparison, choice (C) refers to the findings as an example of what the researchers have found, making it the best answer. Therefore, the correct answer is choice (C).

45. **D** Brian Beal is the main researcher focused on in the passage. He is quoted several times as giving background information on mussels and describing the research questions he and his team studies and the purpose of those questions. Although he does mention the environmental benefits of mussels, his research is dedicated to helping enhance consistent commercial farming of mussels. Although this is partly to help keep mussels from being over-harvested, choice (A) is too limited in its focus on the environment. Although Beal is searching for an efficient way to farm mussels consistently, he himself is not the one who intends to profit. This makes the use of *capitalist* in choice (B)

incorrect. Beal is an *academic*, but he is studying mussels to solve a problem, not to write a book on them, so choice (C) is not correct. As the passage indicates Beal and his team are *conducting field studies to examine the effects of stocking densities on mussel growth and survival*, which best matches a scholar testing hypotheses. Therefore, the best answer is choice (D).

46. **A** This sentence is discussing the timing of transitioning mussels into ocean pens, which would mean a physical movement of the mussels into the pens. The closest meaning of *transition* is physical movement. Choices (B), (C), and (D) are all closer in meaning to "change" than to "movement," so they are all incorrect. The only choice that matches the meaning of "movement" is *shift*, making choice (A) the correct answer.

47. **A** This passage discusses blue mussels and their various values and the issues that have been experienced commercially farming them. It reviews the findings of a research team attempting to increase the consistency of mussel farming practices. Only choice (A) contains a general statement that addresses these aspects of the passage. Choice (B) is too limited as it only touches on the consumption of mussels. Choice (C) is also too limited as it only refers to the ability of mussels to filter feed and makes a claim that is not substantiated in the passage. The information in choice (D) is correct, but it only discusses a single research question the team in the passage is focused on as opposed to the central idea of the entire passage. Therefore, choice (A) is the best answer.

Part III
Writing and Language Test

Chapter 8
Writing and
Language Test
Drill 1

Writing and Language Test

35 MINUTES, 44 QUESTIONS

Turn to Section 2 of your answer sheet to answer the questions in this section.

Questions 1–11 are based on the following passage.

The Economics of the Environment

As each of us tries to be more environmentally conscious, we have to consider certain **1** trade offs. Many of us would love, for instance, to wire our homes for solar electricity, but sometimes it's just not in the budget. We'd love to drive alternative-fuel cars, like those with hydrogen fuel-cells or electric engines, but we may not be able to afford such cars. **2** It would be great to buy sustainably grown vegetables or meats, but sometimes **3** it's just too expensive.

1

Which of the following alternatives to the underlined portion would be LEAST acceptable?
A) concessions
B) compromises
C) allowances
D) swaps

2

A) NO CHANGE
B) We are loving
C) We want to
D) We'd love

3

A) NO CHANGE
B) they're
C) its
D) one's

4 Considerations like these occupy many environmentally conscious people, and the answers are by no means simple. On a much larger scale, these considerations occupy environmental economists.

5 Big questions are like the bread and butter for economists all kinds. First of all, economics doesn't have an obvious relationship to the environment. Second of all, where economics *does* have a relationship to the environment, that relationship seems to be one of conflict rather than conservation. How, we might expect an economist to ask, can a resource be implemented efficiently and with the greatest possible profit margin? There seems to be more emphasis here on **6** how *used* rather than *conserved* environmental resources can be.

4

Which of the following would provide the best transition between the initial discussion in the paragraph and the idea presented in the last line of the paragraph?

A) NO CHANGE

B) Sometimes organic produce can cost twice as much as traditionally farmed produce.

C) Microeconomics is on a small scale; macroeconomics is on a large one.

D) Economists can work in a wide variety of fields and specializations.

5

Which of the following would provide the best introduction to this paragraph?

A) NO CHANGE

B) The job title might seem like a contradiction in terms.

C) There are a few things about environmental economists that are interesting.

D) What are a few things that environmental economists do?

6

A) NO CHANGE

B) conservation rather than usage in the environmental-resource department.

C) how environmental resources can be used rather than conserved.

D) how some of the environment's riches that are used can be conserved.

However, environmental economists cannot be categorized so easily. **7** While they are often interested in the workings of the market, they are interested in finding ways that environmental conservation can work effectively within that market. For **8** instance: if a company is allowed to pollute freely by dumping its waste into a nearby river, that act has negative consequences because it damages other potential market activities: tourist kayaking, camping, clean water, etc. For environmental economists, in fact, pollution is seen as an *anti*-market practice because **9** they have the same selfish effect of cornering the market as do monopolies.

7

Which of the following alternatives to the underlined portion would be LEAST acceptable?

A) Although

B) Whereas

C) Because

D) Though

8

A) NO CHANGE

B) instance, if

C) instance; if

D) instance if:

9

A) NO CHANGE

B) it has

C) the two things have

D) its inefficiency and waste have

In this sense, environmental economists occupy [10] a middle-ground between hardcore environmentalists and those who think people should be free to pollute as much as they want. In order for pollution to come down to absolute non-existence, the economy would essentially have to shut down. If people were not regulated at all, the consequences (economic and otherwise) could be similarly dire. As a result, environmental economists are in the business of trying to find economically and environmentally reasonable amounts of pollution and to advise businesses and politicians accordingly. [11] As we continue to see changes in how the world thinks about protecting the environment, we will see more of the counterintuitive but absolutely essential work of environmental economists.

10

A) NO CHANGE

B) a middle-ground, between hardcore environmentalists, and those who think people should be free to pollute as much as they want.

C) a middle-ground, between hardcore environmentalists, and those who think people should be free to pollute, as much as they want.

D) a middle-ground between hardcore environmentalists, and those who think people should be free to pollute, as much as they want.

11

The author is considering rewriting the previous sentence as follows:

> As a result, environmental economists are in the business of trying to advise businesses and politicians accordingly.

Should the sentence be kept as it is or rewritten?

A) Kept as is, because the sentence does not have sufficient information otherwise.

B) Kept as is, because the sentence sounds more formal without the deletions.

C) Rewritten, because the sentence contains redundant information as written.

D) Rewritten, because the sentence as written is irrelevant to the paragraph as a whole.

Questions 12–22 are based on the following passage.

The Runway to Civil Rights

[1]

12 Because it does mark a kind of leap forward for civil rights, the end of the Civil War was by no means the end of cruel treatment toward African Americans in the United States. In 1896, the U.S. Supreme Court ruled in favor of the practice of what was called "separate but equal" treatment for the races in the United States. **13** The fact of the matter was that things were separate but certainly not equal. African Americans were no longer enslaved, but they were still treated like second-class citizens. Even the anti-lynching laws, which **14** punish the mob killings of African Americans that had been rampant and unpunished since the 1860s, did not appear until the 1940s.

[2]

For the early part of the twentieth century, another manifestation of this legal segregation was in the military. Black and white men could not serve in the same companies, and **15** in particular they were barred from assuming certain military positions. For example, during World War I, **16** sometimes called "The Great War," there was not a single African American pilot in the entire air force.

12

A) NO CHANGE
B) It does
C) While it does
D) Really, it does

13

Which of the following would provide the most detailed support for the claim made in the previous sentence?

A) The case started in Louisiana and went all the way to the Supreme Court!
B) The ruling was not to be overturned until *Brown v. Board of Education* in 1954.
C) The defendant in the case was Homer Plessy, who was considered "black" because he had one African-American great grandparent.
D) Train cars, bathrooms, hotels, even water fountains were marked "White" and "Colored."

14

A) NO CHANGE
B) had punished
C) were punishing
D) punished

15

A) NO CHANGE
B) those in particular
C) black men in particular
D) in particular some

16

Which of the following best maintains the focus of this sentence?

A) NO CHANGE
B) a war fought in large part in the air,
C) which the U.S. joined kind of late,
D) during which President Woodrow Wilson declared war on Germany,

[3]

The Civil Rights decade—the era of **17** Martin Luther King and Malcolm X—is really considered the 1960s. However, that era would not have been possible without the bravery of African American soldiers **18** who fought valiantly in World War II. Radio comedian Jack Benny spoke for many Americans when he said, "When the black man's fight for equal rights and fair play became an issue after the war, I would no longer allow Rochester [a black character on his show] to say or do anything that an audience would consider degrading to the dignity of a modern Afro-American." The bravery of the Tuskegee Airmen and others brought the humanity and patriotism of African Americans to **19** our attention. Even though white Americans should've been much more welcoming much earlier, **20** the Tuskegee Airmen overwhelmed prejudice and led to some real changes.

17
A) NO CHANGE
B) Martin Luther King and Malcolm X, is
C) Martin Luther King, and Malcolm X—is
D) Martin Luther King—and Malcolm X—is

18
A) NO CHANGE
B) who fought with vim and vigor
C) who showed their true guts
D) DELETE the underlined portion.

19
A) NO CHANGE
B) the nation's
C) the national people's
D) people's

20
Which of the following would best conclude this paragraph by restating its main idea?
A) NO CHANGE
B) The Tuskegee Airmen fought hard whether anyone knew it or not.
C) The military is now integrated, and it has been for a while.
D) Prejudice still exists in many forms in the United States today.

[4]

After twenty years of protest, African-American leaders finally began to break down some of this military segregation. In 1939, Appropriations Bill Public Law 18 was passed, allotting some military funding for African American pilots. In time, technical training was available to qualified pilots of all races, and programs like that of Tuskegee, an all-black university in Alabama, came to a new national prominence. With the advanced training they received at Tuskegee, a new crop of pilots, known as the Tuskegee Airmen, were given **21** there rightful place in the Allied victory in the Second World War. **22**

21

A) NO CHANGE
B) they're
C) their
D) DELETE the underlined portion.

22

The best placement for paragraph 4 would be
A) where it is now.
B) before paragraph 1.
C) before paragraph 2.
D) before paragraph 3.

Questions 23–33 are based on the following passage.

Faces Made for Radio

Critics and historians typically set 1953 as the birth year for the TV revolution in the United States. **23** Between 1950 and 1955, the number of households that owned a TV grew a staggering amount, **24** from 4% to 12% of all American households. As a result, television programs (like Jack Benny's or Sid Caesar's) became part of the national conversation.

23

Which of the following maintains the focus of this paragraph and accurate information based on the chart?

A) NO CHANGE

B) From 1950 to 1975,

C) After 1980,

D) Since 2000,

24

Which of the following maintains the focus of this paragraph and accurate information based on the chart?

A) NO CHANGE

B) though after 1965, pretty much everyone had a TV.

C) from a tenth to about two-thirds of all American households.

D) much like cable grew between 1970 and 1975.

Television Set Ownership											
Estimated total number of TV households: 100,800,000											
	1950	1955	1960	1965	1970	1975	1980	1985	1990	1995	2000
% of total households:											
TV households	10	67	87	94	96	97	98	98	98	98	98
% of TV households:											
Multi-set	—	4	12	22	35	43	50	57	65	71	76
Color	—	—	—	7	41	74	83	91	98	99	99
VCR	—	—	—	—	—	—	—	14	66	79	85
Remote Control	—	—	—	—	—	—	—	29	77	91	95
Wired pay cable	—	—	—	—	—	—	—	26	29	28	32
Wired cable	—	—	—	—	7	12	20	43	56	63	68

This birth year doesn't tell the whole story, however. TV did not emerge out of the blue, and the three big stations— **25** NBC, CBS, and also ABC—preexisted TV by a long shot. All three already existed as radio stations throughout the 1930s and **26** 1940s; the only change was that ABC used to be known as "NBC Red." **27** In addition, many of the shows on early television were simply visual adaptations of radio plays that had gained significant followings in the previous decades.

25

A) NO CHANGE
B) NBC, CBS, and ABC
C) NBC, CBS, ABC
D) NBC-CBS-ABC

26

Which of the following alternatives to the underlined portion would NOT be acceptable?
A) 1940s, the only
B) 1940s—the only
C) 1940s. The only
D) 1940s: the only

27

A) NO CHANGE
B) Anyway,
C) Meanwhile,
D) For all that,

This transition period is fascinating because it provides a **28** concrete instance of how shifts in media actually happen. Although the narrative structures and scripts could often be lifted from radio directly, the visual aspects of TV were more complex than many radio performers anticipated. One of the biggest problems was that while radio comedians' *voices* may not have aged, their faces did, and many comedians were out of work because their images could not properly align with **29** the expectations of the viewer. Jim and Marian Jordan, the creators and stars of *Fibber McGee and Molly,* had no choice in the matter: they sold the identities of the characters in the 1940s when the getting was good, and the network replaced **30** them. With younger actors as soon as the show went to TV.

28

Which of the following alternatives to the underlined portion would be LEAST acceptable?

A) tangible

B) definitive

C) hard

D) substantial

29

A) NO CHANGE

B) the expectations of the viewers.

C) the expectation of the viewer.

D) the expectation of the viewer's.

30

A) NO CHANGE

B) them; with

C) them, with

D) them with

The shift to television had some positive social impact as well. Although the voices on the radio may have been racially and ethnically diverse, the same could not be said for the actors. The practice of minstrelsy, white actors mimicking and mocking the voices of African-Americans, was rampant in the radio era. However, when shows like *The Beulah Show*, [31] who's main character was an African-American woman, came to television, no audience would stand the incongruity between sight and sound. As a result, many of the firsts for non-white actors in show business came during the television era [32] when the new medium forced network executives to change with the times.

There's no telling what our own era's shift will bring, or whether that shift will be so [33] nuts. Still, as much as we think we understand the mediascape in which we live, that golden year of 1953 shows us that there may be more to a simple change of medium than we think.

[31]

A) NO CHANGE

B) who is

C) whose

D) their

[32]

Which of the following would provide the most effective conclusion to this paragraph?

A) NO CHANGE

B) though many radio programs would last into the early 1960s.

C) as many white actors were able to handle the transition.

D) despite the obvious lack of non-white talent in the cinema.

[33]

A) NO CHANGE

B) radical.

C) off the wall.

D) crazy.

Questions 34–44 are based on the following passage.

Taking the Express Microbiome Downtown

Anyone who has ever ridden the subway in New York knows that it can be a mysterious and diverse place. People from **34** all walks of life ride the subway, and many have different ideas about what should and shouldn't be done there. If you have food, should you eat it on the subway? Should you sit or stand? **35** I guess it depends: how far are you going to ride?

34

A) NO CHANGE

B) all of life's walks

C) all lives of walking

D) walking all our lives

35

Which of the following would best maintain the style and focus of this paragraph?

A) NO CHANGE

B) Should you hold onto the railings, or is it best to touch nothing at all?

C) How much does it cost to ride the subway versus taking the bus?

D) Does the subway run twenty-four hours a day, seven days a week?

These behavioral questions may never be settled, and there may never be a way to know who is riding next to you. In a recent study, however, a team of scientists [36] have discovered "who" is riding alongside you on the microbial level. [37] A compiled team of researchers led by Christopher Mason, a data geneticist at Weill Cornell Medical College in Manhattan. Mason's team went to all 468 of the stops on the New York subway and the Staten Island Railway, and they swabbed whatever they could find: [38] pretty gross work for most laypeople. They took the swabs back to the lab to discover what life was like on the microbial level in New York's train system.

"The subway kind of looks like skin," said Christopher Mason, by which he meant that most of the bacteria that live on human skin also live on the [39] trains from people's skin. This makes sense, as all the food particles from what those residents like to eat. No matter how clean you are, your food leaves a trail! [40] Living inside the subway, researchers found traces of mozzarella, chickpeas, and just about anything else you can name.

36

A) NO CHANGE
B) are discovering
C) has discovered
D) was discovered

37

A) NO CHANGE
B) Christopher Mason led a research team, a geneticist at Weill Cornell Medical College in Manhattan, with the data.
C) The data were compiled by a research team of Christopher Mason and the Weill Cornell Medical College of Manhattan.
D) A team of researchers led by Christopher Mason, a geneticist at Weill Cornell Medical College in Manhattan, compiled the data.

38

Which of the following would most effectively complete the sentence by providing specific support for the idea presented in the first part of the sentence?
A) NO CHANGE
B) their methods were scientifically sound.
C) there's a lot of disgusting stuff to swab in a subway station.
D) ticket machines, handrails, garbage cans, and seats.

39

A) NO CHANGE
B) trains from homo sapiens.
C) trains.
D) things.

40

A) NO CHANGE
B) In running DNA scans,
C) Fresh off of people's pizza and falafel,
D) Responsible for the subway's foul odor,

The researchers also turned up some bizarre findings. **41** They found traces of the diseases anthrax and plague, but the cells were found to be totally dead. Then, perhaps most curious of all, the researchers found nearly 1,688 organisms or molecules they couldn't identify, quite an odd **42** compliment to the certainty of all the other research. This has left a long and curious path for the researchers to travel and could lead to a new understanding of New York City's **43** diversity, which is some of the most in the world.

In fact, this seemingly frivolous study could have all kinds of future applications. As the study itself claims, "This baseline metagenomic map of NYC could help long-term disease surveillance, bioterrorism threat mitigation, and health management in the built environment of cities." In other words, understanding how a place works on the cellular level may explain **44** the human level. This is a curious study, but it provides an important reminder that the world around us is much more complex than we could ever acknowledge.

41

A) NO CHANGE

B) They found traces of the diseases anthrax and plague, but they were all totally dead.

C) Anthrax and plague were among the traces of disease that they found, but all of them were dead.

D) They were mostly dead, but anthrax and plague were among some of the traces of disease found.

42

A) NO CHANGE

B) complimentary

C) complement

D) complementary

43

The writer wants to add an idea that will emphasize how the new findings will add information for which previous surveys and studies could not account. Which of the following would most effectively add that information?

A) NO CHANGE

B) diversity that the census simply can't capture.

C) diversity, which is economic as well as racial.

D) diversity that spreads across all five of its boroughs.

44

A) NO CHANGE

B) the level of humans.

C) its workings on the level that humans occupy.

D) how it does so on the human level.

Redesigned PSAT

1. Student Information

Your Name: _____
(Print)   Last   First   M.I.

Email Address: _____ Date: _____ / _____ / _____
(Print)   MM   DD   YYYY

Home Address: _____ Apartment No. _____
(Print)   Number and Street

_____
            City   State   Zip Code

High School: _____ Class of: _____

2. Your Name

First 4 letters of last name				FIRST INIT	MID INIT
Ⓐ	Ⓐ	Ⓐ	Ⓐ	Ⓐ	Ⓐ
Ⓑ	Ⓑ	Ⓑ	Ⓑ	Ⓑ	Ⓑ
Ⓒ	Ⓒ	Ⓒ	Ⓒ	Ⓒ	Ⓒ
Ⓓ	Ⓓ	Ⓓ	Ⓓ	Ⓓ	Ⓓ
Ⓔ	Ⓔ	Ⓔ	Ⓔ	Ⓔ	Ⓔ
Ⓕ	Ⓕ	Ⓕ	Ⓕ	Ⓕ	Ⓕ
Ⓖ	Ⓖ	Ⓖ	Ⓖ	Ⓖ	Ⓖ
Ⓗ	Ⓗ	Ⓗ	Ⓗ	Ⓗ	Ⓗ
Ⓘ	Ⓘ	Ⓘ	Ⓘ	Ⓘ	Ⓘ
Ⓙ	Ⓙ	Ⓙ	Ⓙ	Ⓙ	Ⓙ
Ⓚ	Ⓚ	Ⓚ	Ⓚ	Ⓚ	Ⓚ
Ⓛ	Ⓛ	Ⓛ	Ⓛ	Ⓛ	Ⓛ
Ⓜ	Ⓜ	Ⓜ	Ⓜ	Ⓜ	Ⓜ
Ⓝ	Ⓝ	Ⓝ	Ⓝ	Ⓝ	Ⓝ
Ⓞ	Ⓞ	Ⓞ	Ⓞ	Ⓞ	Ⓞ
Ⓟ	Ⓟ	Ⓟ	Ⓟ	Ⓟ	Ⓟ
Ⓠ	Ⓠ	Ⓠ	Ⓠ	Ⓠ	Ⓠ
Ⓡ	Ⓡ	Ⓡ	Ⓡ	Ⓡ	Ⓡ
Ⓢ	Ⓢ	Ⓢ	Ⓢ	Ⓢ	Ⓢ
Ⓣ	Ⓣ	Ⓣ	Ⓣ	Ⓣ	Ⓣ
Ⓤ	Ⓤ	Ⓤ	Ⓤ	Ⓤ	Ⓤ
Ⓥ	Ⓥ	Ⓥ	Ⓥ	Ⓥ	Ⓥ
Ⓦ	Ⓦ	Ⓦ	Ⓦ	Ⓦ	Ⓦ
Ⓧ	Ⓧ	Ⓧ	Ⓧ	Ⓧ	Ⓧ
Ⓨ	Ⓨ	Ⓨ	Ⓨ	Ⓨ	Ⓨ
Ⓩ	Ⓩ	Ⓩ	Ⓩ	Ⓩ	Ⓩ

3. Phone Number

Area Code			Phone number						
⓪	⓪	⓪	⓪	⓪	⓪	⓪	⓪	⓪	⓪
①	①	①	①	①	①	①	①	①	①
②	②	②	②	②	②	②	②	②	②
③	③	③	③	③	③	③	③	③	③
④	④	④	④	④	④	④	④	④	④
⑤	⑤	⑤	⑤	⑤	⑤	⑤	⑤	⑤	⑤
⑥	⑥	⑥	⑥	⑥	⑥	⑥	⑥	⑥	⑥
⑦	⑦	⑦	⑦	⑦	⑦	⑦	⑦	⑦	⑦
⑧	⑧	⑧	⑧	⑧	⑧	⑧	⑧	⑧	⑧
⑨	⑨	⑨	⑨	⑨	⑨	⑨	⑨	⑨	⑨

Writing & Language

SECTION 2

1. Ⓐ Ⓑ Ⓒ Ⓓ
2. Ⓐ Ⓑ Ⓒ Ⓓ
3. Ⓐ Ⓑ Ⓒ Ⓓ
4. Ⓐ Ⓑ Ⓒ Ⓓ
5. Ⓐ Ⓑ Ⓒ Ⓓ
6. Ⓐ Ⓑ Ⓒ Ⓓ
7. Ⓐ Ⓑ Ⓒ Ⓓ
8. Ⓐ Ⓑ Ⓒ Ⓓ
9. Ⓐ Ⓑ Ⓒ Ⓓ
10. Ⓐ Ⓑ Ⓒ Ⓓ

11. Ⓐ Ⓑ Ⓒ Ⓓ
12. Ⓐ Ⓑ Ⓒ Ⓓ
13. Ⓐ Ⓑ Ⓒ Ⓓ
14. Ⓐ Ⓑ Ⓒ Ⓓ
15. Ⓐ Ⓑ Ⓒ Ⓓ
16. Ⓐ Ⓑ Ⓒ Ⓓ
17. Ⓐ Ⓑ Ⓒ Ⓓ
18. Ⓐ Ⓑ Ⓒ Ⓓ
19. Ⓐ Ⓑ Ⓒ Ⓓ
20. Ⓐ Ⓑ Ⓒ Ⓓ

21. Ⓐ Ⓑ Ⓒ Ⓓ
22. Ⓐ Ⓑ Ⓒ Ⓓ
23. Ⓐ Ⓑ Ⓒ Ⓓ
24. Ⓐ Ⓑ Ⓒ Ⓓ
25. Ⓐ Ⓑ Ⓒ Ⓓ
26. Ⓐ Ⓑ Ⓒ Ⓓ
27. Ⓐ Ⓑ Ⓒ Ⓓ
28. Ⓐ Ⓑ Ⓒ Ⓓ
29. Ⓐ Ⓑ Ⓒ Ⓓ
30. Ⓐ Ⓑ Ⓒ Ⓓ

31. Ⓐ Ⓑ Ⓒ Ⓓ
32. Ⓐ Ⓑ Ⓒ Ⓓ
33. Ⓐ Ⓑ Ⓒ Ⓓ
34. Ⓐ Ⓑ Ⓒ Ⓓ
35. Ⓐ Ⓑ Ⓒ Ⓓ
36. Ⓐ Ⓑ Ⓒ Ⓓ
37. Ⓐ Ⓑ Ⓒ Ⓓ
38. Ⓐ Ⓑ Ⓒ Ⓓ
39. Ⓐ Ⓑ Ⓒ Ⓓ
40. Ⓐ Ⓑ Ⓒ Ⓓ

41. Ⓐ Ⓑ Ⓒ Ⓓ
42. Ⓐ Ⓑ Ⓒ Ⓓ
43. Ⓐ Ⓑ Ⓒ Ⓓ
44. Ⓐ Ⓑ Ⓒ Ⓓ

Chapter 9
Writing and Language Test Drill 1: Answers and Explanations

ANSWERS AND EXPLANATIONS

Section 2—Writing and Language Test

1. **D** Since the question is asking for the LEAST acceptable alternative to the underlined portion, then the phrase *trade offs* is correctly used. Eliminate any answer choices that are similar to *trade offs*. Get rid of choices (A), (B) and (C) since each is similar. This leaves choice (D), which means "exchanges." Choice (D) is the best answer.

2. **D** The underlined portion of this sentence is a pronoun, so make sure it is consistent with the non-underlined portion by finding the other nouns and pronouns. The previous sentence uses the partner third-person pronoun *we* a few times, so eliminate choice (A). Eliminate choices (B) and (D) since neither are parallel with the earlier sentence. Choice (D) works because the earlier sentence also uses *we would love* which makes it parallel. Choice (D) is the best answer.

3. **B** The underlined portion of this sentence is a pronoun, so make sure it is consistent with the non-underlined portion by finding the other nouns and pronouns. The partner nouns *vegetables or meats* are used earlier in the paragraph, both of which are plural. Eliminate choices (A), (C) and (D) since each of them are singular. This leaves choice (B), which is the best answer.

4. **A** Notice the question and use POE to find an answer consistent with the information in the paragraph. The author begins this paragraph with *as each of us tries to be more environmentally conscious* and then goes on to discuss the difficulties, so the underlined paragraph is consistent with this information. No comparison is made of *organic* and *traditionally farmed produce*, so eliminate choice (B). Eliminate choices (C) and (D) since the paragraph does not discuss economics nor economists. Choice (A) is the best answer.

5. **B** Notice the question and use POE to find an answer consistent with information in the paragraph. The following sentence states *economics doesn't have an obvious relationship to the environment*, so choice (B) matches this information. Eliminate choice (A) since the passage isn't interested with all types of economists. Also, eliminate choice (C) for its conversational tone. The rest of the paragraph does not discuss what environmental economists do, so eliminate choice (D) since no answers are given to this question. Choice (B) is the best answer.

6. **C** Since the answer choices do not appear to be testing a consistent grammar rule, use POE to find the answer that is the most consistent and concise with the paragraph. Choice (C) is much more concise than the underlined portion, so eliminate choice (A). Choice (B) is also very wordy as it uses nouns instead of verbs to discuss the actions of *environmental resources*, so eliminate it. Eliminate choice (D) since it changes the intended meaning of the sentence. Choice (C) is the best answer.

7. **C** Since the question is asking for the LEAST acceptable alternative to the underlined portion, then the transition *while* is correctly used. *While* indicates a contrast, so eliminate choices (A), (B) and (D) since each also indicates a contrast. This leaves choice (C) as the best answer.

8. **B** Since the answer choices include periods and semicolons, this question is testing STOP punctuation. Draw the vertical line test where the STOP punctuation is and check for complete ideas. The first phrase is an incomplete idea, so eliminate choice (C) because STOP punctuation can only separate two complete ideas. Also, eliminate choices (A) and (D) since colons can only proceed a complete idea. Therefore, choice (B) is the best answer.

9. **D** The underlined portion of this sentence is a pronoun, so make sure it is consistent with the non-underlined portion by finding the other nouns and pronouns. It is not clear what *they* is referring to, so this is an ambiguous pronoun. Eliminate choices (A) and (B). Choice (C) is also unclear since the *two things* are not defined. This leaves choice (D), which clarifies what has an *effect* on the economy.

10. **A** The answer choices contain commas, so find the best answer in which they are correctly used, if at all. In the underlined passage, there is no reason to slow down the ideas in the sentence, so keep choice (A). Eliminate choices (B), (C) and (D) since each uses unnecessary commas to breaks up the flow of ideas in the sentence. Choice (A) is the best answer.

11. **A** Notice the question and use POE to find the best answer consistent with the information in the paragraph. The rewritten sentence is vague since it doesn't state what the economists are trying to advise the politicians and businesses on. Eliminate choices (C) and (D). Neither sentence sounds more formal than the other, so eliminate choice (B). This leaves choice (A), which is the best answer since it clarifies what the economists will advise politicians and businesses on.

12. **C** Look at the answers to see that they contain different conjunctions. Because the two ideas expressed by the sentence are opposites, we should be using a conjunction like *but*. Therefore choice (A) can be eliminated. Without any conduction, however, the sentence has two complete ideas separated by a comma. This would be incorrect. Therefore, you can eliminate choices (B) and (D). Choice (C) is correct.

13. **D** The previous sentence states that the Supreme Court upheld the practice known as "separate but equal." Choice (A) provides no support for the previous assertion, and should be eliminated. Choice (B) discusses the overturning of that ruling, so it cannot support the previous sentence and should be eliminated. Choice (C) mentions the defendant, but does not explain anything about the ruling, and should be eliminated. Choice (D) is correct because it provides an example of the practice known as "separate but equal" as a visible consequence of the ruling.

14. **D** The answer choices indicate that verb tense is being tested, so let the non-underlined portions guide your choice of verb. Past tense is seen in *did not appear until the 1940s,* so choice (D) is consistent. Eliminate choice (A) because it is present tense, choice (B) because it is past participle, and choice (C) because it is present participle.

15. **C** The underlined portion of this sentence is a pronoun, so make sure it is consistent with the non-underlined portion by finding the other pronouns and nouns. Because the partner noun could either be *white men* or *black men,* choices (A), (B), and (D) are ambiguous and therefore incorrect. Choice (C) is the best answer.

16. **B** Notice the question and use POE and find the best answer that maintains the sentences focus on the air force. Choices (A), (C), and (D) make no mention of the air battles fought in WWI, so they are incorrect. Because choice (B) refers to air combat, it is the best answer.

17. **A** Look at the answers to see that comma usage and dash usage are being tested. Because the non-underlined portion is correct, a dash must be used to surround the unnecessary information in the sentence. First, check to see if *the era of Martin Luther King and Malcolm X* is necessary or unnecessary information. If removed from the sentence, it would still make sense, so it's unnecessary information. Therefore, choice (A) is a good answer. It places two dashes around unnecessary information. Choice (B) is incorrect because it uses a dash and a comma. Choice (C) is incorrect because it places a comma before *and* in a list of two people. Choice (D) is incorrect because it places a dash before *and,* which breaks up the list. Choice (A) is the best answer.

18. **D** Whenever you are given the option to delete, determine whether the underlined portion serves a precise role within the passage. In fact, the underlined portion is redundant with *bravery* and should therefore be eliminated. Choices (A), (B), and (C) all express the same idea as bravery. Therefore, choice (D) is the best answer.

19. **B** The underlined portion of this sentence is a pronoun, so make sure it is consistent with the non-underlined portion by finding the other pronouns and nouns. There are no other instances of *our* or *we* in the rest of the sentence, so choice (A) should be eliminated. Because the patriotism of African Americans came to the attention of America, (B) is a good answer. Because choice (C) expresses the same thing as choice (B), but is less concise, choice (C) should be eliminated. Because choice (D) mentions *people* without any indication of which people, it should be eliminated.

20. **A** The main idea of the paragraph in question is that the exploits of African-American soldiers like the Tuskegee airmen helped bring about the civil rights era. Because the underlined sentence expresses the same idea, choice (A) is a good answer. Because it is vital to the paragraph's argument that people knew how hard the Tuskegee Airmen fought, choice (B) is incorrect. Choices (C) and (D) should be eliminated because both discuss the present-day instead of the eras with which the passage is concerned.

21. **C** Look at the answers to see that each contains a different version of *they're, their,* or *there.* Because the underlined word should indicate the Tuskegee Airmen's rightful place, it should be *their,* the possessive form of *they.* This matches choice (C).

22. **D** Because Paragraph Four introduces the Tuskegee Airmen, it should come before any other mentions of that group. Therefore, it cannot be after Paragraph Three and choice (A) is incorrect. Because the first sentence in Paragraph Four refers to *this military segregation,* it must come after some

mention if military segregation. Because the final sentence of Paragraph Two mentions the segregation of the air force, Paragraph Four should come after Paragraph two. Therefore choices (B) and (C) are incorrect. The correct answer is (D).

23. **A** Notice the question and use POE to find an answer consistent with the information in the paragraph and table. Choice (A) matches the information in the graph since the percentages grew from 10% to 67% of households in just five years. Eliminate choice (B) because while the percentage of households who own a TV grew in that time period, it began to stagnate around 1965. Eliminate choice (C) because the percentage of households was pretty flat around this time. No information is given for after 2000, so eliminate choice (D). Choice (A) is the best answer.

24. **C** Notice the question and use POE to find an answer consistent with the information in the paragraph and table. Choice (A) refers to the wrong time period and the numbers represent the percentage of households with pay cable. Eliminate choice (A). Choice (B) is too extreme since the table discusses households, not individual people, so eliminate it. Choice (C) matches the information in the table, so keep it. Eliminate choice (D) because cable's growth from 1970 to 1975 was much smaller than the growth of households owning televisions. Choice (C) is the best answer.

25. **B** Since there are commas in the answer choices, find the answer that uses them correctly. Choice (B) is correct since a comma is used after each item in the list and before the conjunction *and*. Choice (A) is wordy and not parallel. Choices (C) and (D) are sentence fragments. Eliminate these answers and choice (B) is the best answer.

26. **A** Since there are periods and semicolons in the answer choices, this question is testing STOP punctuation. The question also wants the LEAST acceptable alternative to the underlined portion, so it must be correct. A semicolon is STOP punctuation, so eliminate choice (C) since a period is basically the same thing. Also, eliminate choices (B) and (D) since a colon and dash also serve the same purpose, and therefore both cannot be correct. This leaves choice (A), which is correct since a comma cannot separate two complete ideas.

27. **A** This sentence uses the phrase *many of the shows on early television were simply visual adaptations of radio plays* as a means to support the previous sentence that explained how television shows were offshoots of those on the radio. The underlined portion is correctly used, so keep choice (A). Each of the other choices indicates either a contrast or are too conversational. Choice (A) is formal, and therefore the best answer.

28. **C** Since the question is asking for the LEAST acceptable replacement for the underlined portion, then the underlined portion is correct as written. In this context, *concrete* means "something that exists in material form" or "not abstract." Choices (A), (B) and (D) all match this definition. This leaves choice (C), which is a bit of a trap since it would be a common description of the typical use of *concrete*. Choice (C) is the best answer.

29. **B** Notice the answer choices are changing *viewer* from singular to plural. The plural form is correct since television programs would have multiple *viewers* instead of a single *viewer*. Eliminate choices (A), (C) and (D). Choice (B) is the best answer.

30. **D** Since there are periods and semicolons in the answer choices, this question is testing STOP punctuation. Eliminate choices (A) and (B) since a comma and period are basically the same thing. Eliminate choice (C) since there is no reason to use a comma to pause the two incomplete ideas. This leaves choice (D), which is the best answer.

31. **C** Since there are pronouns in the answer choices, look for agreement and ambiguity. Choice (A) is the contraction form of choice (B), so both cannot be correct. Eliminate choices (A) and (B). Choice (D) is incorrect since *their* is plural and the subject is *main character*, which is singular. Choice (C) is the best answer.

32. **A** Notice the question and use POE to find the best answer consistent with information in the paragraph. The paragraph primarily focuses on how television could not hide white actors playing non-white characters as radio could. Therefore, major changes occurred during the television era. Choice (A) is consistent with this information. The longevity of radio programs is unnecessary, so eliminate choice (B). No information is given about how non-white actors handled the transition, so get rid of choice (C) as well. The cinema is not discussed in the passage, so it's unnecessary information. Eliminate choice (D). Choice (A) is the best answer.

33. **B** The change from white to non-white actors playing non-white characters in the television era was a major change, so find an answer that matches this tone. Choices (A), (C) and (D) are incorrect because each basically means the same thing, and each could also be considered offensive since no information indicates that the change was bad. Choice (B), therefore, is the best answer.

34. **A** Since there isn't a consistent grammar rule being tested here, use POE to find the best and most concise answer. Eliminate choice (B) since it changes the meaning and *life* cannot have possession. Choices (C) and (D) are unnecessarily wordy and awkward. This leaves choice (A), which is a common figure of speech and therefore the best answer.

35. **B** Notice the question and use POE to find an answer most consistent with the information in the paragraph. The previous sentences indicate a choice between two distinct things, so eliminate choice (A) since no choice is given. Choice (B) shows a choice that would occur on a subway, so keep it. Buses are not discussed in the paragraph, so eliminate choice (C). Eliminate choice (D) as well since the operating hours of the subway are unnecessary information. Choice (B) is the best answer.

36. **C** Since the answer choices have verbs, use POE to find the answer that has proper agreement and tense with the non-underlined portion of the paragraph. The subject of the sentence is *team*, which is singular, so eliminate choice (A) since *have* is plural. Eliminate choice (B) because the present tense is incorrect. Choice (D) is also incorrect since *was* changes the meaning by suggesting that the *team* was discovered. This leaves choice (C), which is the best answer.

37. **D** Since the answer choices each seem to be saying the same thing, use POE and look for an answer that is clear and concise. Eliminate choice (A) because is a sentence fragment. Eliminate choice (B) since it implies that the *team* is the *geneticist,* which is incorrect. The plural verb *were* does not agree with the singular subject *data,* so eliminate choice (C). This leaves choice (D), which is clear and concise.

38. **D** Notice the question and use POE to find an answer that is consistent with the information in the paragraph. Choices (A) and (C) basically say the same thing and are somewhat informal, so eliminate them. Nothing in the paragraph questions how valid the science is, so eliminate choice (B). Choice (D) works, since it describes how the experiment was conducted and would answer some of the questions presented in the first sentence. Choice (D) is the best answer.

39. **C** Since the answer choices each seem to be saying the same thing, use POE and look for an answer that is clear and concise. Eliminate choices (A) and (B) because each contains unnecessary information. Choice (D) is vague so this leaves choice (C), which is the best, most concise answer.

40. **B** Each answer choice is a modifying phrase and the subject—*researchers*—comes right after the comma, so find the answer choice that refers to them. Eliminate choices (A) and (D) since the *researchers* are not living on the subway, nor they responsible for the odor. Choice (C) implies that the *researchers* are part of the food, so eliminate this choice as well. This leaves choice (B), which is the best answer.

41. **A** Since there isn't a consistent grammar rule being tested in this question, use POE to find an answer that is clear and concise. Choice (A) makes sense, so keep it for now. Eliminate choice (B) because it changes the meaning by implying that the diseases were dead instead of the cells. Choice (C) makes the same error, so eliminate it as well. Eliminate choice (D) since the pronoun *they* could be referring to the *researchers* from the previous paragraph, and they are certainly not dead. Choice (A) is the best answer.

42. **C** This question is testing proper word use, so use the context of the non-underlined portion of the sentence to find the best answer. Eliminate choices (B) and (D) since both are adverbs and do not fit the sentence properly. *Compliment* is the "act of saying something nice," which does not make sense within the context of the sentence, so eliminate choice (A). Choice (C) is the proper use of this word since it means "something that completes something else." Choice (C) is the best answer.

43. **B** Notice the question and use POE to find an answer that is consistent with the information in the paragraph. The correct answer should address a previous survey or study. Only choice (B) does this as the census is a particular study. Choices (A), (C) and (D) each have unnecessary information that does not address the question. Choice (B) is the best answer.

44. **D** Notice the sentence is making a comparison between *a place* and *the level,* which is incorrect. All comparisons must be apples to apples. Eliminate choices (A) and (B). Choice (C) is unnecessarily wordy and passive, so eliminate it as well. Choice (D) makes the correct comparison and is concise. Choice (D) is the best answer.

Chapter 10
Writing and Language Test Drill 2

Writing and Language Test

35 MINUTES, 44 QUESTIONS

Turn to Section 2 of your answer sheet to answer the questions in this section.

DIRECTIONS

Each passage below is accompanied by a number of questions. For some questions, you will consider how the passage might be revised to improve the expression of ideas. For other questions, you will consider how the passage might be edited to correct errors in sentence structure, usage, or punctuation. A passage or a question may be accompanied by one or more graphics (such as a table or graph) that you will consider as you make revising and editing decisions.

Some questions will direct you to an underlined portion of a passage. Other questions will direct you to a location in a passage or ask you to think about the passage as a whole.

After reading each passage, choose the answer to each question that most effectively improves the quality of writing in the passage or that makes the passage conform to the conventions of standard written English. Many questions include a "NO CHANGE" option. Choose that option if you think the best choice is to leave the relevant portion of the passage as it is.

Questions 1–11 are based on the following passage.

The Other Brain Doctors

Who is in charge of your medical care? **1** Doctors and nurses play a big part, obviously, but there is more happening behind the scenes than you might think. A hospital is a business and, like any business, it has a complex infrastructure there to make sure that things run as **2** smoothe as possible. The doctors and nurses do the patient-facing work, and a hospital could not run without them, but the work that goes on administratively is often just as important.

1

Which of the following choices would best answer the question posed at the beginning of this paragraph in a way that is in keeping with the main idea of the paragraph?

A) NO CHANGE

B) A hospital can't run without its doctors, but the real heroes are the nurses.

C) The CEO of a private hospital is beholden to his or her shareholders to make a profit.

D) A hospital needs patients, not that anyone wants you to get sick.

2

A) NO CHANGE

B) smooth

C) smoothing

D) smoothly

Because ▮3▮ medical care inflation has leveled off in the twenty-first century, hospitals feel more and more that they are forced to practice what is called "defensive medicine." The risk of such medicine is relatively low, but it also means that ▮4▮ it is not necessarily getting the best possible care.

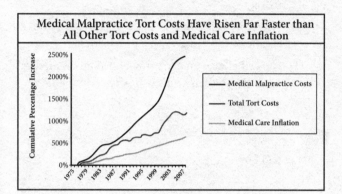

Medical Malpractice Tort Costs Have Risen Far Faster than All Other Tort Costs and Medical Care Inflation

In order to find the balance between risk and safety, hospitals are more and more relying on the work of medical ethicists. ▮5▮ Most hospitals have an ethics board that will draft the hospital's ethical guidelines and advice on those matters where questions of the medical and legal meet. Sometimes these boards will intervene on an individual-patient ▮6▮ basis, as when a patient, is terminally ill, but such patient-facing cases are rare.

3

Which of the following gives accurate information based on the graph?

A) NO CHANGE

B) total tort costs were almost the same as medical-malpractice costs in 2006,

C) medical malpractice costs have risen dramatically since the 1970s,

D) medical malpractice costs have increased nearly 100% since 1975,

4

A) NO CHANGE

B) they are

C) patients are

D) doctors are

5

The writer is considering deleting the phrase *between risk and safety* from the previous sentence and placing the comma after the word *balance*. Should the writer keep or delete the phrase?

A) Keep the phrase, because it details what medical ethicists do at work.

B) Keep the phrase, because it clarifies what is described earlier in the sentence.

C) Delete the phrase, because it adds unnecessary words to a sentence that is already too long.

D) Delete the phrase, because it is grammatically incorrect and does not make sense in the context.

6

A) NO CHANGE

B) basis, as when a patient is terminally ill

C) basis as when a patient is terminally ill,

D) basis, as when a patient is terminally ill,

7 Today, hospitals and universities are beginning to take the question of medical ethics to the next level. Whereas ethics review boards are typically made up of people with a variety of specialties (nurses, social workers, psychologists, lawyers, doctors), a medical ethicist has specific training in **8** their field and usually holds a PhD or an MD/DO. A medical ethicist therefore has a very particularized **9** expertise that gets into the details that allows him or her to comment on a variety of matters, including experimental treatments and high-risk procedures. He or she may be a part of the team of doctors that consults with a family during a hospital stay.

Currently, large academic medical centers **10** of medical ethicists are the primary employers; community hospitals still rely mainly on the ethics board. But this may be changing as more specialization exists for aspiring medical ethicists. After all, the job requires a very specific kind of **11** person—one who can be interested in the one-to-one aspects of patient care but is also interested in the state of the field of medicine and, over and above all of that, the big philosophical questions about right and wrong.

7

Which of the following would best introduce this paragraph by establishing a contrast with the ideas described in the previous paragraph?

A) NO CHANGE

B) However, as mentioned before, the cost of medical malpractice is rising, and the healthcare system is dying.

C) Therefore, a medical ethicist will obviously not see a patient as often as, say, a nurse does.

D) Nevertheless, you can't run a hospital on medical ethicists, so their work is clearly secondary.

8

A) NO CHANGE

B) its

C) they're

D) his or her

9

A) NO CHANGE

B) expertise that is all about the fine-toothed comb

C) expertise that gets him or her into the nitty-gritty

D) expertise

10

The best placement for the underlined portion would be

A) where it is now.

B) after the word *employers* (and before the semi-colon).

C) after the word *hospitals*.

D) after the word *ethics*.

11

A) NO CHANGE

B) person one

C) person; one

D) person. One

Questions 12–22 are based on the following passage.

Oh, Why No More Weimar?

Germany made some big news in the early part of the twentieth century, but not the kind that most countries hope to make. **12** Germanies' aggression in the First World War played a big role in impelling that conflict, and Hitler's rise to power in 1933 led to one of the bloodiest and widest-ranging conflicts of the twentieth century. What is less known, however, is what happened between those two conflicts. We have a tendency to use wars as the primary motivators of history, **13** and the wars are useful because there are so many of them.

In Germany, that in-between period, 1919 to 1933, is what known as the era of the Weimar Republic. **14** It got its name from the city of Weimar, where a national convention produced the new German constitution, one that favored democracy and openness. This constitution was crucial in re-establishing Germany's position in the world, and it saved **15** them from having to follow through on many of the articles of the Treaty of Versailles, a largely punitive document in which Germany essentially pled guilty to the international charges that it had caused the First World War.

12

A) NO CHANGE

B) Germanys'

C) Germany's

D) Germans

13

Which of the following choices would provide the most effective transition between this paragraph and the next?

A) NO CHANGE

B) so all history is in a sense a kind of military history.

C) for people are drawn to conflicts in their own lives and in history.

D) but what happens in between is often just as influential.

14

A) NO CHANGE

B) The Republic got its

C) The Republic got their

D) They got their

15

A) NO CHANGE

B) those of Germany

C) the nation

D) it

16 Weimar may have had its problems, but it was one of the most culturally effervescent periods of the twentieth century. The shapes that art, architecture, cinema, and philosophy were to take for the rest of the century were determined in this forgotten decade and a half. In particular, the *Goldene Zwanziger* ("Golden Twenties"), the period between 1924 and 1929, **17** stand out.

A) NO CHANGE

B) Despite its problems as a culture, Weimar had an effervescent period all the same in the century.

C) In the twentieth century, the Weimar Republic was culturally effervescent and problematic sometimes.

D) With and alongside its cultural effervescence, the Weimar Republic also had some problems in the twentieth century.

A) NO CHANGE

B) stands

C) stood

D) standing

During this period, Gustav Streseman was foreign minister, and he set as his goal the management of Germany's financial straits, characterized in large part by debts to foreign nations and staggering inflation of the German mark. **18** Germany uses the "euro" now, not the mark. Streseman, too, helped the Germany economy blossom again with big loans from the American government, which took German products (including the national railways and the national bank) as collateral. **19** Things were looking up, many of the cultural movements that flourished elsewhere found a new home in Weimar Germany. **20** One of the greatest movements of German architecture, the "Bauhaus," flourished in this period.

18

Which of the following sentences would best maintain the paragraph's focus on the consequences of economic improvement?

A) NO CHANGE

B) Streseman is considered a national hero in Germany.

C) Many German buildings were destroyed in the First World War.

D) With increased financial stability came a cooling of civil unrest.

19

A) NO CHANGE

B) Thus, things

C) Clearly, things

D) As things

20

The writer is considering adding the following parenthetical remark after the word *elsewhere*.

(cinema in the Soviet Union, art in Paris, music in the United States)

Should the writer make this addition here?

A) Yes, because it shows the writer's knowledge of artistic movements.

B) Yes, because it specifies what the writer mentions earlier in the sentence.

C) No, because this information is well-known to all readers.

D) No, because it repeats information given elsewhere in the passage.

Unfortunately, the renaissance of Weimar could not last forever. The American stock market crash flung Germany into a depression **21** deeper than the United States. With this economic crash, a group of belligerent conservatives, including some led by Adolf Hitler, seized power amid the promise that they could restore Germany to its past glories. The rest is an ugly chapter in history, but the Weimar Republic gives a wonderful **22** interlude that is really nice to think about.

21

A) NO CHANGE

B) deep like the United States.

C) deeper than that of the United States.

D) deeper than the country of the United States.

22

A) NO CHANGE

B) interlude, which is "intermezzo" in Italian.

C) interlude, a term often used in music like that of the Weimar composers.

D) interlude.

Questions 23–33 are based on the following passage.

The Wondrous Life of Junot Diaz

Although he's not quite the household name that someone like Stephen King is, Junot Diaz is one of the most exciting, most highly regarded authors in contemporary literature. **23** Diaz won the Pulitzer Prize for Fiction in 2008, for his novel, *The Brief Wondrous Life of Oscar Wao*, and in 2012, he was awarded a MacArthur Genius Grant. What is it about Diaz's work that makes it so relatable?

24 [1] I would argue that part of Diaz's power comes from his late-twentieth century "American" story. [2] Stories about immigrants moving to the United States seem to be relegated to the late nineteenth and early twentieth centuries: most of them take place in New York or Chicago. [3] Diaz gives us an updated version. [4] There, Diaz went to public schools as his family dealt with grinding poverty, an absentee **25** father, and the difficulty of assimilation. [5] All the while, Diaz was a voracious reader and became enthralled with the apocalyptic fantasy worlds of *Planet of the Apes* and *The Day of the Triffids*. [6] Born in the Dominican Republic in 1968, **26** Diaz's family moved to Parlin, New Jersey, in 1974. **27**

23

A) NO CHANGE

B) Diaz won the Pulitzer Prize for Fiction in 2008 for his novel *The Brief Wondrous Life of Oscar Wao*,

C) Diaz won, the Pulitzer Prize for Fiction in 2008, for his novel, *The Brief Wondrous Life of Oscar Wao*,

D) Diaz, won the Pulitzer Prize for Fiction in 2008 for his novel, *The Brief Wondrous Life of Oscar Wao*,

24

Which of the following would best introduce this paragraph by stating the author's main idea?

A) NO CHANGE

B) This is a question that has puzzled the ages—I've got the answer.

C) Junot Diaz is a writer from New Jersey who currently teaches at MIT in Massachusetts.

D) Next time you're inclined to read a book by Dan Brown, try one by Junot Diaz instead.

25

A) NO CHANGE

B) father and the difficulty

C) father, and the difficulty,

D) father, and, the difficulty

26

A) NO CHANGE

B) Diaz

C) Diaz's people

D) the Diaz family

27

The best placement for sentence 6 would be

A) where it is now.

B) after sentence 2.

C) after sentence 3.

D) after sentence 4.

This unique intersection, between the old country and the new, gives Diaz both a particular relatability and a general one. On the one hand, Diaz comes from a newly prominent place: **[28]** the Dominican Republic is a Spanish-speaking country in the Caribbean Sea. This may seem like an insignificant number, but when we consider how very small the Dominican Republic is and how the same number 20 years ago was below 1%, we cannot help but see its significance. Diaz's story is in this way an updated version of the "rags to riches" story of a century ago. The **[29]** difficulties of assimilation may have remained largely the same, but **[30]** there's an entirely new cast of characters trying to navigate them.

28

Which of the following true choices would best support the claim made in the first part of this sentence?

A) NO CHANGE

B) the other country on the island of Hispaniola is Haiti, which suffered a terrible earthquake in 2010.

C) fashion designer Oscar de la Renta is also from the Dominican Republic.

D) Dominican immigrants now make up nearly 3% of new immigrants to the United States.

29

Which of the following alternatives to the underlined portion would be LEAST acceptable?

A) challenges

B) hardships

C) obstructions

D) struggles

30

A) NO CHANGE

B) there've been

C) there was

D) there were

But the challenge of living in [31] a garbage world is certainly more universal as well. Whether he came from the Dominican Republic or not, Junot Diaz had a tough childhood. His home life was not as steady as it could've been. He got interested in books and movies that no one else seemed to care much [32] about. His family didn't understand or acknowledge his real passions. We all know what it's like to feel isolated or misunderstood, and we've all at times felt like we're entering a world completely alien to our own. [33]

31

A) NO CHANGE

B) an unfriendly

C) a major bummer of a

D) a not totally awesome

32

A) NO CHANGE

B) about his

C) about, his

D) about his,

33

At this point, the writer wants to conclude the essay with a general sentence that captures Diaz's achievements. Which of the following choices would best fulfill that goal?

A) We can expect much more greatness from Junot Diaz in the future.

B) Give his books a chance some time!

C) Junot Diaz has managed to capture that feeling on a number of levels.

D) Let's hope that he inspires more writers who are just as good.

Questions 34–44 are based on the following passage.

The Change in Climate Change

[1]

It is now fully accepted that human behavior has **34** messed up the global climate. Whether from transportation or industrial waste, our technologies have changed the globe's natural climate, and we can only hope that the consequences are not as dire as **35** everyone says.

[2]

For those who doubt the claims of climate **36** scientists: a series of new findings may be helpful. It seems that air pollution is nearly as old as civilization itself. Led by Celia Sapart of Utrecht University in the Netherlands, a team of scientists analyzed the ice trapped in certain parts of Greenland. **37** By analyzing the chemical content of this ice, the scientists determined that methane levels had risen artificially as early as the Roman era. Around 100 BCE, the scientists reasoned, the Romans began to domesticate animals. The Chinese Han Dynasty expanded its rice fields. Both places **38** had used metallurgical techniques to produce weapons. The level of methane gas in the atmosphere rose in step.

34

A) NO CHANGE
B) messed with
C) altered
D) boggled

35

A) NO CHANGE
B) many scientists predict.
C) all that.
D) people say.

36

A) NO CHANGE
B) scientists; a series
C) scientists. A series
D) scientists, a series

37

Which of the following would best maintain the focus of this paragraph?
A) NO CHANGE
B) Accomplished as they were in collecting scientific data,
C) From a variety of schools,
D) Going to a sparsely populated island nation,

38

A) NO CHANGE
B) were using
C) had been using
D) used

[3]

It has become almost a cliché that air pollution began with the Industrial Revolution of the mid-1800s, but these researchers show that humans have been polluting the air for far longer than that. Still, we should keep these findings in their proper **39** prospective. Between 100 BCE and 1600 AD, methane emissions in the world rose by approximately 31 million tons per year. Those numbers are minuscule, actually, as **40** the United States produces one sixth of all methane emissions, and some nations produce as much as ten times that much each year.

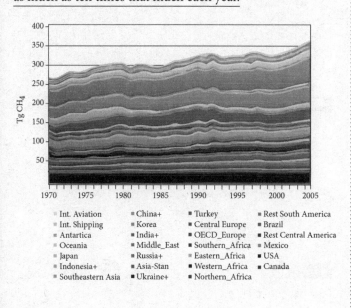

39

A) NO CHANGE

B) prospect.

C) perspective.

D) point of view.

40

Which of the following gives accurate information based on the graph?

A) NO CHANGE

B) the United States produces approximately that much each year, and the industry of international aviation produces the rest.

C) the United States alone produces more than that much each year, and some nations produce as much as eight times that much each year.

D) the United States produces nearly 50 million tons, and China produces almost twenty times that much.

[4]

41 More recently, scientists have analyzed samples from Quelccaya, a glacier in the Andes. The scientists found that prior to the 1530s, there was very little alien material in the ice, apart from the dust and ash from occasional volcanic eruptions. By 1540, however, when colonial mining began to boom in the region, the cores contained a smattering of foreign elements, including chromium, molybdenum, antinomy, and lead. Europeans, especially the Spanish, came to these lands in search of silver, and **42** there technologies for extracting silver came at an environmental cost. For a time, technological advancement and the popularity of mining existed in a loop together, as increases in mining would lead to technological advancement, which would lead to increases in mining... **43**

[5]

Therefore, we should not take this ancient data as a free pass for **44** our own polluting ways. The ancient air pollution should show us instead just how fragile our environment is, and if a bit of small-scale farming and technology was able to alter climate levels in the past, we should see all the more clearly how much damage our heavy industry can do.

41

A) NO CHANGE

B) Scientists have been analyzing more recent Quelccaya, a glacier in the Andes, samples.

C) Samples from more recent scientists are those of Quelccaya, a glacier in the Andes.

D) In more recent science have been the samples from Quelccaya, an Andes glacier.

42

A) NO CHANGE

B) their

C) they're

D) our

43

The best placement for paragraph 4 would be

A) after paragraph 1.

B) after paragraph 2.

C) after paragraph 5.

D) where it is now.

44

A) NO CHANGE

B) their

C) one's

D) your

The Princeton Review

Redesigned PSAT

1. Student Information

Your Name: _____
(Print)   Last   First   M.I.

Email Address: _____ Date: ____ / ____ / ____
(Print)   MM   DD   YYYY

Home Address: _____ Apartment No. _____
(Print)   Number and Street

_____
City   State   Zip Code

High School: _____ Class of: _____

2. Your Name

First 4 letters of last name				FIRST INIT	MID INIT
Ⓐ	Ⓐ	Ⓐ	Ⓐ	Ⓐ	Ⓐ
Ⓑ	Ⓑ	Ⓑ	Ⓑ	Ⓑ	Ⓑ
Ⓒ	Ⓒ	Ⓒ	Ⓒ	Ⓒ	Ⓒ
Ⓓ	Ⓓ	Ⓓ	Ⓓ	Ⓓ	Ⓓ
Ⓔ	Ⓔ	Ⓔ	Ⓔ	Ⓔ	Ⓔ
Ⓕ	Ⓕ	Ⓕ	Ⓕ	Ⓕ	Ⓕ
Ⓖ	Ⓖ	Ⓖ	Ⓖ	Ⓖ	Ⓖ
Ⓗ	Ⓗ	Ⓗ	Ⓗ	Ⓗ	Ⓗ
Ⓘ	Ⓘ	Ⓘ	Ⓘ	Ⓘ	Ⓘ
Ⓙ	Ⓙ	Ⓙ	Ⓙ	Ⓙ	Ⓙ
Ⓚ	Ⓚ	Ⓚ	Ⓚ	Ⓚ	Ⓚ
Ⓛ	Ⓛ	Ⓛ	Ⓛ	Ⓛ	Ⓛ
Ⓜ	Ⓜ	Ⓜ	Ⓜ	Ⓜ	Ⓜ
Ⓝ	Ⓝ	Ⓝ	Ⓝ	Ⓝ	Ⓝ
Ⓞ	Ⓞ	Ⓞ	Ⓞ	Ⓞ	Ⓞ
Ⓟ	Ⓟ	Ⓟ	Ⓟ	Ⓟ	Ⓟ
Ⓠ	Ⓠ	Ⓠ	Ⓠ	Ⓠ	Ⓠ
Ⓡ	Ⓡ	Ⓡ	Ⓡ	Ⓡ	Ⓡ
Ⓢ	Ⓢ	Ⓢ	Ⓢ	Ⓢ	Ⓢ
Ⓣ	Ⓣ	Ⓣ	Ⓣ	Ⓣ	Ⓣ
Ⓤ	Ⓤ	Ⓤ	Ⓤ	Ⓤ	Ⓤ
Ⓥ	Ⓥ	Ⓥ	Ⓥ	Ⓥ	Ⓥ
Ⓦ	Ⓦ	Ⓦ	Ⓦ	Ⓦ	Ⓦ
Ⓧ	Ⓧ	Ⓧ	Ⓧ	Ⓧ	Ⓧ
Ⓨ	Ⓨ	Ⓨ	Ⓨ	Ⓨ	Ⓨ
Ⓩ	Ⓩ	Ⓩ	Ⓩ	Ⓩ	Ⓩ

3. Phone Number

Area Code			Phone number						
⓪	⓪	⓪	⓪	⓪	⓪	⓪	⓪	⓪	⓪
①	①	①	①	①	①	①	①	①	①
②	②	②	②	②	②	②	②	②	②
③	③	③	③	③	③	③	③	③	③
④	④	④	④	④	④	④	④	④	④
⑤	⑤	⑤	⑤	⑤	⑤	⑤	⑤	⑤	⑤
⑥	⑥	⑥	⑥	⑥	⑥	⑥	⑥	⑥	⑥
⑦	⑦	⑦	⑦	⑦	⑦	⑦	⑦	⑦	⑦
⑧	⑧	⑧	⑧	⑧	⑧	⑧	⑧	⑧	⑧
⑨	⑨	⑨	⑨	⑨	⑨	⑨	⑨	⑨	⑨

Writing & Language

SECTION **2**

1. Ⓐ Ⓑ Ⓒ Ⓓ
2. Ⓐ Ⓑ Ⓒ Ⓓ
3. Ⓐ Ⓑ Ⓒ Ⓓ
4. Ⓐ Ⓑ Ⓒ Ⓓ
5. Ⓐ Ⓑ Ⓒ Ⓓ
6. Ⓐ Ⓑ Ⓒ Ⓓ
7. Ⓐ Ⓑ Ⓒ Ⓓ
8. Ⓐ Ⓑ Ⓒ Ⓓ
9. Ⓐ Ⓑ Ⓒ Ⓓ
10. Ⓐ Ⓑ Ⓒ Ⓓ

11. Ⓐ Ⓑ Ⓒ Ⓓ
12. Ⓐ Ⓑ Ⓒ Ⓓ
13. Ⓐ Ⓑ Ⓒ Ⓓ
14. Ⓐ Ⓑ Ⓒ Ⓓ
15. Ⓐ Ⓑ Ⓒ Ⓓ
16. Ⓐ Ⓑ Ⓒ Ⓓ
17. Ⓐ Ⓑ Ⓒ Ⓓ
18. Ⓐ Ⓑ Ⓒ Ⓓ
19. Ⓐ Ⓑ Ⓒ Ⓓ
20. Ⓐ Ⓑ Ⓒ Ⓓ

21. Ⓐ Ⓑ Ⓒ Ⓓ
22. Ⓐ Ⓑ Ⓒ Ⓓ
23. Ⓐ Ⓑ Ⓒ Ⓓ
24. Ⓐ Ⓑ Ⓒ Ⓓ
25. Ⓐ Ⓑ Ⓒ Ⓓ
26. Ⓐ Ⓑ Ⓒ Ⓓ
27. Ⓐ Ⓑ Ⓒ Ⓓ
28. Ⓐ Ⓑ Ⓒ Ⓓ
29. Ⓐ Ⓑ Ⓒ Ⓓ
30. Ⓐ Ⓑ Ⓒ Ⓓ

31. Ⓐ Ⓑ Ⓒ Ⓓ
32. Ⓐ Ⓑ Ⓒ Ⓓ
33. Ⓐ Ⓑ Ⓒ Ⓓ
34. Ⓐ Ⓑ Ⓒ Ⓓ
35. Ⓐ Ⓑ Ⓒ Ⓓ
36. Ⓐ Ⓑ Ⓒ Ⓓ
37. Ⓐ Ⓑ Ⓒ Ⓓ
38. Ⓐ Ⓑ Ⓒ Ⓓ
39. Ⓐ Ⓑ Ⓒ Ⓓ
40. Ⓐ Ⓑ Ⓒ Ⓓ

41. Ⓐ Ⓑ Ⓒ Ⓓ
42. Ⓐ Ⓑ Ⓒ Ⓓ
43. Ⓐ Ⓑ Ⓒ Ⓓ
44. Ⓐ Ⓑ Ⓒ Ⓓ

Chapter 11
Writing and Language Test Drill 2: Answers and Explanations

ANSWERS AND EXPLANATIONS

Section 2—Writing and Language Test

1. **A** Notice the question and use POE to find the best answer that is consistent with the information in the paragraph. Since the main idea of this paragraph is expressed in the final sentence—*the doctors and nurses do the patient-facing work, and a hospital could not run without them, but the work that goes on administratively is often just as important*—find an answer that matches this information. Choice (A) is a good match. Eliminate choice (B) since the paragraph doesn't value judge doctors and nurses. The CEO and shareholders are unnecessary information, so eliminate choice (C). Get rid of choice (D) as well since no mention is made about getting sick.

2. **D** The underlined portion and answer choices indicate the question is interested in the correct use of a similar word. Based on the sentence, an adverb is needed, so choice (D) is a good answer. Since choices (A) and (B) are primary and secondary spellings of the same word, eliminate both answer choices. The present participle is unnecessary in this sentence, so eliminate choice (C) as well. Choice (D) is the best answer.

3. **C** Notice the question and use POE to find an answer with information consistent with the graph. Choice (A) is incorrect since medical care inflation seems to be increasing in the 21st century. Medical tort and malpractice costs are very different from each other in 2006, so eliminate choice (B). Each part of the graph has been rising since the 1970s, so choice (C) is consistent. Malpractice costs have increased nearly 2500% since 1975, so eliminate choice (D). Choice (C) is the best answer.

4. **C** The underlined portion of the sentence is a pronoun, so be sure that it is consistent and clear with other nouns and pronouns in the sentence. Since no information is given in the sentence regarding the pronoun, eliminate choices (A) and (B) since the pronouns are ambiguous. Because *care* is discussed in the paragraph, choice (C) makes sense since that's what patients receive. Eliminate choice (D) since doctors don't receive *care*. Choice (C) is the best answer.

5. **B** Whenever you are given the option to delete, determine whether the underlined portion plays a precise role in the passage. The previous passage describes the *risk of "defensive medicine,"* so this distinction is relevant to the paragraph. Eliminate choices (C) and (D). The phrase *balance between risk and safety* is too vague to describe specifically what medical ethicists do, so eliminate choice (A). This leaves choice (B), which is the best answer.

6. **D** Look at the answers to see that comma usage is being tested. Take a look at the full phrase—*as when a patient is terminally ill*—and you'll notice that this is unnecessary information, so commas must be placed around the whole phrase. Eliminate choices (A), (B) and (C). Choice (D) is the best answer.

7. **A** Notice the question and use POE to find the best answer that is consistent with the information in the paragraph. The paragraph discusses the specific experience and education many medical ethicists have, therefore choice (A) is consistent, so keep it. No mention is made about the death of the healthcare system, so eliminate it. Nurses are not mentioned in the paragraph, so they are unnecessary, which means choice (C) is incorrect. Choice (D) is the direct opposite of what the paragraph is suggesting, so eliminate it. Choice (A) is the best answer.

8. **D** The underlined portion of the sentence is a pronoun, so be sure that it is consistent and clear with other nouns and pronouns in the sentence. The underlined portion is referring to the *medical ethicist,* so a singular pronoun is needed. Eliminate choices (A) and (C). Choice (B) is incorrect since "its" cannot refer to a person, so choice (D) is the best answer.

9. **D** The underlined portion mentions *expertise* and *gets into all the details,* which is redundant information, so eliminate choice (A). Also, eliminate choices (B) and (C) for the same reason. Choice (D) is the most concise, therefore the best answer.

10. **B** Notice the question and use POE to find the best answer that is consistent with the information in the passage. The medical ethicists are not employers, so eliminate choice (A). Choice (B) works since the centers are the employers. Choice (C) doesn't work implying the ethicists are part of the hospital is unnecessary information. Choice (D) would be redundant information, so get rid of it. Choice (B) is the best answer.

11. **A** Since there are periods and semicolons in the answers, check for STOP punctuation. Eliminate choices (C) and (D) since a period and semicolon are STOP punctuation and both cannot be correct. The information in the underlined portion is referring to the person, so it needs to be separated since it's a descriptive phrase. Eliminate choice (B). Therefore, choice (A) is the best answer.

12. **C** The underlined portion in the sentence includes an apostrophe, so look for either contractions or possession. Since the noun *aggression* comes after the apostrophe, look for the answer indicating possession. Eliminate choice (D). Germany doesn't end with an s, so eliminate choices (A) and (B). Choice (C) is the best answer.

13. **D** Notice the question and use POE to find the answer that best links these two paragraphs. The next paragraph opens with the phrase *that in-between period.* Choice (D) is a good match with this information. Eliminate choice (A) since the number of wars in unnecessary information. No information is given in either the first or second paragraph to support choices (B) and (C), so eliminate them. Choice (D) is the best answer.

14. **B** The underlined portion of this sentence includes pronouns, so make sure both are consistent with the non-underlined portion of the sentence. The first use of *it* is ambiguous since there is no indication of what is being referenced. Eliminate choices (A) and (D). Compare choices (B) and (C). Since *republic* is singular, then find the singular pronoun to match. Choice (B) is the best answer.

15. **C** The underlined portion of this sentence includes pronouns, so make sure both are consistent with the non-underlined portion of the sentence. There is no plural antecedent before the pronoun *them*, so eliminate choices (A) and (B). Compare choices (C) and (D). Eliminate choice (D) since *it* is ambiguous since it's not clear whether it refers to either *Germany's position* or its *constitution*. Choice (C) is the best answer.

16. **A** The underlined portion nor the answer choices seem to be testing a consistent grammar rule, so use POE and find the most concise answer without errors. Choice (A) seems okay, so hold onto it. Eliminate choice (B) since it changes the meaning by suggesting Weimar's culture was a problem. Choice (C) doesn't show distinction between the country's effervescence and problems, so eliminate it. Choice (D) is very wordy and not as concise as the underlined portion, so choice (A) is the best answer.

17. **B** The underlined portion of the sentence is a verb, so find the subject and check for agreement. The subject of the sentence is *period,* which is singular, so find the correct verb tense. Eliminate choice (A) since it's plural. Past perfect nor progressive is necessary, so eliminate choices (C) and (D). Choice (B) is the best answer.

18. **D** Notice the question and use POE to find the answer most consistent with the information in the paragraph. Eliminate choice (A) since Germany's current currency is unnecessary information. Choice (B) doesn't indicate any consequences, so eliminate it. Choice (C) is also unnecessary information since the destroyed buildings are not discussed in this paragraph. This leaves choice (D), which is the best answer.

19. **D** The answer choices include conjunction words, so check for agreement or complete ideas. Choice (A) is incorrect since the comma in the sentence separates two complete ideas, and only STOP punctuation can do this. Eliminate choices (B) and (C) for the same reason. The conjunction as in choice (D) is correct since it makes the first part of the sentence before the comma incomplete, and a comma can separate a complete and incomplete idea. Choice (D) is the best answer.

20. **B** Notice the question and use POE to find the answer most consistent with the information in the paragraph. The sentence includes the phrase *many of the cultural movements that flourished elsewhere,* so a description of those movements would be necessary information, so choice (B) looks like a good match. Eliminate choices (C) and (D). The writer's knowledge is unnecessary information, so eliminate choice (A). Choice (B) is the best answer.

21. **C** Notice the comparison word *than* in the sentence, so make sure both things that are compared are the same thing. A *depression* is being compared to the *United States,* which doesn't match, so eliminate choices (A) and (D). Choice (B) is incorrect since the adjective *deeper* is necessary for the structure of the sentence. Choice (C) works, since the pronoun *that* compares to the *depression.* Choice (C) is the best answer.

22. **D** Notice the underlined portion and answer choices contain information after *intermezzo,* so check to see if this information is necessary for the sentence. Choices (A), (B) and (C) each contain unnecessary information, so eliminate them. Choice (D) is the most concise, and therefore the best answer.

23. **B** The underlined portion and answer choices are testing comma usage, so use POE to find an answer with proper use. Eliminate choices (A) and (D) since there is no reason to stop the flow of ideas after *2008.* Choice (B) works since the name of the book is not unnecessary information, so there's no need to place commas around it. Because of that, eliminate choice (D). Choice (B) is the best answer.

24. **A** Notice the question and use POE to find the best answer consistent with the information in the paragraph. Choice (A) is a good fit since the paragraph discusses Diaz's story, which correlates with the previous paragraph that asks why work is so *relatable.* Eliminate choice (B) since there is no indication that this is a timeless question. Eliminate choices (C) and (D) since Diaz's current teaching post or the author Dan Brown is unnecessary information. Choice (A) is the best answer.

25. **A** The underlined portion and answer choices are testing comma usage, so use POE to find an answer with proper use. Since there is a list of items involved, the correct answer will have a comma after each item in the list and before the word *and.* The underlined portion is correct, so choice (A) works. Eliminate choices (B), (C) and (D) since each either omits a comma before an item in the list or adds an unnecessary one after *and* or the last item in the list. Choice (A) is the best answer.

26. **B** The underlined portion comes after the descriptive phrase *born in the Dominican Republic in 1968,* so eliminate choice (A) since it implies that Diaz's entire family was born at that place and time. Choices (C) and (D) make the same mistake. Choice (B) works since it states only Diaz as born at that place and time, so choice (B) is the best answer.

27. **C** Notice the question and use POE to find the proper placement for sentence 6. Since this sentence details when and where Diaz was born, look for other sentences that would come after this time period. Sentence 4 opens with the pronoun *there,* which has to refer to a place. Therefore, it's referring to the *Dominican Republic,* so sentence 6 should come right before sentence 4. Choice (C) is the best answer.

28. **D** Notice the question and use POE to find the best answer that is consistent with the information in the paragraph. Earlier in the sentence it's stated Diaz comes from *a newly prominent place,* so choice (D) is consistent since it discusses the population of the Dominican Republic and the United States (the next sentence further clarifies this relationship). Eliminate choice (A) since the language spoken in the Dominican Republic is unnecessary to the paragraph. Choices (B) and (C) are also unnecessary since the passage discusses neither Haiti nor Oscar de la Renta. Choice (D) is the best answer.

29. **C**   Since the question is asking for the LEAST acceptable alternative to the underlined word, then *difficulties* is correctly used. Eliminate all answer choices that are similar to *difficulties*. Choices (A), (B) and (D) are all similar, so eliminate them. Choice (B) doesn't match, since *obstructions* are physical impediments, whereas the others are abstract. Choice (C) is the best answer.

30. **A**   Since the underlined portion and answer choices include apostrophes, look for contractions or proper possession. Choice (A) fits since it could be replaced with *there is* and the subject is *a new cast,* so the subject and verb agree with each other. Eliminate choice (B) since it's a version of *there have* and the plural, past participle is incorrect. Eliminate choices (C) and (D) since past tense doesn't work here. Choice (A) is the best answer.

31. **B**   Look at the answer choices and there isn't a consistent grammar rule being tested. Compare answer choices and the difference is that *unfriendly* is a proper description of the world Diaz lived in, whereas the other answer choices use slang or hyperbole. Since it's the most clear and direct, choice (B) is the best answer.

32. **A**   Since there is a period in the answer choice, this question is testing STOP punctuation. The period separates two complete ideas, so it is used correctly. Eliminate choices (B), (C) and (D) since no STOP punctuation is used. Choice (A) is the best answer.

33. **C**   Notice the question and use POE to find the best answer that is consistent with information in the passage. No indication is made of what Diaz will do in the future, so eliminate choice (A). Choice (B) doesn't work since the author isn't trying to convince the readers to read Diaz's work. Choice (C) fits since the previous sentence refers to the *feeling* of being *isolated* or *misunderstood*. The passage never discusses other authors, so choice (D) is incorrect. Choice (C) is the best answer.

34. **C**   The underlined portion is using slang language, so look at the context within the paragraph and use POE to find the best answer consistent with the information. The paragraph goes on to say that *our technologies have changed the globe's natural climate* so choice (C) would be a good match. All other answer choices, when taken literally, wouldn't match the information in the paragraph. Choice (C) is the best answer.

35. **B**   The answer choices alternate between pronouns and nouns, so find the choice that is the most clear with the information in the paragraph. The following paragraph states that some might *doubt the claims of climate scientists,* so the *predictions* in the previous paragraph must be those of the scientists. Choice (B) is the best answer.

36. **D**   Since there are answer choices with periods and semicolons, the question is testing STOP punctuation. Eliminate choices (B) and (C) since both a period and semicolon are STOP punctuation, so both cannot be correct. Eliminate choice (A) as well since a complete idea must precede a colon. This leaves choice (D), which is the best answer.

37. **A** Notice the question and use POE to find the best answer consistent with the information in the paragraph. Choice (A) works because the rest of the sentence discusses the rise of *methane levels.* Choice (B) indicates a contrast that is not apparent in the sentence, so eliminate it. No information is given about the types of schools or the population density, so eliminate both choices (C) and (D). Choice (A) is the best answer.

38. **D** Since the answer choices have different verb tenses, the question is testing proper verb tense. Use the rest of the sentence to find information to support the proper tense. The previous sentence uses the simple past tense verb *expanded,* so choice (D) works. Eliminate choices (A) and (C) since past perfect should not be used since there are not two events that started and ended in the past. Eliminate choice (B) since it's present tense. Choice (D) is the best answer.

39. **C** Since the answer choices keep changing the word choice, use POE to find the best word that matches the context in the sentence. Eliminate choices (A) and (B) since both are the adjective and noun form of the same word, which basically means something that is "likely to happen." Eliminate choice (D) since no specific point-of-view is discussed in the passage. Choice (C) means "a way of looking at something," so this fits the sentence, therefore making it the best answer.

40. **C** Notice the question and use POE to find information consistent in the graph. Eliminate choice (A) since the United States produces much less than one-sixth of the world's methane emissions. Choice (B) is incorrect since many other countries contribute to methane emissions. Choice (C) works since the United States is above *31 million tons per year* and some countries use more than eight times as that, such as Indonesia. Eliminate choice (D) since China produces at most just under 300 tons, which is still less than ten times as much as the United States. Choice (C) is the best answer.

41. **A** The answer choices keep changing the location of the word *recent* or *recently,* so use POE to find the best use. Since *recently* is referring to a time period, choice (A) works. Choice (B) is incorrect since the glacier Quelccaya is not recent. Eliminate choices (C) and (D) since neither the scientists nor the science is recent. Choice (A) is the best answer.

42. **B** The underlined portion of this sentence is a pronoun, so make sure it is consistent with the non-underlined portion by finding the other nouns and pronouns. The *technologies* discussed in the sentence are those of the *Europeans,* which is plural, so *their* should be used as an adjective since it's placed right before a noun. Choice (B) is the best answer.

43. **B** Notice the question and use POE to find best answer consistent with the information in the passage. Paragraph 4 opens with *more recently,* and then discusses another scientific study. Therefore, the correct answer will come after another paragraph that discusses a scientific study. Eliminate choices (A) and (C) since no studies are discussed. Keep choice (B) since it mentions that *a team of scientists analyzed the ice trapped in certain parts of Greenland and the scientists determined that methane levels had risen artificially as early as the Roman era.* Keeping it where it is would be awkward since no studies are discussed in paragraph 3. Choice (B) is the best answer.

44.   **A**   The underlined portion of this sentence is a pronoun, so make sure it is consistent with the non-underlined portion by finding the other nouns and pronouns. The sentence begins with we, and the underlined portion is the possessive form of this pronoun, so choice (A) is the best answer.

Part IV
Math Test

Chapter 12
Math Test Drill 1

Math Test – No Calculator

25 MINUTES, 17 QUESTIONS

Turn to Section 3 of your answer sheet to answer the questions in this section.

DIRECTIONS

For questions **1-13**, solve each problem, choose the best answer from the choices provided, and fill in the corresponding circle on your answer sheet. For questions **14-17**, solve the problem and enter your answer in the grid on the answer sheet. Please refer to the directions before question 14 on how to enter your answers in the grid. You may use any available space in your test booklet for scratch work.

NOTES

1. The use of a calculator **is not permitted**.
2. All variables and expressions used represent real numbers unless otherwise indicated.
3. Figures provided in this test are drawn to scale unless otherwise indicated.
4. All figures lie in a plane unless otherwise indicated.
5. Unless otherwise indicated, the domain of a given function *f* is the set of all real numbers *x* for which *f(x)* is a real number.

REFERENCE

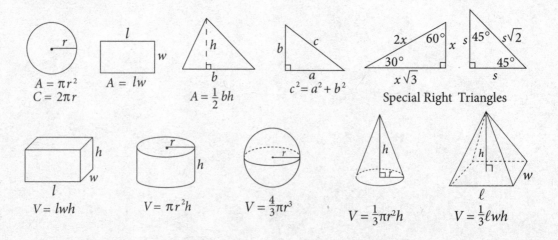

The number of degrees of arc in a circle is 360.
The number of radians of arc in a circle is 2π.
The sum of the measures in degrees of the angles of a triangle is 180.

1

Given that $3\left(\dfrac{x}{2} + 1\right) = 9$, what is x ?

A) 2

B) $\dfrac{8}{3}$

C) 3

D) 4

2

The population of Charlotte, NC, has risen by about 77,000 people every 5 years since 1990. If the population of Charlotte was 430,000 in 1990, which of the following equations could be used to estimate what the population of Charlotte, in thousands, was in 2011 ?

A) $P = 430 + 21(77)$

B) $P = 430 + \dfrac{21}{5}(77)$

C) $P = 430 + \dfrac{5}{21}(77)$

D) $P = \dfrac{430 + 21(77)}{5}$

3

Given that $f(x) = 2x^2 + 2$, what is $f(3) - f(1)$?

A) 20

B) 16

C) 10

D) 4

4

Sandra discovers that her test scores on biology tests are directly proportional to the number of hours she studies and inversely proportional to the number of classes she misses. She determines that her test score, T, can be calculated with the equation $T = \dfrac{x}{ky}$, where k is a constant. If she studied for 6 hours and got a 90 on her test, which of the following expressions represents the number of classes she missed, in terms of k ?

A) $\dfrac{6}{90k}$

B) $\dfrac{90}{6k}$

C) $90(6k)$

D) $\dfrac{90}{6}k$

5

$$x^2 - 8x - d = 0$$

In the above polynomial, the constant d is a negative integer. Which of the following could be the roots of the equation?

A) $x = -2$ and $x = -6$

B) $x = -4$ only

C) $x = -9$ and $x = 1$

D) $x = 7$ and $x = 1$

6

$$\frac{x + 6}{x - 2} > 6$$

If x is an integer, which of the following represents the solution set of x ?

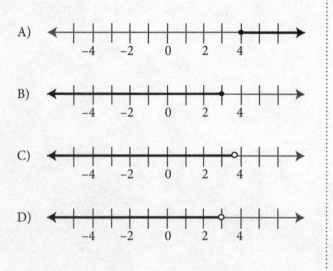

7

$$\frac{b}{A(x - b)} = \frac{x + b}{bA}$$

If $xb < 0$, and $A \neq 0$, which of the following correctly expresses b in terms of x ?

A) $b = \dfrac{-x}{\sqrt{2}}$

B) $b = \dfrac{x}{\sqrt{2}}$

C) $b = \dfrac{x}{4}$

D) $b = \dfrac{x^2}{2}$

8

James is studying the growth rates of trees and needs to determine the height of a tree. He stands 8 feet from the base of the tree and looks at the top of the tree. If his eyes are tilted up 70 degrees when he focuses on the top of the tree, and his eye level is 5 feet high, how tall is the tree?

A) $8 \sin 70° - 5$

B) $\dfrac{8 \sin 70°}{5}$

C) $8 \tan 70° - 5$

D) $8 \tan 70° + 5$

9

Which of the following is equivalent to $\dfrac{ab^2}{\sqrt[3]{a^4 b^2}}$?

A) $a^{\frac{2}{3}} b^{\frac{4}{3}}$

B) $\dfrac{b^4}{\sqrt[3]{ab}}$

C) $\sqrt[3]{\dfrac{b^4}{a}}$

D) $\dfrac{b^{\frac{4}{3}}}{a^{-\frac{1}{3}}}$

10

Before Annie leaves for a trip she determines that if she stops only once for gas, then the number of miles she can drive is given by the equation $f(x, y, z) = \dfrac{yz}{2.5} + xy$. The variables x, y, and z in this equation are the amount of money, in dollars, she brings to spend at the gas station, the number of gallons of gas in her tank when she starts her trip, and the miles per gallon her car gets for the entire trip, respectively. Given this information, how many gallons did Annie buy at the gas station if she drove 420 miles, her gas mileage was 40 miles per gallon, and she started with 9 gallons in the tank?

A) 16.8

B) 3.75

C) 2.5

D) 1.5

11

For two integers, p and q, if the positive difference between p and q is no more than 3, and the sum of p and q is between −12 and 30, which of the following describes all possible values of q ?

A) $-7 \leq q \leq 16$

B) $-8 \leq q \leq 17$

C) $-6 < q < 17$

D) $-7 \leq q \leq 13$

12

If three times the sum of the squares of x and y is four more than three times the square of the difference between x and y, what is the value of xy ?

A) −2

B) $\dfrac{-2}{3}$

C) $\dfrac{2}{3}$

D) 2

13

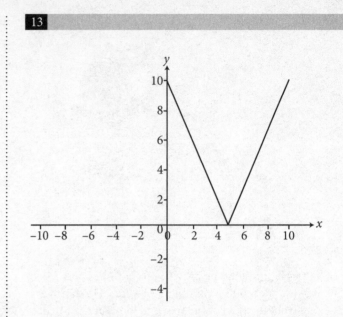

The function $h(x)$ is a reflection of $f(x)$ across the y-axis. If the graph shown above is $h(x) - 5$, which of the following could represent $f(x)$?

A) $f(x) = 2|x - 5| - 5$

B) $f(x) = 2|x + 5| + 5$

C) $f(x) = |x + 5| + 5$

D) $f(x) = |2x - 5| - 5$

DIRECTIONS

For questions 14-17, solve the problem and enter your answer in the grid, as described below, on the answer sheet.

1. Although not required, it is suggested that you write your answer in the boxes at the top of the columns to help you fill in the circles accurately

2. Mark no more than one circle in any column.

3. No question has a negative answer.

4. Some problems may have more than one correct answer. In such cases, grid only one answer.

5. **Mixed numbers** such as $3\frac{1}{2}$ must be gridded as 3.5 or 7/2. (If [3 1 / 2] is entered into the grid, it will be interpreted as $\frac{31}{2}$, not as $3\frac{1}{2}$).

6. **Decimal Answers:** If you obtain a decimal answer with more digits than the grid can accomodate, it may be either rounded or truncated, but it must fill the entire grid.

Answer: $\frac{7}{12}$ Answer: 2.5

Write answer in boxes.

Fraction line

Decimal point

Grid in result.

Acceptable ways to grid $\frac{2}{3}$ are:

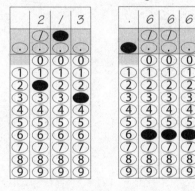

Answer: 201
Either position is correct.

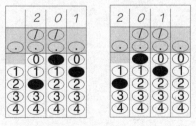

NOTE: You may start your answers in any column, space permitting. Columns you don't need to use should be left blank.

14

If $x^2 - x = 12$ and $x > 0$, what is the value of x?

15

If one-third of m is equal to six less than m, what is m?

16

$$3a - 16 = b$$
$$4a + b = 32$$

What is the value of a in the above system of equations?

17

$$\frac{x}{x-3} + \frac{2x}{x-2} = -\frac{4}{x^2 - 5x + 6}$$

Given the above equation, what is a possible value of $x + 6$?

THIS PAGE IS LEFT INTENTIONALLY BLANK.

Math Test – Calculator

45 MINUTES, 31 QUESTIONS

Turn to Section 4 of your answer sheet to answer the questions in this section.

DIRECTIONS

For questions **1-27**, solve each problem, choose the best answer from the choices provided, and fill in the corresponding circle on your answer sheet. For questions **28-31**, solve the problem and enter your answer in the grid on the answer sheet. Please refer to the directions before question 28 on how to enter your answers in the grid. You may use any available space in your test booklet for scratch work.

NOTES

1. The use of a calculator **is permitted**.
2. All variables and expressions used represent real numbers unless otherwise indicated.
3. Figures provided in this test are drawn to scale unless otherwise indicated.
4. All figures lie in a plane unless otherwise indicated.
5. Unless otherwise indicated, the domain of a given function f is the set of all real numbers x for which $f(x)$ is a real number.

REFERENCE

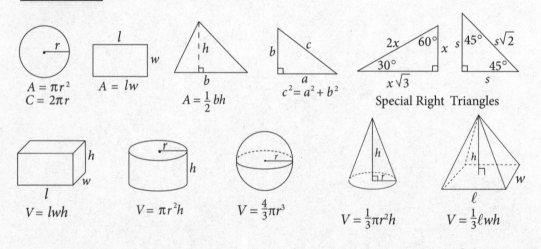

The number of degrees of arc in a circle is 360.
The number of radians of arc in a circle is 2π.
The sum of the measures in degrees of the angles of a triangle is 180.

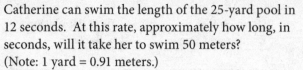

1

Catherine can swim the length of the 25-yard pool in 12 seconds. At this rate, approximately how long, in seconds, will it take her to swim 50 meters? (Note: 1 yard = 0.91 meters.)

A) 13.2

B) 21.8

C) 24

D) 26.4

2

Nick is working on a project and is supposed to take hourly measurements of the temperature. He records the temperature at 2 PM as 78° Fahrenheit, but later realizes that the data needs to be in degrees Celsius. Given that the formula $F = \frac{9}{5}C + 32$ can be used to convert Celsius (C) to Fahrenheit (F), what is the temperature in degrees Celsius at 2 PM?

A) 25.6°

B) 29.3°

C) 61.1°

D) 172.4°

3

Percent of University Community with Health Insurance		
	Male	Female
Undergraduate	75%	83%
Graduate	65%	72%
Faculty and Staff	87%	91%

Roger wants to determine the approximate percentage of residents in his state that have health insurance, so he goes to the state university and asks 500 randomly selected people on campus whether or not they have healthcare. The results are shown in the table above. Which of the following conclusions can be most logically drawn from the data shown above?

A) The number of females at the university with health insurance is greater than the number of males with health insurance at the university

B) Approximately 76% of males in the state have health insurance

C) The faculty and staff at this university are more likely to be insured than the graduate students.

D) Graduate students are less likely to have health insurance than the average resident of the state.

4

If $\frac{3x + 2}{7} = \frac{2x + 5}{7}$, then $x = ?$

A) $-\frac{5}{2}$

B) $-\frac{2}{3}$

C) 3

D) 7

5

Year	% Unemployed
2005	5.3
2006	4.7
2007	4.6
2008	5.0
2009	7.8
2010	9.8
2011	9.2
2012	8.3
2013	8.0
2014	6.6
2015	5.7

The table above shows the percentage of Americans aged 16 and older who were unemployed in the years 2005-2015 (measured annually at the end of January). According to the data above, what was the average (arithmetic mean) percentage of unemployed Americans aged 16 and older in the years 2008-2011, inclusive?

A) 4.57%

B) 6.82%

C) 7.95%

D) 9.21%

6

In a certain safari park in Tanzania, the ratio of wildebeest to gazelles is 4 to 3 and the ratio of elephants to hyenas is 3 to 5. If the ratio of gazelles to elephants is 1 to 1, then what is the ratio of hyenas to wildebeest?

A) 5 to 4

B) 4 to 5

C) 5 to 3

D) 3 to 5

7

Hours Since Experiment Began	Total Population of Bacteria
0	7
1	14
2	28
3	56

A scientist is studying the growth rate of bacteria in a certain colony. Based on the data in the chart above, she determines that the number of bacteria in the colony at any time in the first 3 hours can be modeled by the expression $7 \times b^c$. What does the quantity b represent in the expression?

A) The initial population of the bacteria colony

B) The factor by which the colony multiplies every hour

C) The hours since the experiment began

D) The total population of the bacteria colony at a given time

8

	5mg dose	10mg dose	15mg dose
Nausea	14%	16%	32%
Insomnia	10%	25%	40%
Nausea and Insomnia	6%	12%	15%

Researchers studying a new medication find that it can cause nausea, insomnia, or both in patients who take it. After studying patients in three different groups, each taking a different dose of the medication, the researchers calculate the chance that a patient on the medication will experience these side effects. The results are shown in the table above. If a patient is chosen at random from those with nausea after taking 10 milligrams of the medication, what is the probability that the patient also has insomnia?

A) 0.50

B) 0.64

C) 0.75

D) 0.80

9

Time (seconds)	Height (feet)
0	
1	
2	
3	
4	
5	

The table above shows the height of a projectile that is shot from a 10-foot tall platform. If $H(t)$ represents the height of the projectile in feet, and t represents the time, in seconds, then which of the following functions accurately reflects the projectile's trajectory according to the data above?

A) $H(t) = -x^2 + 4x + 10$

B) $H(t) = x^2 - 4x + 10$

C) $H(t) = -x^2 - 4x + 10$

D) $H(t) = x^2 + 4x - 10$

10

During a sale at a certain clothing store, customers receive a discount of 10% off for purchases that are up to $120 at regular price and 15% for purchases that are $120 or more at regular price. A sales tax of 7% is added after the discount. If Sara's total bill is $103.04, what was the original price of the merchandise she bought?

A) $96.70

B) $99.20

C) $107

D) $113.20

11

Cara has a greenhouse full of pea plants and begins an experiment in which she varies the amount of sunlight that the plants receive. She determines that the average height, in centimeters, of her pea plants t days after she begins the experiment is given by the equation $h = 13 + 0.2t$. Plants that have a height within 15% of this value exhibit "standard" growth. Plants that are taller than this range exhibit "superior" growth, and plants that are shorter than this range exhibit "inferior" growth. If a pea plant has a height of m centimeters after n days it exhibits "superior" growth, but if it has a height of $m - 3$ centimeters, it exhibits "inferior" growth. Which of the following pairs of inequalities could be used to determine possible values of m and n ?

A) $m > 13 + 0.15(0.2n)$

   $m - 3 < 13 - 0.15(0.2n)$

B) $n > 1.15(13 + 0.2m)$

   $n < .85 (13 + 0.2(m - 3)$

C) $m < 1.15 (13 + 0.2n)$

   $m - 3 > .85(13 + 0.2n)$

D) $m > 1.15(13 + 0.2n)$

   $m - 3 < 0.85(13 + .2n)$

12

A function is given by $y = ax + c$, in which a and c are constants and $a > c$. Which of the following could be the graph of y ?

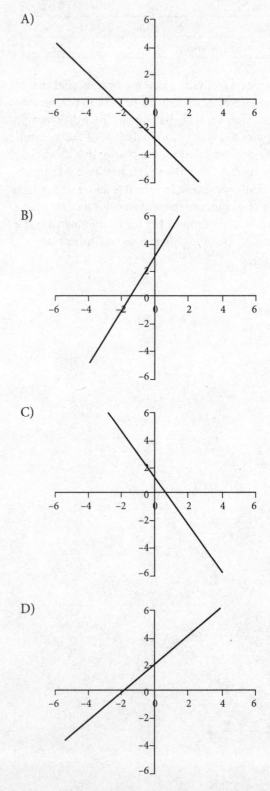

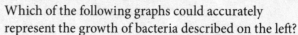

13

A study group of four students took a midterm exam in Botany class. The students' scores had a high score of 85, a range of 25, and a mode of 70. If a student who scored a 95 on the midterm joined the study group, then what would be the average (arithmetic mean) score of all five students on the midterm?

A) 69

B) 76

C) 78

D) 90

▼

Questions 14-15 refer to the following information.

A scientist places 100 bacteria in a petri dish and observes the increase in the number of bacteria over time. She determines that the number of bacteria triples every hour.

14

If m represents the time, in minutes, then which of the following functions could represent the number of bacteria, $N(m)$, over time?

A) $N(m) = 100(3^{60m})$

B) $N(m) = 100(3^m)$

C) $N(m) = 100(60^{3m})$

D) $N(m) = 100\left(3^{\frac{m}{60}}\right)$

15

Which of the following graphs could accurately represent the growth of bacteria described on the left?

A)

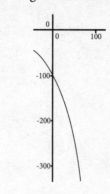

B)

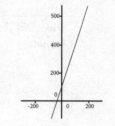

C)

D)

▲

16

If $3x + 5y = 80$ and $24 - y = x$, then which of the following is equivalent to $\dfrac{x}{y}$?

A) 3

B) 5

C) 7

D) 9

17

	Did Donate	Did Not Donate	Total
Had children present	324	36	360
Did not have children present	66	174	240
Total	390	210	600

A social scientist hypothesizes that people are more likely to donate to charities that benefit children if they have children with them when asked to donate. He set up a booth for a children's charity at a craft fair at a mall and asked for donations. He noted whether each person he asked to donate gave money and whether the person was accompanied by any children. The results are shown in the table above. The probability that a person with children donated is how much greater than the probability that a person without children did NOT donate?

A) 0.175

B) 0.245

C) 0.725

D) 0.900

18

$$y = (x - 5)(x + 6)$$
$$y = x + 6$$

The system of equations above has two solutions in the xy-plane. What is the x-coordinate of the midpoint of the two solutions?

A) −6

B) 0

C) 6

D) 12

19

$$F = 3x - 2$$
$$G = x - 1$$

Given the equations above, which of the following is equivalent to $F^3 - G$?

A) $x^3 - 3x^2 + 1$

B) $8x^3 - 12x^2 + 6x - 1$

C) $27x^3 - 54x^2 + 35x - 7$

D) $27x^3 - 54x^2 + 37x - 9$

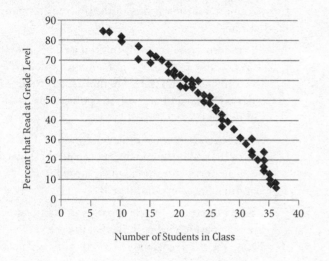

Questions 20-21 refer to the following information.

The scatter plot below shows the relationship between the number of students per third grade class in a metro area and the percentage of the students that read at or above grade level.

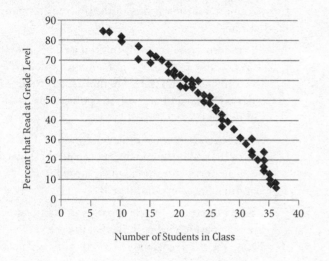

Number of Students in Class

20

For all classes with at least 5 people, which of the following equations, in which n represents the number of students and P represents the percent that read at grade level, most accurately models the above relationship?

A) $P = 85 + 2.5(n)$

B) $P = 85 - 2.5(n - 5)$

C) $P = 88 - \left(\dfrac{n}{4}\right)^2$

D) $P = 88 - \left(\dfrac{n}{2}\right)^2$

21

A school in the metro area has 208 third grade students spread evenly over x classrooms. Approximately 40% of the students in these classes read at a third grade level. If the school had one more third grade classroom approximately what percent of the students would be expected to read at grade level?

A) 23%

B) 41%

C) 50%

D) 60%

22

Shawn purchases 200 shares of a stock at the beginning of 2009. The stock decreases in value by 15% in 2009, then increases 8% per year in 2010 and 2011, and then the total value of the 200 shares increases by $500 in 2012. If the total value of the stock Shawn owns is $2,750 at the end of 2012, what was the approximate price per share when he purchased it?

A) $11.15

B) $11.35

C) $11.61

D) $12.25

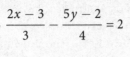
23

$$\frac{2x-3}{3} - \frac{5y-2}{4} = 2$$

$$-4(2x+y) = 27$$

Given the above system of equations, what is the value of $x + y$?

A) $-\dfrac{39}{8}$

B) -3

C) $\dfrac{8}{17}$

D) $\dfrac{9}{8}$

24

On a map Sam's house is 5 centimeters west and 9 centimeters north of Joe's house. If there is a road that runs directly from Sam's house to Joe's house and it takes Sam 45 minutes to drive along this road at 30 miles per hour to Joe's house, approximately how many miles does each centimeter on this map represent?

A) 0.46

B) 1.6

C) 1.8

D) 2.2

25

As part of its effort to predict a recent election, a prominent polling company conducted telephone interviews during which respondents were asked whether they were more likely to vote for Candidate A or Candidate B. Based on the results of this telephone survey, the polling company predicted that Candidate A would likely win the election. Which of the following pieces of information, if true, would cast the most doubt upon the validity of the polling company's prediction?

A) The polling company only interviewed people with landline telephones, but younger voters who only use cell phones are more likely than older voters to affiliate with the political party of Candidate B

B) An independent mail-in survey conducted by one of the polling company's competitors showed that a majority of respondents claimed to favor Candidate A over Candidate B

C) Analyses of the polling company's predictions over the past ten years show that it has a very strong record of correctly predicting the results of major elections

D) The polling company conducted a follow-up telephone interview with the same respondents and asked a more open-ended question: "Which candidate do you plan to vote for in the upcoming election?" and, based on the results of this second interview, concluded that Candidate A was likely to win the election

26

In a Brazilian nature conservancy, park rangers have worked over the past few decades to increase the number of howler monkeys living within the grounds of the conservancy. In the year 1980, the conservancy contained 800 howler monkeys, and in the year 2010 the conservancy contained 1200 howler monkeys. In the equation $1200 = 800 + 30x$, what does the x most likely represent?

A) The total number of howler monkeys added to the conservancy's population from 1980-2010

B) The total number of years that have passed since the park rangers began working to increase the howler monkey population

C) The average yearly increase in the howler monkey population from 1980-2010

D) The minimum number of howler monkeys that must be added for the population in the conservancy to remain constant

27

Which of the following expressions is equivalent to $\dfrac{64^4 - 32^8}{128^2}$?

A) $\dfrac{2^8}{1 + 2^6}$

B) $2^{24} - 2^{-4}$

C) $\dfrac{1 - 2^4}{2^{10}}$

D) $2^{10}(1 - 2^{16})$

DIRECTIONS

For questions 28-31, solve the problem and enter your answer in the grid, as described below, on the answer sheet.

1. Although not required, it is suggested that you write your answer in the boxes at the top of the columns to help you fill in the circles accurately

2. Mark no more than one circle in any column.

3. No question has a negative answer.

4. Some problems may have more than one correct answer. In such cases, grid only one answer.

5. **Mixed numbers** such as $3\frac{1}{2}$ must be grid-ded as 3.5 or 7/2. (If 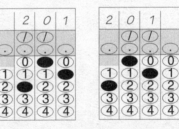 is entered into the grid, it will be interpreted as $\frac{31}{2}$, not as $3\frac{1}{2}$).

6. **Decimal Answers:** If you obtain a decimal answer with more digits than the grid can accomodate, it may be either rounded or truncated, but it must fill the entire grid.

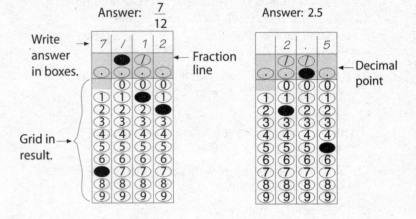

Answer: $\frac{7}{12}$ — Write answer in boxes. — Fraction line — Grid in result.

Answer: 2.5 — Decimal point

Acceptable ways to grid $\frac{2}{3}$ are:

Answer: 201
Either position is correct.

NOTE: You may start your answers in any column, space permitting. Columns you don't need to use should be left blank.

28

$$3y - 9 = \frac{3}{2}x$$

$$y = ax - 3$$

If the system of equations above has no solutions, what is the value of a ?

29

$$y = 2x + 4$$
$$y = (x - 2)^2$$

The system of equations above has two solutions in the xy-plane. What is the sum of the x- and y-coordinates of the solution in Quadrant I ?

Questions 30-31 refer to the following information.

Brian bought a certain 3D printer that has a maximum build volume of 4 inches × 4 inches × 4 inches. It can print objects at different fill levels, which will make the final object more or less dense without changing the volume.

30

If 1 inch equals 25.4 millimeters, and there are 10 millimeters in a centimeter, what is the printer's maximum build volume in cubic centimeters, rounded to the nearest whole number?

31

Brian used the 3D printer to make a tablet stand that weighed 0.2 ounces with a volume of 0.183 cubic inches. If there are 28.35 grams in an ounce and 0.061 cubic inches in a cubic centimeter, at what density did Brian print the stand, in grams per cubic centimeter? (Density = mass / volume)

Redesigned PSAT

Completely darken bubbles with a No. 2 pencil. If you make a mistake, be sure to erase mark completely. Erase all stray marks.

1. Student Information

Your Name: _____
(Print)   Last   First   M.I.

Email Address: _____ Date: ____ / ____ / ____
(Print)   MM   DD   YYYY

Home Address: _____ Apartment No. _____
(Print)   Number and Street

_____
City   State   Zip Code

High School: _____ Class of: _____

2. Your Name

First 4 letters of last name				FIRST INIT	MID INIT

Bubbles A through Z for each column.

3. Phone Number

Area Code			Phone number						

Bubbles 0 through 9 for each column.

Mathematics — No Calculator

SECTION 3

1. Ⓐ Ⓑ Ⓒ Ⓓ
2. Ⓐ Ⓑ Ⓒ Ⓓ
3. Ⓐ Ⓑ Ⓒ Ⓓ
4. Ⓐ Ⓑ Ⓒ Ⓓ
5. Ⓐ Ⓑ Ⓒ Ⓓ

6. Ⓐ Ⓑ Ⓒ Ⓓ
7. Ⓐ Ⓑ Ⓒ Ⓓ
8. Ⓐ Ⓑ Ⓒ Ⓓ
9. Ⓐ Ⓑ Ⓒ Ⓓ
10. Ⓐ Ⓑ Ⓒ Ⓓ

11. Ⓐ Ⓑ Ⓒ Ⓓ
12. Ⓐ Ⓑ Ⓒ Ⓓ
13. Ⓐ Ⓑ Ⓒ Ⓓ

14.

15.

16.

17.

Grid-in answer boxes with bubbles 0 through 9 for questions 14, 15, 16, and 17.

1. Student Information

Your Name: _____
(Print)   Last   First   M.I.

Email Address: _____   Date: _____ / _____ / _____
(Print)   MM   DD   YYYY

Home Address: _____   Apartment No. _____
(Print)   Number and Street

_____
City   State   Zip Code

High School: _____   Class of: _____

2. Your Name

First 4 letters of last name				FIRST INIT	MID INIT

3. Phone Number

Area Code			Phone number						

Mathematics — Calculator Permissible

SECTION **4**

1. Ⓐ Ⓑ Ⓒ Ⓓ
2. Ⓐ Ⓑ Ⓒ Ⓓ
3. Ⓐ Ⓑ Ⓒ Ⓓ
4. Ⓐ Ⓑ Ⓒ Ⓓ
5. Ⓐ Ⓑ Ⓒ Ⓓ
6. Ⓐ Ⓑ Ⓒ Ⓓ

7. Ⓐ Ⓑ Ⓒ Ⓓ
8. Ⓐ Ⓑ Ⓒ Ⓓ
9. Ⓐ Ⓑ Ⓒ Ⓓ
10. Ⓐ Ⓑ Ⓒ Ⓓ
11. Ⓐ Ⓑ Ⓒ Ⓓ
12. Ⓐ Ⓑ Ⓒ Ⓓ

13. Ⓐ Ⓑ Ⓒ Ⓓ
14. Ⓐ Ⓑ Ⓒ Ⓓ
15. Ⓐ Ⓑ Ⓒ Ⓓ
16. Ⓐ Ⓑ Ⓒ Ⓓ
17. Ⓐ Ⓑ Ⓒ Ⓓ
18. Ⓐ Ⓑ Ⓒ Ⓓ

19. Ⓐ Ⓑ Ⓒ Ⓓ
20. Ⓐ Ⓑ Ⓒ Ⓓ
21. Ⓐ Ⓑ Ⓒ Ⓓ
22. Ⓐ Ⓑ Ⓒ Ⓓ
23. Ⓐ Ⓑ Ⓒ Ⓓ
24. Ⓐ Ⓑ Ⓒ Ⓓ

25. Ⓐ Ⓑ Ⓒ Ⓓ
26. Ⓐ Ⓑ Ⓒ Ⓓ
27. Ⓐ Ⓑ Ⓒ Ⓓ

28.

29.

30.

31.

Chapter 13
Math Test
Drill 1: Answers
and Explanations

ANSWERS AND EXPLANATIONS

Section 3—Math Test

1. **D** To solve this equation, isolate x on one side of the equation. First, divide both sides by 3, resulting in $\left(\dfrac{x}{2}\right) + 1 = 3$. Subtract 1 from each side to get $\left(\dfrac{x}{2}\right) = 2$. Finally, multiply both sides by 2 to get $x = 4$, or (D). Alternatively, you can use PITA and plug in each of the answer choices into the equation until one of them works.

2. **B** As you work this problem, keep in mind that the question asks for the population in thousands, so we will drop the last three zeroes off the numbers. The population starts at 430,000, so the increase will be added to the base number of 430. Eliminate (D). The population rises 77,000 every five years. Since there are 21 years from 1990 to 2011, divide 21 by 5 and then multiply by the increase of 77, or answer (B).

3. **B** Plug in 3 and 1 for x in the given function. $f(3)$ is equal to $2(3)^2 + 2$ or 20. $f(1)$ is equal to $2(1)^2 + 2$ or 4. To find the answer, subtract 4 from 20, giving a final answer of 16 or (B).

4. **A** To find the answer, plug in the values given into the equation. Her test score, T, equals 90. She studied 6 hours, which is directly proportional to T, so $6 = x$ (for direct proportion $y = kx$). The equation is now $90 = \dfrac{6}{yk}$. To solve for y, multiply both sides by yk to get $90 = \dfrac{6}{yk}$. Finally, divide both sides by $90k$ to get $y = \dfrac{6}{90k}$ or answer (A).

5. **D** To find the possible roots that work, try them out. Start with (A). If the roots are –2 and 6, then the factored polynomial is $(x + 2)(x + 6)$. FOIL to get $x^2 + 8x + 12$, which does not fit the polynomial given. Try the other three sets of roots. The constant d is a negative number being subtracted (a double negative) so d will become positive in the polynomial. Only (D) results in –8 for the second term and a positive constant.

6. **B** First solve for x. Multiply both sides by $(x - 2)$ to get $x + 6 > 6x - 12$. Subtract x and add 12 to both sides to get $18 > 5x$. Isolate x on one side to get $3.6 > x$. Be careful of choice (C). The question says x must be an integer, so the answer is (B).

7. **A** Multiply both sides by A to get $\dfrac{b}{x-b} = \dfrac{x+b}{b}$. Cross-multiply: $b^2 = (x-b)(x+b)$. Right-hand side is difference of squares: $b^2 = x^2 - b^2$. Add b^2 to both sides: $2b^2 = x^2$. Divide both sides by 2: $b^2 = \dfrac{x^2}{2}$. Take the square root of both sides: $\sqrt{b^2} = \sqrt{\dfrac{x^2}{2}}$. Note you get both positive AND negative roots of b: $b = \pm\dfrac{x}{\sqrt{2}}$. Because $xb < 0$, it must be the case that one of x or b is negative (and the other is positive), so you must have the negative root: $b = -\dfrac{x}{\sqrt{2}}$, which is choice (A).

8. **D** Label the base of the triangle with 8 ft. Use SOHCAHTOA to choose tan as the appropriate trig function. $\tan 70 = \dfrac{x}{8}$ or $x = 8\tan 70$. Remember to add 5 to the answer to account for James's height. The answer is (D).

9. **C** First, rewrite the denominator. Taking the cube root is the same as raising to the $\dfrac{1}{3}$ power. The new denominator then becomes $a^{\frac{4}{3}}b^{\frac{2}{3}}$. Use the properties of exponents (MADSPM). $\dfrac{a}{a^{\frac{4}{3}}} = a^{-\frac{1}{3}}$ and $\dfrac{b^2}{b^{\frac{2}{3}}} = b^{\frac{4}{3}}$. The b value is the numerator, and the a value is the denominator. The only answer choice equivalent to $\dfrac{b^{\frac{4}{3}}}{a^{-\frac{1}{3}}}$ is (C).

10. **D** Be careful with this question; the equation is unnecessary to solve the problem. We know that Annie drove 420 miles total. With the 9 gallons in the tank and a gas mileage of 40 miles per gallon, Annie can drive 360 miles before she needs to stop for more gas. To find how many gallons she purchased, divide the remaining miles (60) by the gas mileage (40), to get 1.5 more gallons, or answer (D).

11. **A** Try the numbers in the answer choices (if it helps, first write out the inequalities: $|p - q| < 3$ and $-12 < p + q < 30$). Start with the largest possible value of q, which occurs in (B) and (C). If q equals 17, then p can equal any number between 14 and 20 (for the first equation to remain true). Then check to see if any of the p values will also make the second equation true by testing 14 and 20 in the second: neither $17 + 20$ nor $17 + 14$ is less than 30. Eliminate (B) and (C). Check $q = 16$: p is between 19 and 13, which does work ($13 + 16 = 29$, which is < 30). Since we want to include all of the values of q that work, we eliminate (D) and choose (A).

12.   **C**   Begin by translating the question into an equation: $3(x^2 + y^2) = 4 + 3(x - y)^2$. Distribute the 3 and FOIL the $(x - y)^2$ to get $3x^2 + 3y^2 = 4 + 3x^2 - 6xy + 3y^2$. Eliminate $3x^2$ and $3y^2$ from both sides to get $0 = 4 - 6xy$. Isolate xy to get the answer $\dfrac{2}{3}$ or answer choice (C).

13.   **B**   First, pick a point on the current function. We know that $h(x) - 5$ is the graph of $h(x)$ moved down five units (5 is subtracted from every y-coordinate). If $h(x) - 5$ has the point $(5, 0)$, then that point on $h(x)$ will be $(5, 5)$. Next, translate the point across the y-axis, reversing the sign of the x value, to get $(-5, 5)$. Now check to see what functions contain this point by plugging in -5 for x. Two answer choices, (B) and (C), give us a y value of 5. Try a new point. $(0, 10)$ becomes $(0, 15)$ for $h(x)$. It's the same point on $f(x)$ as well. Plug in 0 for x in the remaining answer choices. Only (B) gives the correct y value of 15.

14.   **4**   Move the 12 to the other side and factor to get $(x - 4)(x + 3) = 0$. x equals 4 and -3. The question states x > 0, so the correct answer is 4.

15.   **9**   Write out the equation: $\left(\dfrac{1}{3}\right)m = m - 6$. Multiply both sides by 3 to get rid of the fraction, resulting in $m = 3m - 18$. Subtract 3m from both sides to get $-2m = -18$. Divide by -2 to get $m = 9$.

16. $\dfrac{48}{7}$ **or 6.85 or 6.86**

       Rewrite the first equation so it looks like the second equation: $3a - b = 16$. Then add the two equations together. The b's cancel out, leaving $7a = 48$. Divide both sides by 7 to get $a = \dfrac{48}{7}$.

17. $\dfrac{20}{3}$ **or 6.67**

       Start by factoring the denominator of the right side of the equation to get $\dfrac{x}{x-3} + \dfrac{2x}{x-2} = \dfrac{-4}{(x-3)(x-2)}$. With a common denominator of $(x - 3)(x - 2)$, add the fractions to get $\dfrac{x(x-2) + 2x(x-3)}{(x-3)(x-2)} = \dfrac{-4}{(x-3)(x-2)}$. Distribute the x and the $2x$ to get $\dfrac{x^2 - 2x + 2x^2 - 6x}{(x-3)(x-2)} = \dfrac{-4}{(x-3)(x-2)}$. Simplify the numerator to get $\dfrac{3x^2 - 8x}{(x-3)(x-2)} = \dfrac{-4}{(x-3)(x-2)}$.

       Because the denominators of the two fractions are the same, the numerators of the two fractions on either side of the equal sign must be equal to each other. Therefore, $3x^2 - 8x = -4$. Bringing all terms over to the left side gives us $3x^2 - 8x + 4 = 0$. Factoring $3x^2 - 8x + 4 = 0$ gives us

$(3x-2)(x-2)=0$. From this, we get $x=\dfrac{2}{3}$ or $x=2$. However, plugging in $x=2$ back in to the original equation would result in two of the fractions becoming undefined, so $x=2$ is discarded.

Therefore, $x=\dfrac{2}{3}$ and, thus, $x+6=\dfrac{2}{3}+6=\dfrac{20}{3}$.

Section 4—Math Test

1. **D** Start by converting 50 meters to yards by using a proportion: $\dfrac{1 \text{ yard}}{0.91 \text{ meters}}=\dfrac{x \text{ yards}}{50 \text{ meters}}$. Cross-multiply to get $0.91x=50$. Divide both sides by 0.91 to get 54.95 yards. Next, set up a proportion to determine how long it will take Catherine to swim 54.95 yards: $\dfrac{25 \text{ yards}}{12 \text{ seconds}}=\dfrac{54.95 \text{ yards}}{x \text{ seconds}}$. Cross-multiply to get $25x=659.34$. Divide both sides by 25 to get $x=26.37$, which is closest to choice (D).

2. **A** Plug in 78 for F in the equation: $78=\dfrac{9}{5}C+32$. Subtract 32 from both sides: $46=\dfrac{9}{5}C$. Multiply both sides by 5 to clear the fraction: $230=9C$. Finally, divide both sides by 9 to get $25.56=C$, which is closest to choice (A).

3. **C** Consider each answer choice and work Process of Elimination (POE). For choice (A), you would need to know how many males and how many females are at the university. It may be the case that there are many more times as many males as females, which would make the number of males with health insurance greater (despite the lesser percentage). Eliminate choice (A). Choice (B) would require you to assume that the university is reflective of the state and that averaging the three groups would result in a good reflection of the state as a whole. Each of these alone are questionable assumptions; both together means you should eliminate (B). Choice (D) can similarly be eliminated, as it makes an inference about the average resident of the state. Choice (C) simply compares the groups surveyed and makes a safe inference based on how likely it is a particular member of one group is insured, so choice (C) is the best response.

4. **C** Start by multiplying both sides by 7 to clear the fractions. This gives you $3x+2=2x+5$. Next, subtract $2x$ from both sides: $x+2=5$. Finally, subtract 2 from both sides to get $x=3$, which is choice (C).

5. **C**   In order to find the average percentage of unemployed Americans in the years 2008-2011, simply find the relevant years in the table and extract the data you need. The average for these four years will be the sum divided by the number of things: $\frac{5.0 + 7.8 + 9.8 + 9.2}{4} = \frac{31.8}{4} = 7.95$, which matches answer choice (C).

6. **A**   This question can be solved by plugging in numbers. If you say that there are 4 wildebeest and 3 gazelles, and the ratio of gazelles to elephants is 1 to 1, then there would also be 3 elephants (and thus 5 hyenas). The ratio of hyenas to wildebeest would therefore be 5 to 4, answer choice (A).

7. **B**   Knowing the growth formula can help here. The *formula is final amount = original amount (multiplier)*$^{\text{number of changes}}$, so b is the growth multiplier. Without knowing the formula, find the answer using Process of Elimination and Plugging In. At a time of 0, or when the experiment began, there were 7 bacteria in the colony. The 7 is already represented in the expression, so b would not also be 7. Eliminate (A). The entire expression $7 \times b^c$ represents the total population at any time, according to the question, so eliminate (D). Therefore, b is either the growth factor or the number of hours. Plug in some numbers from the chart to determine which it is. To test (B), plug in 14 for the total population and 1 for c, which would be the time if b is the growth factor. The equation becomes $14 = 7 \times b^1$. Divide both sides by 7 to get $2 = b^1$, so $b = 2$. If the growth multiplier is 2, the population would double every hour, and the chart shows that it does. The correct answer is (B).

8. **C**   Probability is defined as the number that fit the requirement divided by the total number of things. In this case, there are no numbers, so plug in. Plugging in 100 on percent questions is the easiest way to go. If 100 people took the medication, 16 of them would have taken the 10 milligram dose and had nausea. This number is the "total" for the probability and is therefore the denominator of the fraction. Of those 16 people, 12 of them would have both nausea and insomnia, so that is the numerator. The probability, then, is $\frac{12}{16} = 0.75$, which is choice (C).

9. **A**   The best way to approach this question is to plug the values from the table into the functions in the answer choices to determine which one matches. Only answer (A) works for all of the values in the table.

10. **C**   Plug In the Answers! Choice (B) is more obnoxious than choice (C) (because (B) has a decimal), so start with choice (C). If the item was $107, then Sarah receives a discount of 10%, or $0.10 \times 107 = \$10.70$, making the post-discount price $107 - 10.70 = \$96.30$. Next, you must apply 7% sales tax. 7% of $96.30 is $0.07 \times 96.30 = \$6.74$. This is added to the total: $96.30 + 6.74 = \$103.04$. This matches what the question indicates, so choose (C).

11. **D** Start with the "superior" growth scenario. If the average height is $13 + 0.2t$, and superior growth is greater than 15% more than the average, then superior growth is greater than $13 + 0.2t + 0.15 (13 + 0.2t)$, which simplifies to $1.15(13 + 0.2t)$. Because a plant with growth of m is superior, then $m > 1.15(13 + 0.2t)$. Only choice (D) has this inequality. (Note that choice (B) switches the variables; very tricky!)

12. **A** In the form $y = mx + b$, m represents the slope and b represents the y-intercept. Therefore, if the form is instead $y = ax + c$, a is slope and c is y-intercept. Therefore, in this case the slope must be greater than the y-intercept. It's easier to determine the y-intercept first, so start there and then determine the slope for each answer choice. In choice (A), the y-intercept is at $(0, -3)$, so the y-intercept and therefore the value of c is -3. The line goes through $(-3, 0)$ and $(0, -3)$, which makes the slope $\dfrac{-3 - 0}{0 - (-3)} = -1$, so $a = -1$. $-1 > -3$, so choice (A) works; choose (A).

13. **B** For the four original students, because the mode was 70, there must be at least two students with a 70. If the highest score was an 85 and the range of scores was 25, then the lowest score was $85 - 25 = 60$. This means the original four scores were 60, 70, 70, 85. With the new student, the five scores are 60, 70, 70, 85, and 95. To find the average, add the scores and divide by the number of scores (5): $\dfrac{60 + 70 + 70 + 85 + 95}{5} = 76$, which matches choice (B).

14. **D** Since the number of bacteria triples every hour, that means that the number of bacteria triples every 60 minutes. Since the m in the functions represents the number of minutes, you need to divide m by 60 to represent the number of hours. Only choice (D) matches. Alternatively, you could plug in numbers such as to determine how many bacteria there would be after $\dfrac{120 \text{ minutes}}{2 \text{ hours}}$ (and then find which answer choice matches your target answer).

15. **C** The question states that the number of bacteria triples every hour; this is an exponential relationship. Choice (B) is linear and choice (D) is quadratic, so both can be eliminated. The number of bacteria is increasing, not decreasing, so eliminate (A) and choose (C).

16. **B** Start by rearranging the second equation in order to get all of the variables on one side: $x + y = 24$. Next, multiply the second equation by 3: $3(x + y = 24)$ gives you $3x + 3y = 72$. Subtract this equation from the first equation as follows and then solve for y:

$$\begin{aligned} 3x + 5y &= 80 \\ -(3x + 3y &= 72) \\ \hline 2y &= 8 \\ y &= 4 \end{aligned}$$

Now that you know the value for y, use $x + y = 24$ to determine that $x = 20$. The value of $\frac{x}{y}$ is thus $\frac{20}{4} = 5$, which is choice (B).

17. **A** Start by Ballparking—most people with children donated and most without children did not. Therefore, the difference in probabilities can't be very large, so (C) and (D) are too big. Now, make the two probabilities and find the difference. Probability is defined as the number that fit the requirement divided by the total number of things. For those with children, 324 of the 360 people in that category donated, so the probability is $\frac{324}{360} = 0.9$. For those without children, 174 of the 240 people in that category did not donate, so the probability is $\frac{174}{240} = 0.725$. Now subtract the probabilities to get $0.9 - 0.725 = 0.175$, which is choice (A).

18. **B** Graphing these two equations on a graphing calculator can be a quick way to find the solutions or points of intersection. Another option is to set them equal to each other and solve. The first equation can be rewritten as $y = x^2 + x - 30$, so when the equations are set equal to each other, it becomes $x^2 + x - 30 = x + 6$. Subtract x and 6 from both sides to get $x^2 - 36 = 0$. Factor the left side to get $(x + 6)(x - 6) = 0$. The values of x that make the equation true are -6 and 6. The x-coordinate of the midpoint will be the average of these two values, so $\frac{-6 + 6}{2} = \frac{0}{2} = 0$, which is (B). Don't waste time finding the y-coordinates of the solutions if it's not necessary!

19. **C** Don't do all this complicated polynomial multiplication and subtraction; whenever there are variables in the question and answer choices, plug in! If $x = 2$, then $F = 3(2) - 2 = 6 - 2 = 4$ and $G = 2 - 1 = 1$. Therefore, $F^3 - G = 4^3 - 1 = 64 - 1 = 63$. Plug $x = 2$ into the answer choices to see which equals the target number of 63. Choice (A) becomes $2^3 - 3(2)^2 + 1 = 8 - 12 + 1 = -3$. This does not match the target number, so eliminate (A). Choice (B) becomes $8(2)^3 - 12(2)^2 + 6(2) - 1 = 64 - 48 + 12 - 1 = 27$. Eliminate (B). Choice (C) becomes $27(2)^3 - 54(2)^2 + 35(2) - 7 = 216 - 216 + 70 - 7 = 63$. Keep (C), but check (D) just in case. Choice (D) becomes $27(2)^3 - 54(2)^2 + 37(2) - 9 = 216 - 216 + 74 - 9 = 65$. Eliminate (D) and choose (C).

20. **C** Plug In a point from the graph. At 35 students, about 10 percent of the students that read at grade level, so make $n = 35$ and eliminate answers which aren't close to 10. (You don't have an exact point nor a line of best fit to go on, so you need to keep answers which are close). Choice (A) becomes $P = 85 + 2.5(35) = 172.5$; way off, so eliminate (A). Choice (B) becomes $P = 85 - 2.5(35 - 5) = 10$;

keep (B). Choice (C) becomes $P = 88 - \left(\dfrac{35}{4}\right)^2 = 11.44$; close enough, so keep (C). Choice (D) becomes $P = 88 - \left(\dfrac{35}{2}\right)^2 = -218.25$; definitely wrong, so eliminate (D). Try another point: at 20 students, about 60 percent of students read at grade level. You only need to test choices (B) and (C). Choice (B) becomes $P = 85 - 2.5(20 - 5) = 47.5$. This is quite far off; eliminate (B) and choose (C).

Alternatively, you may note that the graph must be a negative exponential function, which allows you to eliminate choices (A) and (B), as both are linear relationships. This leaves choices (C) and (D) to Plug In on.

21. **C**   First, use the graph to determine how many students per classroom would result in 40% of the students reading at grade level. The graph is at 40% at approximately 28 students per classroom. If there are total of 208 students, that means there are approximately $\dfrac{208}{28} = 7.43$ classrooms. (Obviously there are either 7 or 8 classrooms, but you are dealing with approximate values here, so it's OK). If another classroom were added, there would be about 8.43 classrooms, meaning there are students $\dfrac{208}{8.43} = 24.67$ per classroom. Returning to the graph, at about 25 students approximately 50% of the students read at grade level. This matches choice (C).

22. *B*   Plug In the Answers! Start with choice (B). If Shawn purchased 200 shares at $11.35 a share, then he has a total value of 200 × 11.35 = $2,270 at the beginning. If the stock decreases by 15%, then its value is 85% of the start, or 0.85 × 2,270 = $1,929.50. If it increases by 8% in 2010, then its value is 108% of the 2009 value, or 1.08 × 1,929.50 = $2,083.86. The value increases again in 2011, so the stock is now worth 1.08 × 2,083.86 = $2,250.57. In 2012, $500 is added to the value to give 2,250.57 + 500 = $2,750.57. Because the problem wanted the approximate price per share when Shawn purchased the stock, this is really close (less than 1% off), so choose (B).

23. **A**   Start by simplifying the first equation. Multiply the equation by 12 (least common multiple of 3 and 4) to clear the fractions. You get $4(2x - 3) - 3(5y - 2) = 24$. Distribute for each parenthesis: $8x - 12 - 15y + 6 = 24$ (be careful with the negative on the second parenthesis!). Combine like terms: $8x - 15y - 6 = 24$. Add 6 to both sides to get $8x - 15y = 30$. Next, distribute the –4 in the second equation to get $-8x - 4y = 27$. Stack the equations to see what's going on:

$$8x - 15y = 30$$
$$-8x - 4y = 27$$

Note if you add the equations the x terms will cancel. So do that to get $-19y = 57$. Divide both sides by –29 to get $y = –3$. Plug this value into the simplified version of the second equation: $–8x – 4(–3) = 27$. Multiply to get $–8x + 12 = 27$. Subtract from both sides: $–8x = 15$. Divide both sides by –8: $x = –\dfrac{15}{8}$. Add this to the value of y: $–3 + \left(–\dfrac{15}{8}\right) = –\dfrac{39}{8}$, which matches choice (A).

24. **D** Start by drawing a picture of Sam's and Joe's houses:

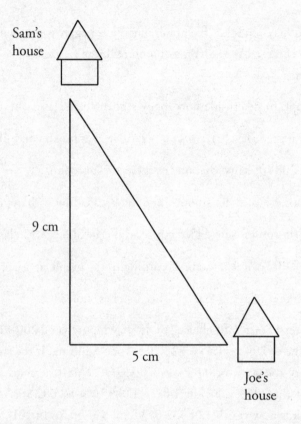

The distance in centimeters on the map can by found by using the Pythagorean Theorem: $5^2 + 9^2 = c^2$, where c is the distance from Joe's house to Sam's house. Solve for c: $25 + 81 = c^2$; $106 = c^2$; $\sqrt{106} = c$. Next, you need to find the distance in miles from Joe's house to Sam's house. 45 minutes is $\dfrac{45}{60} = 0.75$ hours, so driving at 30 miles per hour means the houses are $0.75 \times 30 = 22.5$ miles apart. Finally, you need to determine how many miles each centimeter represents, so set up a proportion: $\dfrac{22.5 \text{ miles}}{\sqrt{106} \text{ cm}} = \dfrac{x \text{ miles}}{1 \text{ cm}}$. Divide the left side to get 2.19, which is closest to choice (D).

25. **A** If answer (A) is true, then it would provide evidence that calls into question the methodology of the polling company. If the respondents to the initial interview were older and more likely to belong to a particular political party, then the polling company is not basing its predictions on a representative sample of the voting population. This makes choice (A) the best answer for calling the results into question.

26. **C** Since the period from 1980-2010 encompasses 30 years, you can conclude that in the equation provided, $30x$ represents the number of howler monkeys added to the conservancy's population during that time period. The x itself, however, is the average number of howler monkeys added to the park's population each year for that 30-year time period—choice (C).

27. **D** The best place to start is to rewrite all parts of the expression such that they have the same base.

Since all of the numbers are multiples of 2, you can rewrite everything in terms of 2 as follows:
$$\frac{64^4 - 32^8}{128^2} = \frac{\left(2^6\right)^4 - \left(2^5\right)^8}{\left(2^7\right)^2} = \frac{2^{24} - 2^{40}}{2^{14}} = \frac{2^{24}(1 - 2^{16})}{2^{14}} = 2^{10}(1 - 2^{16})$$, which is choice (D).

28. $\frac{1}{2}$ **or 0.5**

These are linear equations, since no variable has an exponent on it. For two linear equations to have no solutions, they must be parallel. Parallel lines have the same slope. Put the first equation into $y = mx + b$ form to see the slope more easily. Add 9 to both sides to get $3y = \frac{3}{2}x + 9$, then divide both sides by 3 to get $y = \frac{1}{2}x + 3$. Therefore, for the lines to have the same slope, $a = \frac{1}{2}$.

29. **22** Graphing these two equations on a graphing calculator can be a quick way to find the solutions or points of intersection. Another option is to set them equal to each other and solve. The second equation can be rewritten as $y = x^2 - 4x + 4$, so when the equations are set equal to each other, it becomes $x^2 - 4x + 4 = 2x + 4$. Subtract $2x$ and 4 from both sides to get $x^2 - 6x = 0$. Factor the left side to get $x(x - 6) = 0$. The values for x that make this true are 0 and 6. When $x = 0$, the solution is on the y-axis and not in Quadrant I, so the point in question is at $x = 6$. Plug that value into the first equation to get $y = 2(6) + 4 = 16$. The solution is at (6, 16), and the sum of the coordinates is $6 + 16 = 22$.

30. **1,049** Convert the dimension given in inches to millimeters, using the conversion rate given.
$$\frac{25.4\ mm}{1\ inch} = \frac{x}{4\ inches}$$

Cross-multiply and solve for x to find that the 3D printer can print objects 101.6 millimeters on each side. Now convert this measurement into centimeters by setting up another proportion:
$$\frac{10\ mm}{1\ cm} = \frac{101.6\ mm}{x}$$

Cross-multiply to get $10x = 101.6$, then divide by 10 to get $x = 10.16$ centimeters per side. Volume = length × width × height, so multiply the three sides in centimeters to get the volume in cubic centimeters. $10.16^3 = 1,048.772$, so rounded to the nearest whole number, the answer is 1,049.

31. **1.89** Convert the ounces to grams using the given conversion rate:

$\dfrac{1\ ounce}{28.35\ grams} = \dfrac{0.2\ ounces}{mass}$. Cross-multiply to find that the *mass* of the stand is 5.67 grams. No convert the cubic inches to cubic centimeters:

$\dfrac{1\ cm^3}{0.061\ in^3} = \dfrac{volume}{0.183\ in^3}$. Cross-multiply to get $0.061(volume) = 0.183$, then divide both sides by 0.061 to get $volume = 3cm^3$. Now plug these values into the formula for density to get

$density = \dfrac{mass}{volume} = \dfrac{5.67\ grams}{3cm^3} = 1.89$

Chapter 14
Math Test Drill 2

Math Test – No Calculator

25 MINUTES, 17 QUESTIONS

Turn to Section 3 of your answer sheet to answer the questions in this section.

DIRECTIONS

For questions **1-13**, solve each problem, choose the best answer from the choices provided, and fill in the corresponding circle on your answer sheet. For questions **14-17**, solve the problem and enter your answer in the grid on the answer sheet. Please refer to the directions before question 14 on how to enter your answers in the grid. You may use any available space in your test booklet for scratch work.

NOTES

1. The use of a calculator **is not permitted**.
2. All variables and expressions used represent real numbers unless otherwise indicated.
3. Figures provided in this test are drawn to scale unless otherwise indicated.
4. All figures lie in a plane unless otherwise indicated.
5. Unless otherwise indicated, the domain of a given function f is the set of all real numbers x for which $f(x)$ is a real number.

REFERENCE

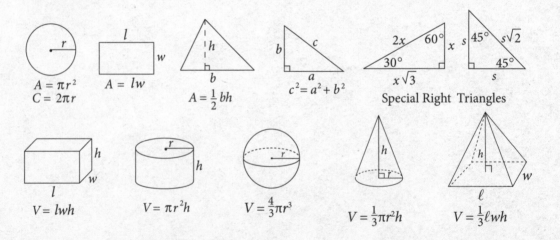

The number of degrees of arc in a circle is 360.
The number of radians of arc in a circle is 2π.
The sum of the measures in degrees of the angles of a triangle is 180.

1

Kate buys a car for $25,000 that depreciates 10% per year. Which of the following shows the value of the car, in dollars, after t years?

A) $25,000(.9)^t$

B) $25,000 - 10t$

C) $25,000(1.1)^t$

D) $25,000 - .1t$

2

John is traveling to Singapore for a days for a conference. He expects to spend 40 Singapore dollars on food per day. Which of the following inequalities shows all the possible values in US dollars, represented by x, that John could exchange for Singapore dollars and have at least enough money to spend on food for the whole conference? (Note: 1 US dollar = 1.3 Singapore dollars.)

A) $1.3x \leq 40a$

B) $x \geq 1.3(40a)$

C) $1.3x \geq 40a$

D) $x \geq 1.3(40+a)$

3

When Bryan caters a meal he charges a flat fee to reserve the date plus an additional price per person. He charges a discounted rate for children. The amount that Bryan charges when he caters is given by the function $P = m + 25a + 10b$. What does m represent in this equation?

A) The price per adult that Bryan charges

B) The flat fee Bryan charges

C) The number of hours that Bryan works

D) The price per child

4

The kinetic energy (KE) of an object is calculated by the equation $KE = \frac{1}{2}mv^2$ where m is the mass of the object and v is the velocity. Which of the following equations would solve for the mass of the object in terms of v and KE ?

A) $m = \dfrac{KE}{2v^2}$

B) $m = \dfrac{2KE}{v^2}$

C) $m = KE - v^2$

D) $m = KEv^2$

5

Which of the following is equal to $x^{\frac{2}{3}}$?

A) $\dfrac{x^2}{3}$

B) $\sqrt{x^3}$

C) $\dfrac{x^{\frac{5}{3}}}{x}$

D) $\dfrac{x^2}{x^3}$

6

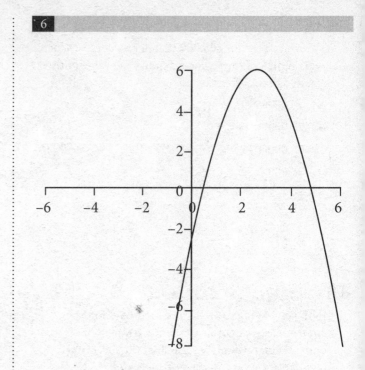

The graph above represents the equation $y = c(x - d)^2 + e$, where c, d, and e are constants. Which of the following must be true?

A) $e > 0 > c > d$

B) $c > 0 > d > e$

C) $e > 0 > d > c$

D) $e > d > 0 > c$

7

Kelly's car has 12 gallons of gas in it when she starts her trip. After she travels a hours at a speed of b miles per hour, she has 7 gallons left. If Kelly's car averages 29 miles per gallon for this trip, which of the following expresses a in terms of b ?

A) $a = \dfrac{5(29)}{b}$

B) $a = \dfrac{b}{7(29)}$

C) $a = 5(29)b$

D) $a = \dfrac{7(29)}{b}$

8

Given that $\dfrac{y + 3}{x - 2} = \dfrac{x + 2}{y - 3}$, which of the following expressions must be equal to 1 ?

A) $\dfrac{(y - 3)^2}{(x - 2)^2}$

B) $\dfrac{x^2 + 4}{y^2 - 9}$

C) $\dfrac{x^2 - 4}{y^2 - 9}$

D) $\dfrac{y^2 - 3}{x^2 - 2}$

9

If the expression $\dfrac{x^2 - 5x + 6}{x^2 - 6x + 8}$ can be rewritten as

$\dfrac{x^2 + 2x - 15}{C}$, what is C ?

A) $x^2 + 9x + 20$

B) $x^2 + x - 20$

C) $x^2 - x - 20$

D) $x^2 - 9x - 20$

10

If c is a constant and the equation $\dfrac{1}{8}cx - 2 = \dfrac{16 - cx}{2c}$

has infinitely many solutions, which of the following

is the value of c ?

A) −4

B) 0

C) 2

D) 4

11

$$-14 \text{ m/s} < V_f < 28 \text{ m/s}$$
$$8 \text{ m/s} < V_i < 14 \text{ m/s}$$

An object travels for 4 seconds with a constant acceleration and the object's initial and final velocities are represented by the above two inequalities. Which of the following expresses the set of all possible accelerations for the object? (Note: An object's final velocity is given by the equation $V_f = V_i + at$, in which V_i, a, and t represent the object's initial velocity, acceleration, and time, respectively.)

A) $-28 \text{ m/s}^2 < a < 20 \text{ m/s}^2$

B) $-7 \text{ m/s}^2 < a < 5 \text{ m/s}^2$

C) $-5.5 \text{ m/s}^2 < a < 3.5 \text{ m/s}^2$

D) $1.5 \text{ m/s}^2 < a < 3.5 \text{ m/s}^2$

12

$$x^2 - 2ax + 3a = 0$$

Given that $x = 2$ is a solution to the above equation, what is the value of a ?

A) -4

B) $-\dfrac{4}{7}$

C) $\dfrac{4}{7}$

D) 4

13

In the 2008 presidential election, then-Senator Barack Obama received 52.9% of the popular vote, and in 2012 he received approximately 51.1% of the popular vote. Approximately 3.2 million less people voted in 2012 than 2008, and 3.5 million more people voted for Obama in 2008 than in 2012. Which of the following sets of equations could be used to solve for the number of voters, in millions, that participated in the 2008 and 2012 elections?

A) $.529x = .511y + 3.5$

   $x + 3.2 = y$

B) $.529x - 3.2 = .511y$

   $x = y + 3.5$

C) $.529x = .511y + 3.5$

   $x = y + 3.2$

D) $.529x + .511y = 3.5$

   $x + y = 3.2$

DIRECTIONS

For questions 14-17, solve the problem and enter your answer in the grid, as described below, on the answer sheet.

1. Although not required, it is suggested that you write your answer in the boxes at the top of the columns to help you fill in the circles accurately

2. Mark no more than one circle in any column.

3. No question has a negative answer.

4. Some problems may have more than one correct answer. In such cases, grid only one answer.

5. **Mixed numbers** such as $3\frac{1}{2}$ must be gridded as 3.5 or 7/2. (If 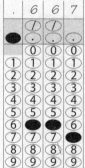 is entered into the grid, it will be interpreted as $\frac{31}{2}$, not as $3\frac{1}{2}$).

6. **Decimal Answers:** If you obtain a decimal answer with more digits than the grid can accomodate, it may be either rounded or truncated, but it must fill the entire grid.

Answer: $\frac{7}{12}$ Answer: 2.5

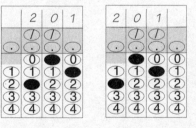

Acceptable ways to grid $\frac{2}{3}$ are:

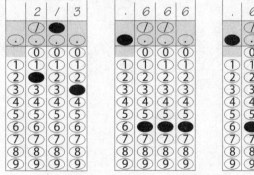

Answer: 201
Either position is correct.

NOTE: You may start your answers in any column, space permitting. Columns you don't need to use should be left blank.

14

Eugene wants to discover the density of an unknown metal with a mass of 70 grams, so he places it in a rectangular container of water whose base has an area of 8 cm². The metal sinks to the bottom and the water in the container raises 5 centimeters. What is the density, in grams per centimeter, of the object? (Note: Density = Mass / Volume)

15

If $2x + 3y = 13$ and $3x + 2y = 12$, what is the value of $3x + 3y$?

16

$$P = 10(10 - d)^2$$

The equation above shows the number of points a contestant in a game of darts can earn per dart thrown. Contestants receive points on a throw only if they hit the circular dartboard that has an area of 100π cm², and the points a contestant receives. P, on each throw depend on the distance, d, in centimeters, from the center bulls-eye the dart lands (closer darts receive more points). If a turn consists of 3 throws, what is the maximum number of points that a contestant can earn on a turn?

17

Given that $\left(\dfrac{x^2 + 3x - 10}{x^2 - 4} \right)\left(\dfrac{16x + 32}{x^2 + 10x + 25} \right) = 3$, what is x ?

THIS PAGE IS LEFT INTENTIONALLY BLANK.

Math Test – Calculator

45 MINUTES, 31 QUESTIONS

Turn to Section 4 of your answer sheet to answer the questions in this section.

DIRECTIONS

For questions **1-27**, solve each problem, choose the best answer from the choices provided, and fill in the corresponding circle on your answer sheet. For questions **28-31**, solve the problem and enter your answer in the grid on the answer sheet. Please refer to the directions before question 28 on how to enter your answers in the grid. You may use any available space in your test booklet for scratch work.

NOTES

1. The use of a calculator **is permitted**.
2. All variables and expressions used represent real numbers unless otherwise indicated.
3. Figures provided in this test are drawn to scale unless otherwise indicated.
4. All figures lie in a plane unless otherwise indicated.
5. Unless otherwise indicated, the domain of a given function *f* is the set of all real numbers *x* for which *f(x)* is a real number.

REFERENCE

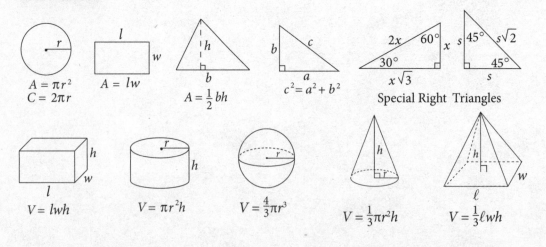

$A = \pi r^2$
$C = 2\pi r$

$A = lw$

$A = \frac{1}{2}bh$

$c^2 = a^2 + b^2$

Special Right Triangles

$V = lwh$

$V = \pi r^2 h$

$V = \frac{4}{3}\pi r^3$

$V = \frac{1}{3}\pi r^2 h$

$V = \frac{1}{3}\ell w h$

The number of degrees of arc in a circle is 360.
The number of radians of arc in a circle is 2π.
The sum of the measures in degrees of the angles of a triangle is 180.

1

$$y = x^2 - x - 20$$

The quadratic equation above has two real solutions. Which solution is smaller?

A) $x = -5$

B) $x = -4$

C) $x = 0$

D) $x = 4$

2

	Enrolled in Chemistry	Enrolled in Physics	Enrolled in Biology
11th Grade	62	36	75
12th Grade	24	54	18

What percent of students enrolled in Physics are in the 11th grade?

A) 20%

B) 30%

C) 40%

D) 50%

3

Reaction A: $A + D \rightarrow P$	$P = kt$
Reaction B: $D + C \rightarrow P$	$P = k^t$

Madison is completing two separate chemical reactions to obtain product P. Both reactions start with product P at zero concentration, at $t = 0$ in seconds. In the first reaction, the concentration of P increases linearly with time, with the rate constant $k = 1.3$. In the second reaction, P increases exponentially with the rate constant $k - 1.1$. Which of the following statements best represents the two reactions to form product P?

A) When $t = 10$, reaction A has produced approximately 5 times as much product as reaction B.

B) When $t = 10$, reaction B has produced approximately 5 times as much product as reaction A.

C) When $t = 10$, reaction A has produced approximately 10 times as much product as reaction B.

D) When $t = 10$, reaction B has produced approximately 10 times as much product as reaction A.

4

$$y = -\frac{1}{2}x + 4$$

Given the linear equation above, at which value of x does the line cross the x-axis?

A) $x = -2$

B) $x = 2$

C) $x = 4$

D) $x = 8$

5

If $\dfrac{\left(\sqrt{3}\right)(x+3)(x-2)}{x-2} = 0$, what are all possible real values of x ?

A) $-3, 0, 2$

B) $-3, 0$

C) $0, 2$

D) 0

6

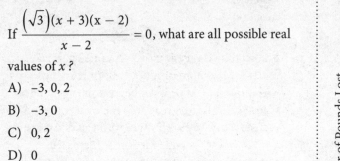

Average Hours of Exercise per Day

A group of medical students studied 50 participants over a two month period to determine the effects of exercise on weight loss. The scatterplot above shows the relationship between the average number of hours a participant exercised per day and the total weight the participant lost over the two month period. If x represents the average hours of exercise per day, which of the following expressions give the line of best fit for the number of pounds lost in two months?

A) $10x - 15$

B) $5x + 15$

C) $15 - 10x$

D) $x^2 + 10$

Questions 7-8 refer to the information below.

The table shows the employment data for four states for the year 2008. The workforce is the total number of people who could be employed. The unemployment rate is the percentage of the workforce who are not employed.

	Michigan	Minnesota	Ohio	Wisconsin
Unemployment Rate	8.3	5.4	6.6	4.8
Workforce	9,542,000	5,005,000	12,485,000	5,862,000

7

According to the table above, how many people were employed in Michigan in 2008?

A) 791,986

B) 8,750,014

C) 9,542,000

D) 114,963,855

8

According to the table above, which of the following conclusions can be properly drawn about the employment in the four states in 2008?

A) Michigan had the greatest number of unemployed people because it has the highest unemployment rate.

B) Minnesota had both the fewest number of people unemployed and the fewest number of people employed.

C) Ohio did not have the greatest number unemployed people because it did not have the greatest unemployment rate.

D) Wisconsin had the fewest number of unemployed people because it has the lowest unemployment rate.

9

Line l has an x-intercept of 3. Which of the following could be the equation of line l?

A) $y = 2x - 6$

B) $y = 3x$

C) $y = x + 3$

D) $y = \dfrac{x}{3} + 1$

10

A class is polled on where to take their next field trip. 45% of the class wants to go to the arboretum, 35% of the class wants to go to the planetarium, and 20% of the class wants to go to the aquarium. If there are 80 students in the class, how many do not want to go to the planetarium?

A) 28

B) 36

C) 52

D) 64

11

A continuous reaction produces carbon dioxide at a rate of 0.02 pounds per minute. After 15 minutes, how many grams of carbon dioxide have been produced? (Note: 1 pound = 453.6 grams)

A) 9.1 grams

B) 30.2 grams

C) 68.0 grams

D) 136.1 grams

12

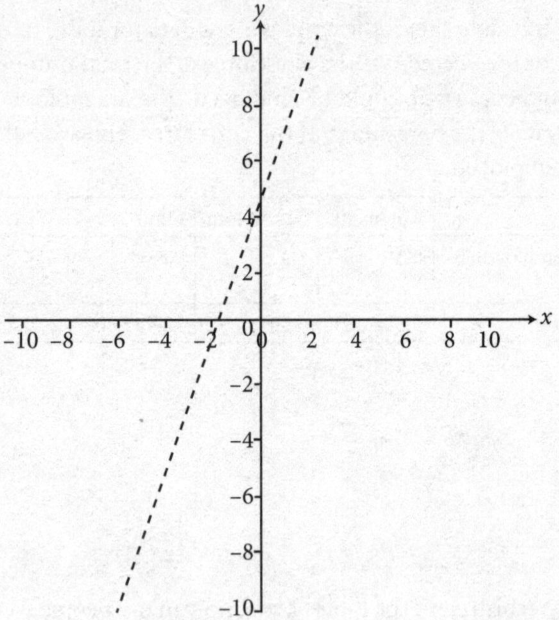

Which of the following equations best represents the chart above ?

A) $y > 3x - 4$

B) $y > 3x + 4$

C) $y < 3x - 4$

D) $y < 3x + 4$

13

Sara and her partner James studied the population growth of a certain bacterium in petri dishes. They determined that no matter how many bacteria a petri dish initially had, the population tripled every four days. If B represents the population after d days, which of the following expressions represents the population of a petri dish that started with s bacteria?

A) $B = s + \dfrac{3d}{4}$

B) $B = 3s^{4d}$

C) $B = s(3)^{\frac{d}{4}}$

D) $B = 3^{\frac{d}{4}} + s$

14

The MacRuff storage facility has decided to conserve energy by limiting the amount of energy for lighting to 22 joules per day. The storage facility has 60 lightbulbs that each consume 110 watts of energy per hour. If 1 joule equals 3,600 watts, what is the maximum number of minutes MacRuff storage facility can keep all the lights on without exceeding its limit?

A) 12

B) 300

C) 720

D) 43,200

15

$$x - \frac{y}{5} = 2$$

$$24x + 2y = 82$$

If (x, y) is a solution to the system of equations above, what is the value of x ?

A) –5

B) 3

C) 5

D) There are no real x values for the solution

16

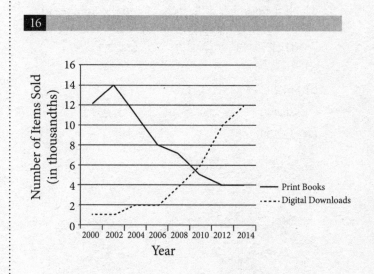

The graph above shows the number of print books and the number of digital downloads sold, in thousands, by the Literary Wonders publishing company from the year 2000 to the year 2014. The number of print books sold in the year for which print book sales were highest was approximately what percent greater than the number of digital download sales in the year for which digital download sales were highest?

A) 14%

B) 17%

C) 67%

D) 71%

17

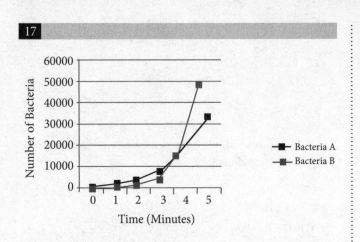

Time (Minutes)

The graph above shows the growth patterns of two different bacteria over time. The growth of Bacteria A is given by the equation $N(t)=1000(2^t)$ and the growth of Bacteria B is given by the equation $P(t)=200(3^t)$, where t represents the time, in minutes, since the beginning of the bacteria's growth. At the time for which the number of Bacteria A and the number of Bacteria B were equal, how many total bacteria (A and B) were present?

A) 16,000

B) 16,200

C) 20,400

D) 32,200

18

Yasmine, a college sophomore, is driving home to visit her parents for winter break. Her college dorm is 225 miles from her parents' house. If she stops at a rest stop one third of the way to her parents' house and drives at an average speed of 50 miles per hour for the remainder of the trip, then which of the following expressions represents the remaining distance Yasmine still has to drive in terms of t, the time in minutes after leaving the rest stop?

A) $150 - \dfrac{5t}{6}$

B) $225 - 50t$

C) $225 - \dfrac{5t}{6}$

D) $150 - 50t$

19

Frank is working on a statistics project for his math class. For his project, he categorizes each rubber band in an unopened package. 30% of the rubber bands were small length, 40% of the bands were medium length, and 30% were categorized as long. Of the long bands, 15% were single width, 70% were double width, and 15% were triple width. Of the double width, half were dark brown and the other half were light brown. If Frank counted 9 dark brown, triple width, long rubber bands in the bag, how many bands total did the bag contain?

A) 120

B) 300

C) 400

D) 800

20

If the equation $\dfrac{2x-8}{\sqrt{12}}$ is most nearly equal to $C - \dfrac{4\sqrt{3}}{3}$, then what is C in terms of x ?

A) $-\dfrac{\sqrt{3}}{3}x$

B) $\dfrac{\sqrt{3}}{3}x$

C) $x\sqrt{3}$

D) $3x$

21

Census Year	Population
1920	7,989
1930	10,136
1940	11,659
1950	19,056
1960	22,993

The Census data for a rural town in Kansas is shown above. In which of the following decades did the town experience the highest percent growth?

A) 1920–1930 with 21% growth

B) 1920–1930 with 27% growth

C) 1940–1950 with 39% growth

D) 1940–1950 with 63% growth

22

Regina sells cars, for which she receives a yearly salary. Since 2004, Regina has received a raise each year. She also gets a yearly bonus of $500 for each car she sells after the first 300. Her total pay, P, in dollars, for any year after 2004 can be expressed as $P = 35,000 (1 + 0.05y) + 500x$. Which of the following is the best interpretation of the expression?

A) x represents the number of cars sold after the first 300

B) x must be greater than 300

C) y must be greater than 2004

D) y represents the current year

23

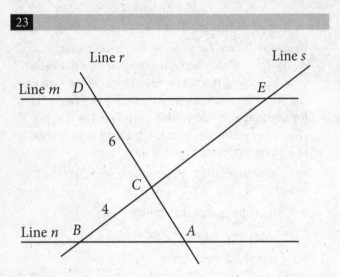

Line r
Line s
Line m   D   E
6
C
4
Line n   B   A

In the figure above, line m is parallel to line n and line r is perpendicular to line s. If $\overline{DE} = \dfrac{5}{2}\,\overline{BC}$, which of the following could be used to find the measure of $\angle BAC$?

A) $\sin^{-1}\left(\dfrac{3}{5}\right)$

B) $\cos^{-1}\left(\dfrac{3}{5}\right)$

C) $\tan^{-1}\left(\dfrac{4}{3}\right)$

D) $\tan^{-1}\left(\dfrac{5}{2}\right)$

24

In a recent election for president, the citizens of the country of Prelandia chose among three different candidates. The ratio of those who voted for Candidate G to those who voted for Candidate H was 4 to 5, while the ratio of those who voted for Candidate H to those who voted for Candidate J was 10 to 17. If half of the people who voted for Candidate H had instead voted for Candidate J, what would have been the ratio of those who voted for Candidate J to those who voted for Candidate G?

A) 17 to 4

B) 8 to 5

C) 22 to 5

D) 11 to 4

25

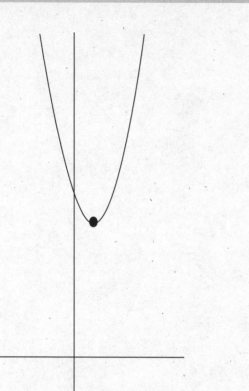

The graph of the function $f(x) = x^2 - 2x + 8$ is shown above. Point P (not shown) represents the vertex of the graph. If the graph is first reflected across the line $y = 3$ and then reflected across the y-axis, what are the new coordinates of point P?

A) $(-1, 7)$

B) $(1, -1)$

C) $(-1, -1)$

D) $(1, 7)$

26

The equation for line m is $y = -\dfrac{1}{5}x + 9$ and the equation for parabola n is $y = x^2 - 2x - 9$. If line r is perpendicular to line m and has a y-intercept of -21, then what are the points of intersection of parabola n and line r?

A) $(-3, -6)$ and $(-4, -1)$

B) $(-3, 6)$ and $(-4, 1)$

C) $(3, -6)$ and $(4, -1)$

D) $(3, 6)$ and $(4, 1)$

27

Under 18
18 and Older

The data above show the approximate number of United States residents in selected years between 1920 and 1970. The average population of adults 18 years and older from 1940 to 1970, inclusive, was approximately what percent of the mode of the population of children under 18 from 1930 to 1960, inclusive?

A) 2.47%

B) 247%

C) 36%

D) 111.25%

DIRECTIONS

For questions 28-31, solve the problem and enter your answer in the grid, as described below, on the answer sheet.

1. Although not required, it is suggested that you write your answer in the boxes at the top of the columns to help you fill in the circles accurately

2. Mark no more than one circle in any column.

3. No question has a negative answer.

4. Some problems may have more than one correct answer. In such cases, grid only one answer.

5. **Mixed numbers** such as $3\frac{1}{2}$ must be gridded as 3.5 or 7/2. (If ⟨3 1 / 2⟩ is entered into the grid, it will be interpreted as $\frac{31}{2}$, not as $3\frac{1}{2}$).

6. **Decimal Answers:** If you obtain a decimal answer with more digits than the grid can accomodate, it may be either rounded or truncated, but it must fill the entire grid.

Answer: $\frac{7}{12}$ Answer: 2.5

Write answer in boxes. → Fraction line ← Decimal point

Grid in → result.

Acceptable ways to grid $\frac{2}{3}$ are:

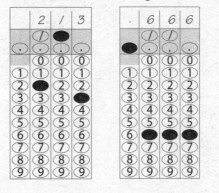

Answer: 201
Either position is correct.

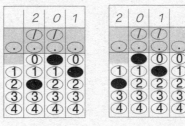

NOTE: You may start your answers in any column, space permitting. Columns you don't need to use should be left blank.

28

The amount of solvent, in milliliters, remaining in a beaker can be modeled by the expression 500 – 0.4*t*, when *t* is in seconds. At what value of *t* will the beaker be empty?

29

$$6x - 4 = \frac{y}{3}$$

$$\frac{y}{2} - 10 = x + 7$$

What is the average of the *x*- and *y*-values of the point of intersection of the two equations listed above, rounded to the nearest tenth?

Questions 30-31 refer to the following information

A chocolatier in Los Angeles decides to offer a special gift box for Valentine's Day. The gift box consists of a variety of different chocolates: 20% are dark chocolate, 15% are white chocolate, 35% are mint chocolate, and the rest are chocolate truffle.

30

If there are 6 chocolate truffles in the gift box, then how many mint chocolates does the gift box contain?

31

If the information in question 30 still holds true, then what is the difference between the number of dark chocolates and the number of white chocolates?

Redesigned PSAT

1. Student Information

Your Name: _____
(Print)   Last   First   M.I.

Email Address: _____ Date: ___/___/___
(Print)   MM   DD   YYYY

Home Address: _____ Apartment No. _____
(Print)   Number and Street

_____
                City   State   Zip Code

High School: _____ Class of: _____

2. Your Name

First 4 letters of last name				FIRST INIT	MID INIT
Ⓐ	Ⓐ	Ⓐ	Ⓐ	Ⓐ	Ⓐ
Ⓑ	Ⓑ	Ⓑ	Ⓑ	Ⓑ	Ⓑ
Ⓒ	Ⓒ	Ⓒ	Ⓒ	Ⓒ	Ⓒ
Ⓓ	Ⓓ	Ⓓ	Ⓓ	Ⓓ	Ⓓ
Ⓔ	Ⓔ	Ⓔ	Ⓔ	Ⓔ	Ⓔ
Ⓕ	Ⓕ	Ⓕ	Ⓕ	Ⓕ	Ⓕ
Ⓖ	Ⓖ	Ⓖ	Ⓖ	Ⓖ	Ⓖ
Ⓗ	Ⓗ	Ⓗ	Ⓗ	Ⓗ	Ⓗ
Ⓘ	Ⓘ	Ⓘ	Ⓘ	Ⓘ	Ⓘ
Ⓙ	Ⓙ	Ⓙ	Ⓙ	Ⓙ	Ⓙ
Ⓚ	Ⓚ	Ⓚ	Ⓚ	Ⓚ	Ⓚ
Ⓛ	Ⓛ	Ⓛ	Ⓛ	Ⓛ	Ⓛ
Ⓜ	Ⓜ	Ⓜ	Ⓜ	Ⓜ	Ⓜ
Ⓝ	Ⓝ	Ⓝ	Ⓝ	Ⓝ	Ⓝ
Ⓞ	Ⓞ	Ⓞ	Ⓞ	Ⓞ	Ⓞ
Ⓟ	Ⓟ	Ⓟ	Ⓟ	Ⓟ	Ⓟ
Ⓠ	Ⓠ	Ⓠ	Ⓠ	Ⓠ	Ⓠ
Ⓡ	Ⓡ	Ⓡ	Ⓡ	Ⓡ	Ⓡ
Ⓢ	Ⓢ	Ⓢ	Ⓢ	Ⓢ	Ⓢ
Ⓣ	Ⓣ	Ⓣ	Ⓣ	Ⓣ	Ⓣ
Ⓤ	Ⓤ	Ⓤ	Ⓤ	Ⓤ	Ⓤ
Ⓥ	Ⓥ	Ⓥ	Ⓥ	Ⓥ	Ⓥ
Ⓦ	Ⓦ	Ⓦ	Ⓦ	Ⓦ	Ⓦ
Ⓧ	Ⓧ	Ⓧ	Ⓧ	Ⓧ	Ⓧ
Ⓨ	Ⓨ	Ⓨ	Ⓨ	Ⓨ	Ⓨ
Ⓩ	Ⓩ	Ⓩ	Ⓩ	Ⓩ	Ⓩ

3. Phone Number

Area Code			Phone number						
⓪	⓪	⓪	⓪	⓪	⓪	⓪	⓪	⓪	⓪
①	①	①	①	①	①	①	①	①	①
②	②	②	②	②	②	②	②	②	②
③	③	③	③	③	③	③	③	③	③
④	④	④	④	④	④	④	④	④	④
⑤	⑤	⑤	⑤	⑤	⑤	⑤	⑤	⑤	⑤
⑥	⑥	⑥	⑥	⑥	⑥	⑥	⑥	⑥	⑥
⑦	⑦	⑦	⑦	⑦	⑦	⑦	⑦	⑦	⑦
⑧	⑧	⑧	⑧	⑧	⑧	⑧	⑧	⑧	⑧
⑨	⑨	⑨	⑨	⑨	⑨	⑨	⑨	⑨	⑨

Mathematics — No Calculator

SECTION 3

1. Ⓐ Ⓑ Ⓒ Ⓓ
2. Ⓐ Ⓑ Ⓒ Ⓓ
3. Ⓐ Ⓑ Ⓒ Ⓓ
4. Ⓐ Ⓑ Ⓒ Ⓓ
5. Ⓐ Ⓑ Ⓒ Ⓓ

6. Ⓐ Ⓑ Ⓒ Ⓓ
7. Ⓐ Ⓑ Ⓒ Ⓓ
8. Ⓐ Ⓑ Ⓒ Ⓓ
9. Ⓐ Ⓑ Ⓒ Ⓓ
10. Ⓐ Ⓑ Ⓒ Ⓓ

11. Ⓐ Ⓑ Ⓒ Ⓓ
12. Ⓐ Ⓑ Ⓒ Ⓓ
13. Ⓐ Ⓑ Ⓒ Ⓓ

14.

	⊘	⊘	
⊙	⊙	⊙	⊙
⓪	⓪	⓪	⓪
①	①	①	①
②	②	②	②
③	③	③	③
④	④	④	④
⑤	⑤	⑤	⑤
⑥	⑥	⑥	⑥
⑦	⑦	⑦	⑦
⑧	⑧	⑧	⑧
⑨	⑨	⑨	⑨

15.

	⊘	⊘	
⊙	⊙	⊙	⊙
⓪	⓪	⓪	⓪
①	①	①	①
②	②	②	②
③	③	③	③
④	④	④	④
⑤	⑤	⑤	⑤
⑥	⑥	⑥	⑥
⑦	⑦	⑦	⑦
⑧	⑧	⑧	⑧
⑨	⑨	⑨	⑨

16.

	⊘	⊘	
⊙	⊙	⊙	⊙
⓪	⓪	⓪	⓪
①	①	①	①
②	②	②	②
③	③	③	③
④	④	④	④
⑤	⑤	⑤	⑤
⑥	⑥	⑥	⑥
⑦	⑦	⑦	⑦
⑧	⑧	⑧	⑧
⑨	⑨	⑨	⑨

17.

	⊘	⊘	
⊙	⊙	⊙	⊙
⓪	⓪	⓪	⓪
①	①	①	①
②	②	②	②
③	③	③	③
④	④	④	④
⑤	⑤	⑤	⑤
⑥	⑥	⑥	⑥
⑦	⑦	⑦	⑦
⑧	⑧	⑧	⑧
⑨	⑨	⑨	⑨

The Princeton Review

Redesigned PSAT

Completely darken bubbles with a No. 2 pencil. If you make a mistake, be sure to erase mark completely. Erase all stray marks.

1. Student Information

Your Name: _____
(Print)   Last   First   M.I.

Email Address: _____ Date: ____ / ____ / ____
(Print)   MM   DD   YYYY

Home Address: _____ Apartment No. _____
(Print)   Number and Street

_____
City   State   Zip Code

High School: _____ Class of: _____

2. Your Name

First 4 letters of last name				FIRST INIT	MID INIT

(Bubbles A through Z for each column)

3. Phone Number

Area Code			Phone number						

(Bubbles 0 through 9 for each column)

Mathematics — Calculator Permissible

SECTION 4

1. Ⓐ Ⓑ Ⓒ Ⓓ
2. Ⓐ Ⓑ Ⓒ Ⓓ
3. Ⓐ Ⓑ Ⓒ Ⓓ
4. Ⓐ Ⓑ Ⓒ Ⓓ
5. Ⓐ Ⓑ Ⓒ Ⓓ
6. Ⓐ Ⓑ Ⓒ Ⓓ

7. Ⓐ Ⓑ Ⓒ Ⓓ
8. Ⓐ Ⓑ Ⓒ Ⓓ
9. Ⓐ Ⓑ Ⓒ Ⓓ
10. Ⓐ Ⓑ Ⓒ Ⓓ
11. Ⓐ Ⓑ Ⓒ Ⓓ
12. Ⓐ Ⓑ Ⓒ Ⓓ

13. Ⓐ Ⓑ Ⓒ Ⓓ
14. Ⓐ Ⓑ Ⓒ Ⓓ
15. Ⓐ Ⓑ Ⓒ Ⓓ
16. Ⓐ Ⓑ Ⓒ Ⓓ
17. Ⓐ Ⓑ Ⓒ Ⓓ
18. Ⓐ Ⓑ Ⓒ Ⓓ

19. Ⓐ Ⓑ Ⓒ Ⓓ
20. Ⓐ Ⓑ Ⓒ Ⓓ
21. Ⓐ Ⓑ Ⓒ Ⓓ
22. Ⓐ Ⓑ Ⓒ Ⓓ
23. Ⓐ Ⓑ Ⓒ Ⓓ
24. Ⓐ Ⓑ Ⓒ Ⓓ

25. Ⓐ Ⓑ Ⓒ Ⓓ
26. Ⓐ Ⓑ Ⓒ Ⓓ
27. Ⓐ Ⓑ Ⓒ Ⓓ

28.

29.

30.

31.

(Grid-in bubbles 0 through 9 for each)

Chapter 15
Math Test
Drill 2: Answers
and Explanations

ANSWERS AND EXPLANATIONS

Section 3—Math Test

1. **A** Whenever there are variables in the question and in the answers think Plugging In. Let $t = 2$. After 1 year the value of the car will be $25,000 - 25,000(.1) = 25,000 - 2,500 = 22,500$. The value of the car after 2 years will be $22,500 - (0.1)(22,500) = 22,500 - 2,500 = 20,250$. In the answers plug 2 in for t to see which answer will equal 20,250. Choice (A) becomes $25,000(0.9)^2 = 25,000(.81) = 20,250$. Keep (A) but check the remaining answers just in case. Choice (B) becomes $25,000 - 10(2) = 25,000 - 20 = 24,980$. Eliminate (B). Choice (C) becomes $25,000(1.1)^2 = 25,000(1.21) = 30,250$. Eliminate (C). Choice (D) becomes $25,000 - 0.1(2) = 25,000 - 0.2 = 24,999.80$. Eliminate (D). The correct answer is (A).

2. **C** Use Process of Elimination. The question asks for "at least how much money." At least translates to $\geq$. Therefore, eliminate (A). For a days John needs $40 \times a = \$40a$ Singapore dollars per day. Set up the following proportion to calculate the amount in US dollars: $\dfrac{1\ US}{1.3\ Singapore} = \dfrac{x\ US}{40\ a}$. Cross multiply to get $1.3x = 40a$. To calculate "at least substitute the = sign with $\geq$ to get $1.3x \geq 40a$. The correct answer is therefore, (C).

3. **B** Use Process of Elimination to solve. According to the question the total amount that Bryan charges includes a flat fee plus a charge for each person. The "each person" part of the equation can be further split up into a charge for each adult and a charge for each child. Immediately eliminate (C) because there is no information in the question related to the number of hours Bryan works. Looking at the numbers in the equation, the value of $25a$ will change based on what a is. Likely a stands for the number of adults in attendance. Likewise the value of $10b$ will change based on the value of b. Likely the b stands for the number of children in attendance. This leaves m which must be the flat fee. The correct answer is, therefore, (B).

4. **B** Multiply both sides of the equation by 2 to get $2KE = mv^2$. Divide both sides of the equation by v^2 to get $\dfrac{2KE}{v^2} = m$. The correct answer is (B).

5. **C** Use Process of Elimination to solve. Choice (A) cannot be reduced any further. Eliminate (A). For fractional exponents the numerator is equal to the power and the denominator is equal to the type of root. Therefore, (B) can be rewritten as $x^{\frac{3}{2}}$. Eliminate (B). When dividing fractions, subtract the exponents. Therefore, (C) can be rewritten as $x^{\frac{5}{3}-1} = x^{\frac{2}{3}}$. The correct answer is (C).

6. **B** The vertex form of a parabola is expressed by the equation $y = a(x - h)^2 + k$ where (h, k) is the vertex. In this problem the variables have changed so that $y = c(x - d)^2 + e$. Therefore, the vertex is (d, e). Look at the graph and notice that both coordinates of the vertex are positive. Therefore, eliminate (A), (C), and (D) because all of these answers make either d or e, or both, negative. The correct answer is (B).

7. **A** She travels 145 miles, but the question does not ask for the number of miles traveled—that is just the first step. The question asks for the relationship between a and b and since a is the number of hours and b is the speed. Since $d = rt$, $145 = ab$ and $a = 145/b$. Thus, the correct answer is (A).

8. **C** Cross-multiplying the fractions gets $y^2 - 9 = x^2 - 4$. These expressions could then get broken down further into $(y + 3)(y - 3) = (x + 2)(x - 2)$. However, in previewing the answer choices, all of them still have the variables represented with an exponent. Therefore, because $y^2 - 9 = x^2 - 4$, choice (C) must be correct since any expression that is divided by another that is equal in value will always result in a value of 1.

9. **B** Start by factoring the first fraction to get $\dfrac{x^2 - 5x + 6}{x^2 - 6x + 8} = \dfrac{(x-3)(x-2)}{(x-4)(x-2)}$. Reduce the fraction to get $\dfrac{x-3}{x-4}$. According to the question then $\dfrac{x-3}{x-4} = \dfrac{x^2 + 2x - 15}{C}$. Whenever there are variables in the question and in the answers think Plugging In. Plug $x = 5$ into the equation to get $\dfrac{5-3}{5-4} = \dfrac{5^2 + 2(5) - 15}{C}$. Solve both sides of the equation to get $\dfrac{2}{1} = \dfrac{25 + 10 - 15}{C}$ and $2 = \dfrac{20}{C}$.

Solve for C to get $2C = 20$ and $C = 10$. In the answers plug 5 in for x to see which answer equals 10.

Choice (A) becomes $5^2 + 9(5) + 20 = 25 + 45 + 20 = 90$. Eliminate (A). Choice (B) becomes $5^2 + 5 - 20 = 25 + 5 - 20 = 10$. Keep (B) but check the remaining answers just in case. Choice (C) becomes $5^2 - 5 - 20 = 25 - 5 - 20 = 0$. Eliminate (C). Choice (D) becomes $5^2 - 9(5) - 20 = 25 - 45 - 20 = 40$. Eliminate (D). The correct answer is (B).

10. **A** An equation will have an infinite number of solutions when one side of the equation is equal to the other side. Whenever you have variables in the question and numbers in the answers think Plugging In the Answers. Start with the middle numbers. Eliminate (B) because plugging in 0 would cause the left side of the equation to have 0 in the denominator of a fraction which can never happen. Try (C). In (C) $c = 2$ and the equation becomes $\dfrac{1}{8}(2)x - 2 = \dfrac{16 - (2)x}{2(2)}$. Simplify both sides

of the equation to get $\frac{1}{4}x - 2 = \frac{16-(2)x}{4}$. Multiply both sides of the equation by 4 to get $x - 8$ = 16 − 2x. Solve for x to get 3x − 8 = 16, 3x = 24, and x = 8. Eliminate (C). It may not be clear which direction to go from here so just pick a direction. In (A) c = −4 and the equation becomes $\frac{1}{8}(-4)x - 2 = \frac{16-(-4)x}{2(-4)}$. Simplify both sides of the equation to get $-\frac{1}{2}x - 2 = \frac{16+4x}{-8}$. Multiply both sides of the equation by −8 to get 4x + 16 = 16 + 4x. Because both sides of the equation are identical, the equation has an infinite number of solutions. The correct answer is (A).

11. **B** The equation can be rearranged as $\frac{V_f - V_i}{t} = a$. Since the question says that the object travels

for 4 seconds, it can be written as $\frac{V_f - V_i}{4} = a$. Now, in order to find the minimum and maxi-

mum values of a, you need to try all four combinations of the inner and outer bounds. So plug in

−14 m/s for V_f and try it with both 8 m/s and 14 m/s for $V_i = \frac{-14-8}{4} = -5.5$ m/s^2 and

$\frac{-14-14}{4} = -7$ m/s^2. Now try V_f= 28 m/s with both 8 m/s and 14 m/s for $V_i = \frac{28-8}{4} = 5$ m/s^2

and $\frac{28-4}{4} = 3.5$ m/s^2. Since these represent all of the extremes, we can see that the lowest value

is -7 m/s and the highest value is 5 m/s, choice (B).

12. **C** Plug 2 in for x in the equation to get $2^2 - 2(a)(2) + 3a = 0$. Simplify the left side of the equation to get 4 − 4a + 3a = 0 and 4 − 7a = 0. Solve for a to get −7a = −4 and $a = \frac{4}{7}$. The correct answer is (C).

13. **C** In the answers x and y relate to the two years 2008 and 2012. All of the answers put .529 with x and .511 with y. According to the question in the 2008 presidential election, Obama received 52.9% of the popular vote, and in 2012 he received approximately 51.1% of the popular vote. Therefore, x = 2008 and y = 2012. According to the question 3.2 million fewer people voted in 2012 than 2008. This translates to x = y + 3.2. Only (C) includes this equation. The correct answer is (C).

14. **1.75 or $\frac{7}{4}$**

If the base of the container has an area of 8 cm^2 and it is rectangular, then when it raises by 5 inches, the total volume change was 8 × 5= 40 cm^3. Therefore, the volume of the metal is 40 cm^3. Since density = mass/volume, the density is 70/40, which is 1.75.

15. **15** Whenever there are two equations with the same variables think Simultaneous Equations. Place the two equations on top of each other and add them together to get:

$$2x + 3y = 13$$
$$+\underline{(3x + 2y) = 12}$$
$$5x + 5y = 25$$

Divide the entire equation by 5 to get $x + y = 5$. Multiply the entire equation by 3 to get $3(x + y) = 3(5)$, and $3x + 3y = 15$. The correct answer is 15.

16. **3,000**

The maximum number of points achieved on any throw occurs when $d = 0$. The points when $d = 0$ can be calculated as $P = 10(10 - 0)^2 = 10(100) = 1000$. Therefore, over 3 throws the maximum number of points is $3 \times 1000 = 3,000$. The correct answer is 3,000.

17. $\dfrac{1}{3}$ **or .333**

Start by factoring the top and bottom of each fraction to get: $\left(\dfrac{(x+5)(x-2)}{(x+2)(x-2)}\right)\left(\dfrac{16(x+2)}{(x+5)(x+5)}\right) = 3$.

Reduce the left fraction to get $\left(\dfrac{(x+5)}{(x+2)}\right)\left(\dfrac{16(x+2)}{(x+5)(x+5)}\right) = 3$. Reduce diagonally to get $\dfrac{16}{x+5} = 3$.

Multiply both sides by $x + 5$ to get $16 = 3(x + 5)$. Distribute the 3 to get $16 = 3x + 15$. Solve for x to get $1 = 3x$ and $x = \dfrac{1}{3}$. The correct answer is $\dfrac{1}{3}$.

Section 4—Math Test

1. **B** Factor the equation to get $0 = (x - 5)(x + 4)$. Therefore, either $x - 5 = 0$ and $x = 5$, or $x + 4 = 0$ and $x = -4$. The smaller of the two possible x-values is -4. Therefore, the correct answer is (B).

2. **C** The total number of students enrolled in physics can be calculated as $36 + 54 = 90$. The question can be translated as $\dfrac{x}{100} \cdot 90 = 36$. Solve for x to get $\dfrac{x}{10} \cdot 9 = 36$, $\dfrac{x}{10} = 4$, and $x = 40$. The correct answer is (C).

3. **A** Each of the answer choices asks about what happens when $t = 10$. Start by working out each reaction with this value. Reaction A would yield a concentration of $1.3 \times 10 = 13$. Reaction B would yield $(1.1)^{10} \approx 2.593$. $13 \div 2.593 \approx 5$. Therefore, the correct answer is (A).

4. **D** When the line crosses the x-axis, the y-value is equal to 0 and the line equation becomes $0 = -\dfrac{1}{2}x + 4$. Solve for x to get $-4 = -\dfrac{1}{2}x$ and $x = 8$. The correct answer is (D).

5. **D** Use Process of Elimination to solve this question. The denominator of a fraction can never be 0. Therefore, x cannot be equal to 2. Eliminate (A) and (C). The square root of a negative number yields a result that is an imaginary number. Therefore, x cannot be -3 since one of the terms in the numerator is $\sqrt{x}$. On this basis eliminate (B). Therefore, the correct answer is (D).

6. **A** Use Process of Elimination. You can see that the graph is linear, so eliminate (D). Also, the slope is positive, so you cannot have a negative coefficient in front of x. Eliminate (C). Lastly, if you extend the line of best fit over to the y-axis, you can see that the y-intercept is negative. Therefore, eliminate (B), the answer must be (A).

7. **B** Use Process of Elimination to solve this question. According to the table the total number of people who could be employed in Michigan is 9,542,000. On this basis eliminate (D) since the number of people employed cannot be larger than the number of people who could be employed. Also, eliminate (C) because Michigan has an unemployment rate of 8.3% which means that not all people who could be employed are employed. Given that the unemployment rate is 8.3%, the employment rate must be $100 - 8.3 = 91.7\%$. $9,542,000 \times .917 = 8,750,014$. Therefore, the correct answer is (B).

8. **B** Use Process of Elimination to solve this question. Having the highest unemployment rate does not automatically imply that the state has the most number of people unemployed. Remember that to find the number of people unemployed, the unemployment rate is multiplied by the workforce. Therefore, the final value is driven as much by the unemployment rate as it is the number of people in the workforce. On this basis eliminate (A) and (C). Likewise, the lowest unemployment rate does not automatically equate with the fewest number of unemployed people. On this basis eliminate (D). The correct answer is (B).

9. **A** The x-intercept is where the line crosses the x axis. At that point the y-value is 0. Plug the point $(3, 0)$ into each of the answer choices to see which equation works. Choice (A) becomes $0 = 2(3) - 6$. Solve the right side of the equation to get $0 = 6 - 6$, and $0 = 0$. This equation works and therefore the correct answer is (A).

10. **C** According to the question 45% of the class wants to go to the arboretum and 20% of the class wants to go to the aquarium. This means that $45 + 20 = 65\%$ of the class does not want to go to the planetarium. $0.65 \times 80 = 52$. Therefore, the correct answer is (C).

11. **D** After 15 minutes $0.02 \times 15 = 0.3$ pounds of carbon dioxide is produced. To convert to grams set up the following proportion: $\dfrac{1\ pound}{453.6\ grams} = \dfrac{0.3\ pounds}{x\ grams}$. Cross multiply to get $x = 453.6 \times 0.3 = 136.08$. Therefore, the correct answer is (D).

12. **B** Use Process of Elimination. Shading above the line means the equation should include the > sign. On this basis eliminate (C) and (D). The equation of a line is $y = mx + b$ where b denotes the y-intercept. In the graph the y-intercept is 4. Therefore, eliminate (A). The correct answer is (B).

13. **C** Whenever the question and the answer choices include variables think Plugging In. If $s = 2$, and $d = 4$ then the value of B will be 6. Plug 2 in for s and 4 in for d in the answers to see which equation equals 6. Choice (A) becomes $B = 3^{\frac{4}{4}} + 2 = 3 + 2 = 5$. Eliminate (A). Choice (B) becomes $B = 3(2^{4 \times 4})$ $= 3(2^{16}) = 3(65,536) = 196,608$. Eliminate (B). Choice (C) becomes $B = 2 + \frac{3(4)}{4} = 2 + 3 = 5$. Keep (C) but check the remaining answer choice just in case. Choice (D) becomes $B = 2\left(3^{\frac{4}{4}}\right) = 2(3) = 6$. Eliminate (D). The correct answer is (C).

14. **C** 60 lightbulbs will use $60 \times 110 = 6,600$ watts per hour. Set up the following proportion to convert the wattage to joules: $\frac{1 \ joule}{3,600 \ watts} = \frac{x \ joules}{6,600 \ watts}$. Cross multiply to get $3,600x = 6,600$. Solve for x to get $x \approx 1.83$. Therefore, the 60 lightbulbs at the MacRuff storage facility use approximately 1.83 joules per hour. The maximum amount of energy MacRuff has is 22 joules. $22 \div 1.83 \approx 12$ hours. $12 \times 60 = 720$ minutes. Therefore, the correct answer is (C).

15. **B** Whenever there are variables in the question and numbers in the answers think Plugging In the Answers. Start with (B). If $x = 3$ then the second equation becomes $24(3) + 2y = 82$. Solve for y to get $72 + 2y = 82$, $2y = 10$, and $y = 5$. Plug 3 in for x and 5 in for y in the first equation to get $3 - \frac{5}{5} = 2$. Solve the left side of the equation to get $3 - 1 = 2$ and $2 = 2$. Since the numbers work the correct answer is (B).

16. **B** According to the graph, print book sales were highest in 2002. The number of print books sold in 2002 was 14,000. Digital download sales were highest in 2014. The number of digital download sales in 2014 was 12,000. This question is asking for percent change, which can be calculated as follows: $\frac{14,000 - 12,000}{12,000} = \frac{2,000}{12,000} = \frac{1}{6} \approx 17\%$. Therefore, the correct answer is (B).

17. **D** The number of Bacteria A and Bacteria B are equal at 4 minutes. At 4 minutes the graph shows each of the bacteria populations to be equal to approximately 16,000. $16,000 + 16,000 = 32,000$. Choice (D) is the closest possible answer and therefore the correct answer.

18. **A** The rest stop is $\frac{1}{3}$ of the way to Yasmine's parents' house, so the rest stop is 75 miles from her dorm. Therefore, Yasmine still has 150 miles to drive. Now, Plug-In a value for t. Since t represents the minutes that Yasmine has driven since leaving the rest stop and Yasmine's speed is given in

miles per hour, Plug-In $t = 60$. After 60 minutes, Yasmine will have driven an additional 50 miles, so she would have 100 miles left to drive. If you plug in $t = 60$ into the answers, only (A) will equal 100.

19. **C** Whenever the question includes unknown quantities and the answers are numbers think Plugging In the Answers. Start with (B). If the bag contains a total of 300 rubber bands then the bag contains $0.3 \times 300 = 90$ long rubber bands of which $0.15 \times 90 = 13.5$ are triple width. Since it is impossible to have half of a rubber band, eliminate (B). Try (C). If the bag contains 400 rubber bands then there are $0.3 \times 400 = 120$ long rubber bands of which $0.15 \times 120 = 18$ are triple width. Half of these or $\frac{1}{2} \times 18 = 9$ are dark brown. This matches the information in the question and therefore the answer is (C).

20. **B** First, rationalize the expression by multiplying both the numerator and the denominator by $\sqrt{12}$. This yields $\frac{(2x - 8)\sqrt{12}}{12}$. We can also rewrite $\sqrt{12}$ as $\sqrt{4(3)} = 2\sqrt{3}$. Distribute this on the numerator and now we have $\frac{4x\sqrt{3} - 16\sqrt{2}}{12}$. Split the numerator to make two terms: $\frac{4x\sqrt{3}}{12} - \frac{16\sqrt{2}}{12}$. Since the second term simplifies to $\frac{4\sqrt{3}}{3}$ then the first term must be C. Reduce the fraction by dividing the numerator and denominator by 4 and C equals $\frac{x\sqrt{3}}{3}$, which is (B).

21. **D** Between 1920 and 1930 the population grew by 2147 people. Since the population in 1920 was 7989, then the percent change was 2147/7989 times 100, which is 27%. Eliminate (A). Between 1940 and 1950 the population grew by 7397 people. The percent change for this decade would be 7397/11659 times 100, which is 63%. This is higher than 27%, so the answer is (D).

22. **A** Use Process of Elimination to solve this question. The current year, e.g. 2015 would not be a number used to calculate her total pay. Therefore, eliminate (D). Likewise the year Regina started getting raises would not be included in the equation to calculate her total pay. Therefore, eliminate (C). The $500 bonus, which is connected to x in the equation, is paid out after the first 300 cars she sells. If Regina sold 290 cars x would be equal to 0 because she would not have sold more than 300 cars and therefore the bonus would not apply. On this basis eliminate (B). The correct answer is (A).

23. **B** First, since the problem says that line r is perpendicular to line s, we know that angles DCE and BCA are both right angles. Also, since $DE = \frac{5}{2} BC$ and $BC = 4$, then DE must be 10. We now have both the adjacent side and the hypotenuse for angle EDC so we can set up the following equation: $\cos EDC = \frac{6}{10}$. Since lines m and n are parallel, we also know that angle BAC is equivalent to angle EDC. Therefore, $\cos BAC = \frac{3}{5}$, which is (B).

24. **D** Whenever the question includes unknown values think Plugging In. According to the question $\frac{G}{H} = \frac{4}{5}$ and $\frac{H}{J} = \frac{10}{17}$. Since both ratios include H plug in a number for H that will make both ratios easy to work with. Let's make $H = 10$. Then the number of votes for each candidate would be as follows:

Votes for G	Votes for H	Votes for J
8	10	17

Therefore, if half of the votes given to H were moved to J, the new vote tallies would be:

Votes for G	Votes for H	Votes for J
8	5	22

The ratio of those who voted for J to those who voted for G would be 22 to 8, which reduces to 11 to 4. Therefore, the correct answer is (D).

25. **C** Get the parabola into vertex form of $(x - 1)^2 + 7$ by completing the square, so the vertex is (1, 7), then do the two reflections. The first brings the point to (1, –1) then the second brings it to (–1, –1).

26. **C** Lines that are perpendicular to each other have slopes that are the negative reciprocal of each other. The equation of a line is $y = mx + b$ where m denotes the slope and b denotes the y-intercept. Therefore, the equation for line r, which is perpendicular to line m, is $y = 5x - 21$. To find the x-values of the points of intersection between line r and the parabola set the two equations equal to each other to get $x^2 - 2x - 9 = 5x - 21$. Set the equation to 0 to get $x^2 - 7x + 12 = 0$. Factor the right side of the equation to get $(x - 3)(x - 4) = 0$. Solve for x to get $x = 3$, and $x = 4$. Eliminate choices (A) and (B) because the x-value in those answer choices is incorrect. Plug x into the equation for line r to get $y = 5(3) - 21 = 15 - 21 = -6$. Therefore, one of the points of intersection is (3, –6). Eliminate (D). The correct answer is (C).

27. **B** First, solve for the average population of adults 18 and older from 1940–1970 by adding up the four values and dividing by 4. The average is 111.25. The mode is the value that occurs most frequently and between 1930 and 1960, inclusive. Since 45 occurs twice for children under the age of 18, the mode is 45. Lastly, the question asks what percent 111.25 is of 45, so divide 111.25 by 45 and multiply by 100. The answer is (B).

28. **1250**

The beaker will be empty when $0.4t = 500$. Solve for t to get $t = 1250$. The correct answer is 1250.

29. **21.3** Start by eliminating the fractions in the two equations. Multiply the first equation by 3 to get $18x - 12 = y$. Multiply the second equation by 2 to get $y - 20 = 2x + 14$. Solve the equation for y to get $y = 2x + 34$. To find the x-value of the point of intersection, set the two equations equal to each other to get $18x - 12 = 2x + 34$. Solve for x to get $16x = 46$ and $x = 2.875$. Plug 2.875 in for x into the equation $y = 2x + 34$ to get $y = 2(2.875) + 34 = 39.75$. Calculate the average of x and y as follows: $\frac{39.75 + 2.875}{2} = \frac{42.625}{2} = 21.3125$. Calculated to the nearest tenth the value becomes 21.3. The correct answer is 21.3.

30. **7** According to the question 20% of the chocolates are dark chocolate, 15% are white chocolate, and 35% are mint chocolate. 20 + 15 + 35 = 70%, which means that 30% of the total number of chocolates are chocolate truffle. The total number of chocolates in the box can be calculated as follows: $6 = 0.3 \times$ total. Total = 20 chocolates. Therefore, the number of mint chocolates in the box is $0.35 \times 20 = 7$. The correct answer is 7.

31. **1** There are 20 chocolates in the box. (See question 30 for an explanation of how to arrive at this information). Therefore, the number of dark chocolates is $0.2 \times 20 = 4$ and the number of white chocolates is $0.15 \times 20 = 3$. The difference is $4 - 3 = 1$. The correct answer is 1.

The Princeton Review

BONUS MATERIALS

COLLEGE INSIDER

Admissions and Financial Aid Advice

While *Workout for the New PSAT* will prepare you for your exam, *College Insider* will help you navigate what comes next. The bonus materials included here contain invaluable information about finding your best fit college, wending your way through the financial aid process, figuring out post-college plans, extra drills, and more. We wish you the best of luck on your studies and preparation for college.

Contents

Part 1

25 Tips to Help You Pay Less for College

by Kalman A. Chany, author of
Paying for College Without Going Broke
(Random House/Princeton Review Books)

GETTING FINANCIAL AID

1. Learn how the financial aid process works. The more and the sooner you know about the process, the better you can take steps to maximize your aid eligibility.

2. Apply for financial aid no matter what your circumstances. Some merit-based aid can only be awarded if the applicant has submitted financial aid application forms.

3. Don't wait until you receive an acceptance letter from your top choice school to apply for financial aid. Do it when applying for admission.

4. Complete all the required aid applications. All students seeking aid must submit the FAFSA (Free Application for Federal Student Aid); however, other forms may also be required by individual schools. Check with each college to see what's required and when.

5. Get the best scores you can on the SAT or ACT as they are used not only in decisions for admission but also financial aid. If your scores and other stats exceed the school's admission criteria, you are likely to get a better aid package than a marginal applicant.

6. Apply strategically to colleges. Your chances of getting aid will be better at schools that have generous financial aid budgets.

7. Don't rule out any school as too expensive. A generous aid award from a pricey private school can make it less costly than a public school with a lower sticker price.

8. Take advantage of education tax benefits. A dollar saved on taxes is worth the same as a dollar in scholarship aid. Look into Coverdells, education tax credits, and loan deductions.

SCHOLARSHIPS AND GRANTS

9. Get the best score you can on the PSAT, since it is the National Merit Scholarship Qualifying Test (as we covered in detail back in Chapter 3) and is also used in the selection of students for other scholarships and recognition programs.

10. Check your eligibility for grants and scholarships in your state. Some (but not all) states will allow you to use such funds out of state.

11. Look for scholarships locally. Find out if your employer offers scholarships or tuition assistance plans for employees or family members. Also look into scholarships from your church, community groups, and high school.

12. Look for outside scholarships realistically: They account for fewer than five percent of aid awarded. Research them at **princetonreview.com** or other free sites. Steer clear of scholarship search firms that charge fees and "promise" scholarships.

PAYING FOR COLLEGE

13. Invest wisely. Considering a 529 plan? Compare your own state's plan, which may have tax benefits with other states' programs. Get info at **savingforcollege.com**.

14. If you have to borrow, first pursue federal education loans (Perkins, Stafford, PLUS). Avoid private loans at all costs.

15. Never put tuition on a credit card. The debt is more expensive than ever given recent changes to interest rates and other fees some card issuers are now charging.

16. Try not to take money from your parent or guardian's retirement account or 401(k) to pay for college. In addition to likely early distribution penalties and additional income taxes, the higher income will reduce your aid eligibility.

PAYING LESS FOR COLLEGE

17. Attend a community college for two years and transfer to a pricier school to complete the degree. Plan ahead: Be sure the college you plan to transfer to will accept the community college credits.

18. Look into "cooperative education" programs. Over 900 colleges allow students to combine college education with a job. It can take longer to complete a degree this way but graduates generally owe less in student loans and have a better chance of getting hired.

19. Take as many Advanced Placement (AP) courses as possible and get high scores on AP exams. Many colleges award course credits for high AP scores. Some students have cut a year off their college tuition this way.

20. Earn college credit via "dual enrollment" programs available at some high schools. These allow students to take college-level courses during their senior year.

21. Earn college credits by taking CLEP (College-Level Examination Program) exams. Depending on the college, a qualifying score on any of the thirty-three CLEP exams can earn students three to twelve college credits.

22. Stick to your major. Changing colleges can result in lost credits. Aid may be limited/not available for transfer students at some schools. Changing majors can mean paying for extra courses to meet requirements.

23. Finish college in three years if possible. Take the maximum number of credits every semester, attend summer sessions, and earn credits via online courses. Some colleges offer three-year programs for high-achieving students.

24. Let Uncle Sam pay for your degree. ROTC (Reserve Officer Training Corps) programs available from U.S. Armed Forces branches (except the Coast Guard) offer merit-based scholarships up to full tuition via participating colleges in exchange for military service after you graduate.

25. Better yet: Attend a tuition-free college!

Part 2

7 Essential Tips for Writing Your College Essay

Most selective colleges require you to submit an essay or personal statement. It may sound daunting to represent your best self in only a few hundred words, and it will certainly take a substantial amount of work. But it's also a unique opportunity that can make a big difference at decision time. Admissions committees put the most weight on your high school grades and your test scores. However, colleges receive applications from many worthy students and use your essay (along with your letters of recommendation and extracurricular activities) to find out what sets you apart from the other talented candidates.

1. What Does Set You Apart?

Your background, interests, and personality combine to make you more than just a GPA and a standardized test score. The best way to tell your story is to write a personal, thoughtful essay about something that has meaning for you. If you're honest and genuine, your unique qualities will shine through.

2. Sound Like Yourself!

For examples of strong application essays, check out The Princeton Review's book, *College Essays that Made a Difference.*

Admissions counselors have to read an unbelievable number of essays. Many students try to sound smart rather than sounding like themselves. Others write about a subject they don't care about, but that they think will impress admissions brass. Don't write about the same subjects as every other applicant. You don't need to have started a company or discovered a lost Mayan temple. Colleges are simply looking for thoughtful, motivated students who will add something to the freshman class.

3. Write About Something that's Important to You.

It could be an experience, a person, a book—anything that has had an impact on your life. Don't just recount—reflect! Anyone can write about how they won the big game or the time they spent in Rome. Describe what you learned from the experience and how it changed you.

4. Be Consistent and Avoid Redundancies.

What you write in your application essay or personal statement should not contradict any other part of your application, nor should it repeat it. This isn't the place to list your awards or discuss your grades or test scores. Answer the question being asked. Don't reuse an answer to a similar question from another application.

5. Use Humor with Caution!

Being funny is a challenge. A student who can make an admissions officer laugh never gets lost in the shuffle. But beware: What you think is funny and what an adult working in a college thinks is funny might be very different. We caution against one-liners, limericks, and anything off-color.

6. Start Early and Write Several Drafts.

Set the essay aside for a few days and read it again. Put yourself in the shoes of an admissions counselor: Is the essay interesting? Do the ideas flow logically? Does it reveal something about the applicant? Is it written in the applicant's own voice?

7. Ask for Feedback!

Have at least one other person edit your essay—a teacher or college counselor is best. And before you send it off, triple check to make sure your essay is free of spelling or grammar errors. We recommend asking a second person to proofread your essay, as spellcheck and grammar software won't pick up every typo. It can be tricky to spot mistakes in your own work, especially after you've spent so much time writing and rewriting.

Part 3

Planning the Perfect College Visit

WHY SHOULD YOU DO A CAMPUS VISIT?

A campus visit won't tell you everything you need to know about life at your prospective college, but it will give you a richer, more detailed view than you would get from surfing websites, browsing brochures, watching videos, or reading college guides. Every school has its own culture, its own unique way of doing things, something you can't divine from a brochure! And even though you won't learn all there is to know from a brief visit, you'll get a sense of the "big picture" issues that define life on a campus. You'll probably get enough of a sense of those issues to determine whether the school is a good fit for you.

Spend a weekday on campus while classes are in session and you'll get a feel for the rhythm of life there, the attitudes of the students toward their studies, and—if you get the chance to attend a few classes—some idea of the atmosphere in the classrooms. Visit over a weekend and you'll experience the school's social life (or lack thereof). You'll also find students relaxing and taking it easy, making it easier to approach them with any questions you may have about the school.

Let's look at some of the benefits of a campus visit:

You'll Get a Feel for the Type of Student Who Attends the School

For many students, whom they go to school with is just as important as where they go to school and what they study. You may think this is a frivolous concern, but it's not; your fellow students will be your peers, friends, and possible rivals throughout your tenure at the school. If you're a bad fit with the student body, you could be in for four miserable years (fewer, probably, because most "bad fits" eventually transfer out; regardless, being the "sore thumb" at a school is an unpleasant scenario that you'll probably want to avoid).

There are lots of different issues to consider as you assess a student body. First, note the degree of similarity among students. Do they all look alike, or is the population diverse? Consider not just racial diversity but also economic diversity, religious diversity, and diversity of personality types. Are you more comfortable surrounded by people just like yourself, or do you want a college that will give you the opportunity to encounter people with different backgrounds and perspectives? More specifically, think about:

- *Personality type:* Do you see lots of students in sweats and sneakers? Or are most students decked out in alpaca sweaters, skinny jeans, or pearls? Is the campus an ocean of polo shirts?

The way students dress can tell you about more than their economic status; it can also tell you about the group or personality type with which they associate. You'll be surprised at how many students you will immediately identify as jocks, hippies, preps, nerds, or other social groups. You've probably encountered most of these personality types in high school. Which type reigns supreme on campus, if any? Is this a group you're comfortable spending four years among? Keep in mind, of course, that you can't judge a book entirely by its cover. Before you draw any definitive conclusions about students' personalities, talk with some students. You may well find that college students don't fit your assumptions as neatly as do your peers in high school.

- *Intellectualism:* Observe students in class, at the library, and in conversation as they walk across campus. Do you get the sense that students study primarily for the sake of learning? Or is their primary goal to score a high-paying job? If you're the type who wants to stay up all night discussing Plato, you won't likely be happy at a school full of pre-professionals with little interest in pure academics. Conversely, if your only goal is to get great grades in order to get into the best med, law, or b-school, you probably won't be happy at a school with a bunch of philosophizing dreamers.

- *Class/Status:* Is the parking lot filled with new sports cars and SUVs? Or are most of the cars clunkers (if they are, make sure you haven't stumbled onto the faculty parking lot by mistake!)? Do students dress as though they do all their shopping at high-priced, name-brand stores? Do the men and women seem especially fashion-conscious? Are they wearing nice but affordable clothing? Are students flashing a lot of high-priced gadgets or the newest, hottest technology? Ask yourself, "Can I envision myself as part of this community?" For many students, answering this question means having to think about class issues and the social circles they feel the most comfortable navigating.

- *Religion:* Are students religious? Are there frequent and obvious demonstrations of religious belief across campus? Deeply religious students may find the rampant secularism of many college campuses off-putting. Students with a more secular bent will likely have a hard time adjusting to life on deeply religious campuses, particularly those with strict behavioral codes or those where students openly proselytize.

- *Sexuality/Gender Issues:* To what extent do couples display affection on campus? Do you see indicators of an active and accepted gay community (e.g., posters for LGBT-friendly events)? Here's another area where it can be important to find a good personal fit. Socially conservative students may be uncomfortable on a campus with a large and active gay community, such as New York University or Smith. Conversely, gay students may be uncomfortable on campuses with profoundly conservative social attitudes.

While it's important for the school's academic program to be the right fit for you, it's just as important for the campus community to be a good fit, too. A college visit, even a brief one, will give you a good sense of who your classmates will be and whether you'll be comfortable among them. Yes, it's true: You really can't know exactly what a school is going to be like until you get there. Even your own opinion of your college experience will change as you grow more accustomed to being on campus. In the meantime, as you're searching, trust your instincts. The real "scoop" lies not so much in the specific information you receive, as in the applicability of the information to your interests, needs, and wants.

So know your priorities. Exactly what type of atmosphere are you looking for? Urban or rural? Big or small? Laid-back or focused? Getting a handle on what will make you happy and settled at college is half the battle.

You'll Get a Feel for the Academic Atmosphere and Whether it's a Good Fit for You

Academics are the primary reason you're attending college, so you want to know whether you and the school you're considering are a good academic fit. The quality of the school's academic life and the intensity of student-teacher relationships will strongly impact your experience at college. Look for clues about both during your campus visit.

If possible, attend a class or two during your visit (make sure to arrange for this with the Admissions Office well in advance). If asked for your preference, request to sit in on a class that is required for all freshmen so that you'll get a better sense of what your first year will be like—or, alternatively, try to pick a low-level class within the subject you're planning to major in, if you've already decided that. When you're there, keep your eyes and ears open. Are the classes huge or small? Is the teacher a full professor or a graduate student? Is the class format lecture, lab, discussion, or a hybrid of several formats? Are student contributions to the class interesting? Are students furiously scribbling notes? Are they asking questions? Is "Will this be on the test?" the only question any of them asks? Answer these questions and you'll get a pretty good sense of how students approach their studies at the school and whether you'll be comfortable with that approach.

If you can't attend a class, at least take time to walk around campus and to observe the students and faculty. Pay close attention to students as they travel to and from class. Are they in a hurry? Do they look stressed? Or are they walking at a leisurely pace, conversing, and laughing? Do faculty members talk with students as they walk across campus? Do you even see faculty members walking across campus, or are they missing from the picture? If faculty members are conspicuously absent, it could mean that they have numerous commitments off campus (e.g., conferences, serving on corporate boards, or teaching at more than one school) that would leave them less time to devote to undergraduates on campus.

You'll get a Feel for Extracurricular Life

Your college experience will consist of more than studying and hanging out with friends. There will be all sorts of clubs and organizations available for participation, and you may want to join one or more, which is why it's important to explore the extracurricular life of a school. What do students do when they're not in class, in the library, or hanging around the dorms with friends? Look for the following:

- *Active clubs and organizations:* All schools have some clubs and organizations, but what those are exactly will vary from school to school. You can find out which clubs are registered on campus by visiting the student activity center, where a list of the school's organizations is usually posted. In addition, most schools list all their clubs and organizations on their websites and many provide separate sites for each group. Look for posters announcing meetings and events to determine which groups are most active.

- *Greek organizations:* Does the school have a Greek scene? How active is it? Is it simply one aspect of campus life or is it the dominant feature? Are lots of students wearing T-shirts and sweatshirts emblazoned with the names of their houses? Are there posters around campus announcing upcoming parties at Greek houses? Ask students—Greeks and independents alike—about the school's fraternity and sorority scene. Their answers will reveal what you can expect from the social scene on campus.

- *The party scene:* The Greek scene and the party scene are synonymous at some schools, but not at all of them. Some schools have no Greek organizations while others place strict restrictions on Greek parties, forcing the party scene elsewhere. At many schools the Greek houses are the locus of parties for underclassmen, while students of drinking age prefer local bars or even smaller parties at their apartments or houses. And some schools have minimal party scenes: military academies, single-sex schools, and religious schools are the most likely candidates, but small schools with large commuter populations or a large in-state population (at some schools, in-state students leave campus for the weekend immediately after their last class of the week) can also be relatively party-free. Whether you're looking for a year-round Mardi Gras, a cloister, or something in between, you should consider the school's party scene when choosing your undergraduate institution. Even if you have no interest in partying—especially if you have no interest in partying, really—the intensity of the party scene will have a big impact on your life at school. During your visit, survey the campus for evidence of an active party scene: dumpsters full of empties, posters advertising huge blowout parties, or bleary-eyed students in pajamas straggling across campus in the early afternoon. Better still, schedule a weekend visit so you can experience the party scene firsthand.

- **The arts:** Some schools house well-known museums and frequently host touring theatrical, musical, and dance productions. Others host regular student theatrical and musical productions, galleries displaying student and faculty art, and a steady diet of movies, old and new. Still others have practically no arts scene at all; there's no interest on campus, so it doesn't exist. If your idea of fun is a Truffaut double feature or a night of experimental theatre, make sure you find a school that can accommodate you. Scan the bulletin boards for notices about upcoming arts events. Survey the campus map for evidence of art-specific buildings, such as student galleries, art and dance studios, and concert halls.

- **Athletics:** Most schools have some form of an athletic program, but the degree to which athletics are a major campus focal point varies greatly from school to school. At some schools, football or basketball season is the high point of the school year; students are passionate about their teams and build their schedules around games, camping out to get tickets and tailgating enthusiastically for hours before the start of an event. You'll see evidence of students' devotion at these sports-happy schools in the form of banners, pennants, bumper stickers, and T-shirts, just to name a few examples. At other schools, athletics are an afterthought, and if you ask students about the football team they're likely to respond, "We have a football team?" If college athletics are important to you, you probably shouldn't attend such a school.

- *The neighborhood around campus and the school's hometown:* Try to save time to tour the town or city in which the school is located. If you can't, at least take a walk around the surrounding neighborhood to see what sort of off-campus housing, restaurants, clubs, and retail shops are easily accessible. If you visit enough schools, you'll probably notice that campus life is generally much more active in schools located in smaller towns. At big-city schools—in New York City, Boston, and Chicago, for example—students tend to seek their fun off-campus, and with good reason: Few schools could compete with all the options that a big city offers.

WHEN IS THE BEST TIME TO VISIT COLLEGES?

There are two timing issues to consider in this question: the best time in the school's schedule, and the best time for you as a high schooler. Let's look at both.

Best Times To Visit During The College Academic Year

The best time to visit a school is when the school is in session. Yes, it's probably easier to visit during the summer when you're on vacation, but the trouble is that the school is on break then, too. You'll be able to see the campus and take a tour, but you won't be able to attend classes (summer classes are nothing like classes held during the regular academic year) and you won't get to see what the campus looks like when it's full of students. You won't get to see the students (or most of the professors and administrators, for that matter), so you won't be able to get a sense of how well you'll fit into the campus community. You won't get a good feel for the school and so will miss out on the most important part of your campus visit.

During the school year, avoid visiting during school holidays such as Thanksgiving and Spring Break. Also, try not to visit during exam periods or reading periods (the few days or week of study time that precedes final exams, during which no classes are scheduled). It'll be difficult to attend a class during those times, and students will be preoccupied with exams and probably a little frazzled. They won't be in the mood to chat, because they won't have the time. Visit during these periods and you'll get a skewed impression of the school. You'll probably walk away thinking the students are all basket cases!

Keep in Mind:
Before you embark on a college visit, be sure to check out our comprehensive *Best Colleges* guides and our website **PrincetonReview.com** to get some preliminary information about the schools you may want to visit.

Be sure to check out the school's website and academic calendar to figure out which are the best days to visit.

Fitting a College Visit Into Your High School Schedule

Exploit your vacation time and off days. When is your spring break? Use it to visit colleges that aren't on break at the same time. Check your school's calendar for three-day weekends; some colleges don't observe national holidays so you can use those weekends for a Sunday overnight visit and attend some college classes on Monday. Remember that overnight visits should be scheduled well in advance as they require extra planning both on your part and on the part of the school.

As for your own schedule, when is the best time in your high school career to visit colleges? The short answer is that, essentially, any time is good once you start seriously considering college choices. In practice this can depend on what your goals for the trips are, where you already are in the college application process and, of course, financial constraints.

Some students prefer to wait until they've already applied and have heard back from schools, using visits to help make their decision between schools where they've already been accepted. This can also help avoid spending money on visiting a school where they aren't accepted. In this case, you'd necessarily need to plan visits in the spring of your senior year.

In an ideal world, though, you could visit schools earlier in the process in order to decide where you want to apply. During your sophomore year and the autumn semester of your junior year, you should try to visit lots of different types of schools—big schools, small schools, urban campuses, suburban/rural campuses, private liberal arts schools, public universities—to see what options are available to you. Intensify your efforts during the spring semester of junior year and throughout senior year, and also intensify your focus; hone in on those schools about which you are most serious. While you're a junior and during the autumn semester of senior year, you should try to pay daytime visits to all the schools on your short list, while trying to schedule overnight visits for at least some of the schools that interest you most.

When you reach the end of your visits and it comes time to compare the schools you visited, remember to take into account the time of year you went. Most campuses are at their most alluring in the early autumn and late spring. Conversely, some schools can be pretty austere, even forbidding, in the height of winter. Don't let the season of your visit unduly influence your final decision positively or negatively.

HOW TO ASK THE RIGHT QUESTIONS

No matter how the information session is organized, at some point you'll get a chance to ask questions. Do so! It gives you a chance to learn about something that truly interests you and also provides an opportunity to impress the session leader with what an articulate and thoughtful person you are.

Lots and lots of questions are listed later, but here are a few rules of thumb when asking questions:

Ask About Something that Is of Particular Interest to You

Do you hope to study abroad in a particular country? Ask about the availability of international education programs. Are you interested in pursuing independent study in a particular field? Ask about the opportunities and resources that will be available to you. Would you like to get related work/internship experience while at school? Ask about available cooperative learning programs.

Don't Ask about Data and Other Information that Can Be Easily Found in the School's Promotional Material

Asking about average SAT scores, the number of volumes in the school library, the student:teacher ratio, etc., communicates that you are too lazy to find this readily accessible information yourself. It also suggests that you're asking a question simply for the sake of it, which fails to demonstrate genuine interest in attending that particular school.

If You Are Accompanied by Your Parents, Politely Suggest that They Let You Ask Most of the Questions

The school is considering you for admission, not your parents and those that ask long-winded questions designed mostly to show off how much they know about the school may think they are making a good impression, but their effect is actually the opposite.

Be Polite

Present yourself well: Don't slouch, don't chew gum, and speak politely. If your parents are with you, don't bicker with them. And for goodness' sake, don't tell the person conducting the information session that the school is your "safety" or that you'll only attend if you receive a monster scholarship (true stories). Remember: tact is key.

GUIDELINES FOR PARENTS

Be supportive, be positive, and be patient: A college visit is a stressful time for everyone. Behave in a way most likely to minimize stress.

Schedule Plenty of Extra Time in Your Itinerary

Nothing creates stress more effectively than running late for important appointments. Plan to spend at least three hours on each campus you visit. Build plenty of buffer time into your travel plans to and from campuses and to and from appointments on campus. Follow these guidelines and you shouldn't find yourself constantly rushing from one place to the next. Worst-case scenario, you'll have some extra time on one of the campuses you're visiting—that's a win-win. Use the extra time to check out popular campus hangout spots.

Don't Try to Run the Show

From the planning of the trip through its execution, consult with your child about the itinerary. Is he or she ready for on-campus interviews? How many campuses does he or she feel capable of assimilating in one day? Once on campus, resist the temptation to advocate for your child or to manage the on-campus experience. Give your child plenty of opportunities to explore on his or her own. And under no circumstances should you try to participate in your child's on-campus interview. It sends a terrible message to the school (i.e., our child is not self-sufficient enough to handle this experience) and almost always produces bad results.

Utilize Your Child's Free Time Efficiently

While your child is exploring campus on his or her own, make your own inquiries. Check out the surrounding area to see whether it looks safe. Search for reasonably priced restaurants and shopping near campus. Visit dormitories, dining halls, computer labs, science labs, arts facilities, and whatever else might be of interest to your child.

Take Pictures

Let's face it—this is way too embarrassing for your kid to be seen doing (your students will be focused on fitting in, not standing out!), but you, on the other hand, can snap away without any embarrassment. These photos will go a long way toward helping your child compare schools later.

Talk to Other Parents

Find out what other parents think about the school, what concerns they have, and what their questions are. Listening to them will help clarify some of your own concerns—you may even learn about a new scholarship, a new college financing program, or the name of another great school for your child to consider!

GUIDELINES FOR STUDENTS

Set Goals in Advance

What exactly do you hope to learn from your visit? Know before you go and you'll get a lot more out of it. Make a list of questions you want to answer during your trip (and check out the lists provided for you at the end of this book). You may not get to ask all your questions, but just having a list will help focus your observations while on campus.

Wear Comfortable Shoes but Dress Nicely

You'll be doing a lot of walking, so choose shoes that won't turn your feet into hamburger meat. Otherwise, dress nicely; remember, you're a guest in someone else's home and you should carry yourself accordingly. This doesn't mean you need to dress in a three-piece suit; wearing a tasteful shirt or blouse and clean pants (jeans or khakis) or a skirt is completely fine. A presentable outfit is especially important if you've scheduled an on-campus interview.

Don't Be Afraid to Ask Questions during Your Tour

Don't be shy. You're on campus to find out what you need to know; asking questions is the best way to get that done. Don't hog the tour guide's attention but don't be a wallflower either.

Don't Be Unduly Influenced by the Tour Guide

Your tour guide may seem really cool, or may seem like a total dork. Either way, the guide is just one of many students who attend the school; don't judge the school based on this one person. Try to meet as many other students as you can to get a broad picture of the student body. Visit the student center and the dining hall. Introduce yourself to students and ask if they wouldn't mind answering questions. If possible, schedule an overnight visit with a stay in a host student's dorm room (many colleges offer this—just talk to the admissions office when you're scheduling your visit).

Keep a Journal

We don't mean you actually have to take notes while you're visiting campus, although it's not a bad idea! At the very least, you should record your observations and insights about each campus you visit at the end of each day. You'll probably be visiting a lot of campuses and a journal will help you remember what you liked and didn't like about each school you visited.

Try to discreetly snap some pictures of the campus. Maybe you can recruit your parents to be the "real" tourists, but even if not, take pictures of things about the campus that you really like so you can look back on the day when it's time to make decisions about which schools to take off your list.

PLANNING YOUR TRIP: 9 STEPS TO A SUCCESSFUL VISIT

The logistics of organizing a multi-stop, multi-day trip can be a daunting task. Following the nine steps outlined below makes it a lot easier.

Step 1: Determine When You Are Free to Take a Trip

Check your school calendar to figure out when you have weeks off, three-day weekends, etc. If you plan to miss a day or two of school in order to accommodate your trip, figure out when your exams are scheduled and make sure you're not traveling during those days or during the week before.

Step 2: Identify All the Schools You Want to Visit and then Group Them by Geographic Area

Collate the academic schedules of the schools you wish to visit with the dates of your planned trip. If possible, plan to visit the geographic region whose schools mesh best with your travel days. Try to avoid visiting campuses during holidays (e.g., Thanksgiving, Christmas, and Spring Break), reading periods, and exam periods.

Step 3: Create an Itinerary

Map out the locations of the schools you plan to visit. If you have to fly to visit colleges, try to coordinate general geographic regions, and figure out if you'll be able to rent a car to drive between locations. If driving, try to map a course that connects the schools in a single loop in order to minimize driving time. Even if you're interested in three schools within a half-hour of each other, plan to visit no more than two schools per day.

Step 4: Tinker with the Itinerary

Now that you know where you're going, look closely at the map. Are there other schools you might consider that are along your route? Make a note to squeeze in a quick visit to one or more schools. Also, take time to find out whether there are some fun sights to see along the way. Yeah, this trip is about seeing schools, but that doesn't mean you can't have a little fun, time permitting.

Step 5: Call the Admissions Offices of the Schools You Plan to Visit

Schedule an interview if you choose to. Find out what time tours begin and end. If you're scheduling more than one campus visit per day, make sure to leave extra time at each school to wander around campus, talk with students, and explore the neighborhood and town surrounding the school.

Step 6: Create a Daily Schedule

Start with the appointments you've made and then figure out when you have to arrive and leave each school in order to make it to all your appointments. Use an online itinerary planner (such as Google Maps, Rand McNally, or mapquest.com) to estimate your travel time between schools.

Step 7: Make your Overnight Arrangements

Find places to stay. If you're planning on staying on campus, make sure to contact the school and make arrangements at least two weeks in advance. Calling a month in advance is better; two months in advance, better still. If you travel with your parents, they will probably need to find a place to stay off campus. Contact the school to ask for recommendations. Schools sometimes have prearranged discount rates with local hotels and motels.

Step 8: Write Out or Print Out Your Entire Itinerary

Be sure it at least includes maps to and from schools and hotels, driving directions, and all the phone numbers you may need, etc. Research any local dining and shopping establishments you're interested in visiting and print out their names, addresses, and telephone numbers.

Step 9: Write out a list of questions you want to ask at the schools

This is the only way to avoid that "Rats, I wish I'd asked about..." feeling that comes about an hour after you've left the campus. We have lists and lists of questions at the end of this book to help you make sure you get all the information you need—be sure to read them through, adding any questions particular to *you*.

When you finally hit the road, don't forget to enjoy yourself. Yes, college visits are important and should be taken seriously, but they are also wonderful adventures to new and exciting places. Soak it all in and be grateful that you're smart enough and capable enough to be looking forward to a college education. It's easy to take all that for granted, but you don't have to step back too far to gain some perspective and realize what a fortunate position you're in. So don't be afraid to have a little fun on your trip; you've earned it!

KEY PLACES TO VISIT

Remember to leave time after the tour/information session to walk around campus on your own. Although the promotional material, the tour, and the information session will all be helpful, they all represent an image of the school packaged by public relations professionals. You want to spend some time seeing the school without that filter. Visit whatever buildings you can access without school identification. High on your list of "must visit" places should be the main freshman dormitory (you'll probably be living there if you attend) and the dining hall (buy lunch and try to imagine eating this food every day of the week; also, try to work your way into a group of current students chatting among themselves on campus so you can ask them about the school); finally, make sure you visit the general information library (this is where books for required courses will be on reserve and thus is a place where you could spend a lot of your freshman year). You should also check out the student union, the athletic facilities, and any other facilities you expect to use. Are all these facilities up-to-date and well maintained? Can you imagine yourself happy in this setting? You should also spend some time exploring the neighborhood around campus.

You should try to attend at least one class while on campus. This will require some extra planning, as you will probably need to schedule your classroom visit in advance with the admissions office. Ideally, the school will send you to a class that's required for all freshmen. Unless the professor calls specifically on you, do not try to participate in the class. You are just there to observe, not to overwhelm your future classmates with your brilliance. Stay for the entire class no matter how boring it is; it's rude to get up and leave a class that's in session. And this may go without saying, but please remember to turn off your cell phone before you enter the classroom!

That's a whole lot of activity to cram into one visit, which is one of the reasons admissions professionals advise against visiting more than two campuses in one day. The other reason is sensory overload—visit more than two schools in a day and they all start to blend into one amorphous blob! Take notes during your visits (or immediately after) so that you can remember what you liked and disliked about each school. If you visit a lot of schools, you will have a hard time remembering which details pertain to which school if you don't take notes.

Your campus visit presents an incredible opportunity to get more information on life at college from the real experts—the students in attendance. Don't be shy about going up to a student and asking them the tough questions—you'll be happy you did.

THE ESSENTIAL TIP LIST FOR GETTING THE MOST OUT OF YOUR COLLEGE VISIT

It's sometimes helpful to have everything boiled down to the basics, this section condenses our most essential tips for getting the most out of your college visit into one place. If your college visits are spread out over a long period of time and you don't have time to go back and re-read a section, or you want a quick reminder about what to look for right before you hit a campus, just visit this section for a refresher!

Visit As Many Colleges As You Can

If possible, visit every college that you are strongly considering. Many students change their minds after a college visit. That's great—it means the visit has done its job. And this is obviously preferable to changing your mind after you enroll!

Mind the Calendar

Schedule your visit while school is in session. You won't get a realistic idea of student life in August (or if you attend during a special event like Spring Fling).

Meet the Experts

Talk to the current students—they may soon be your peers. If they have a problem or grievance, they will probably share it with you and if they love their school, they won't be shy about it either. Specific questions yield far more interesting (and helpful) answers. Here are a few questions to ask:

- What are the best reasons to go here?

- Why made you choose this school over others that you were considering?

- What do you do on weekends?

- What do you love about this college?

- What things frustrate you about this college?

- What do students complain about most?

- Did you have friends that were going here before you?

- Have you changed your major? (If so, why?)

- Are students friendly?

Meet the Other Experts

Stop by the admissions office and introduce yourself. Let them know what interests you about the school so they can direct you to the best place for further investigation. Collect contact information and send a brief, friendly email thanking them for taking the time to talk to you. If there is a sign-up sheet, add your name! Colleges do keep track of which applicants have demonstrated genuine interest in the school. Some schools will let you interview with an admissions rep during your campus visit. If this opportunity is available, don't pass it up.

Take the Campus Tour

Although it's the most obvious thing to do, the official campus tour is worth your while. (Find out if you need to register to get a spot.) It gives the school a chance to show its best face, like the newly built theater or their rooftop planetarium. While you're walking around, check out the flyers and bulletin boards and pick up a school newspaper to get a sense of what's going on ... then venture out on your own. The official tour will probably steer you clear of the school's less attractive features, like the shoddy dining hall or the tiny gymnasium. Take your own unofficial tour by wandering around campus. If there are any facilities that are important to you, find them and have a look for yourself. Make sure your destinations include the freshmen dormitories.

Be a Student for a Day (or Night)

Some schools sponsor overnight programs in which you can stay with a current student. This is a great opportunity to get a deeper sense of campus life and interact with your potential future friends and roommates. Even if you don't stay over, most schools will allow you to sit in on lectures. Browse the course catalogue before you arrive, or ask the admissions office what classes are in session that day.

Save the Best for Last

You'll get better at visiting colleges with practice. As you compare schools, you pick up on the aspects you like and the aspects you're not so fond of. You also figure out the right questions to ask as well as the best campus spots to gauge student life. For that reason, visit your favorite schools last, so you'll be in the best position to make comparisons to the others on your list.

Don't Rush to Judgment

Be careful not to rush to judgment if the weather's bad or the class you attended is boring. There are bound to be sunny days and more interesting classes. At the same time, trust your gut. Sometimes it's love at first sight. Other times, something feels wrong (even if you can't put your finger on it).

Keep a Record of Every College Visit

We recommend jotting down a few notes after every college visit. This may seem pointless, but trust us—after visiting the ninth or tenth school, you'll have a hard time remembering which one had the killer cafeteria or the great library. Keep track of the details you like and the stuff that you don't like, and when more questions arise (as they most definitely will) you can fire off an email for an answer rather than visiting a second time. Your notes will be helpful when you decide where to apply (and, after you're admitted, where to go). They should be candid and real. They're for you—not your parents or college counselor. Be honest with yourself and trust your gut.

CHEAT SHEET: THE MOST IMPORTANT QUESTIONS TO ASK WHILE ON CAMPUS

We've compiled some of the most useful questions to ask while you're visiting colleges and grouped them by subject. Some are no-brainers—you're going to need to know about dorms pretty much everywhere—but not all of these questions will apply for every school, and you may also already be familiar with the answers from a college's admissions brochure.

We encourage you to read through the lists below and use them both as checklists and as jumping-off points for thinking about the *specific* questions you might have. Your college-specific questions can be prompted either by the particular features of a school (for instance, is there a program that appealed to you in the college brochure that you want to know more about?) or about how you might fit in there (e.g., if your hobby is photography, do you want to know if there's a darkroom available on campus?).

Feel free to photocopy this list and take it with you when you're visiting schools. Use the space underneath each question as well as the sidebars to write in your answer. Even if you don't want to take actual notes while touring the campus, looking through this list on your way back from a visit can help you recall what you saw and heard before it slips your mind.

Academics

- What are the most prominent majors and programs?

- Are those majors more difficult to get accepted into?

- Do they offer the major in my area of interest?

- How large or small are the classes?

- What is the student/faculty ratio (especially for the freshman class)?

- Are there freshman seminars?

- How much contact is there between students and professors?

- Are professors required to teach undergraduate courses or do they mostly focus on research?

- Are classes taught by graduate students, especially freshman classes?

- Are there research opportunities with professors?

- What is the Honors Program like?

- Is there a special winter or summer term?

- Who are the best professors?

- What is the quality of the student advising?

- Is there tutoring help on campus?

- How do we contact the office that helps students with learning disabilities?

- How do we contact the office that helps international students?

Administration

- How hard/easy is it to work with the administration?

- How hard/easy is it to work with the financial aid office?

- Does it seem like there is a lot of red tape or bureaucracy?

- How hard/easy is it to register for classes?

- How hard/easy is it to change classes/majors/departments?

- Is it easy to get face-time with administrators?

Dorm/Housing

- How many dorms are there?

- How are the dorms different from each other?

- What are the options (co-ed, suite-style, freshman, houses, honors)?

- Are students required to live on campus?

- Do most freshmen live on campus?

- Is there guaranteed housing for freshmen?

- What's the off-campus housing situation like?

- How are roommates paired up?

- What if that roommate doesn't work out?

- How many roommates per room for different dorms?

- What are the laundry facilities like?

- Are there curfews?

- What kind of security/entry is there for dorms?

- Are there refrigerators/microwaves/group kitchens?

- Are there dedicated study areas?

- Are there dorm events?

- Do the dorms close down during holidays?

Food

- What are the on-campus food options?

- What are the hours for the on-campus food options?

- What are the local/off-campus food options?

- Are there vegetarian/vegan options?

- How much of the food is bought locally?

- Is there a meal plan?

- How does the meal plan work (is there a debit card or is there a per-meal card)?

- How much is the meal plan?

- How is the meal plan billed/paid for?

Extracurricular and Social Activities

- How many clubs, activities, and athletics are at the college?

- How do you sign up for clubs?

- What are the most popular student groups on campus?

- What is there to do on the weekends?

- Are there fraternities and sororities?

- How prominent are fraternities and sororities on campus?

- How prominent is drinking on campus?

- How prominent are drugs on campus?

- What activities are there that don't involve drinking and drugs?

- What kind of events are planned by the campus activities board?

- Are there lots of religious events?

- What kinds of events are school-sponsored?

- What kinds of speakers come to campus?

- What kinds of bands come to campus?

- Do students hang out on campus on the weekends or do they hit up local venues?

- Are there many student theater productions?

Athletics

- What kind of intercollegiate sports are prominent on campus?

- How do you purchase student tickets for sports events?

- What kind of intramural sports are prominent on campus?

- What kinds of sports facilities are available on campus?

- How much scholarship money goes to student athletes?

- What kinds of sports facilities and activities are there in the local community?

- Do athletes have special housing?

- Are admissions requirements different for athletes?

Technology

- How much of campus is Wi-Fi enabled?

- Are classrooms set up for laptops?

- Are there online classes?

- Do professors generally post class notes?

- How much of teacher-student interaction is online?

- How many computer labs are there on campus?

- Are computer labs open 24 hours?

- Are textbooks available as eBooks?

Surrounding Town

- How well does the college get along with the surrounding town?

- What is the local social scene like?

- What is the crime rate in town?

- What are the job prospects like in the local town?

- What are the larger companies in town?

- Do they recruit interns from this college?

- What kinds of public transportation are available in town?

- Where is the local shopping center?

- Where is the closest grocery store?

- What other colleges are around here?

- What other towns/cities are around here?

Transportation

- Are freshmen allowed to have cars on campus?

- What is parking like?

- How much commuter parking is there?

- How much residential parking is there?

- How much does parking cost?

- Are there trolley or bus routes on campus?

- Is there transportation from campus to local areas?

- How late does that transportation run?

- Is there a bike-share program on campus?

- Is theft from cars a problem on campus?

- Is a car necessary to get around the town?

- How much will parking tickets cost?

- Is there a shuttle from campus to the airport?

- Are there late-night shuttles or taxis available?

- Is there a car-share program on campus (Zipcar)?

Study Abroad

- What percentage of students study abroad at some point during their four years?

- What countries do students go to?

- How do you sign up for study abroad?

- How do those credits count toward graduation?

- About how much does it cost?

- Does financial aid cover study abroad?

Financial

- How much is tuition?

- What other charges are there (for example, room and board, fees, computers)?

- What types of scholarships or financial aid is available?

- When are the deadlines for the forms?

- What do you need to do to apply?

- Are there jobs available on or near campus if you want to work? How easy or difficult is it to secure one?

Internships/Career

- What percentage of students receive jobs in their field of interest after graduation?

- Is there a job or career placement program?

- What internship programs or opportunities are available?

Politics

- Are students mostly conservative on campus?

- Are students mostly liberal on campus?

- Are students very politically active on campus?

Religion

- How actively religious are students on campus?

- What is the dominant religion on campus?

- How strict are the rules on campus?

- How tolerant are students of non-religious students?

Holidays/Festivities

- What is the holiday schedule for the school?

- Are the dorms closed over long holidays?

- Are there options for holiday housing?

- What are the Homecoming festivities like?

- What are holiday festivities like?

- What are some of the campus traditions?

Campus Media

- Is there a college radio station?

- Is there a campus newspaper or news website?

- Are there other student publications?

Students

- How happy are students?
- How nice are students?
- How much diversity is there on campus?
- Are students athletic-minded?
- Are students arts-minded?
- Are students involved in lots of clubs and activities?
- Is this mainly a commuter campus?
- Do students generally stay around campus on weekends?
- How tolerant are students of LGBT students?
- Where can I find the best food/coffee on campus?
- What is the school's best-kept secret?
- Can I get anything for free on campus?
- How often do you attend campus events?

Alumni

- How involved are alumni with students?
- How active is the alumni association?
- Are there alumni mentors for students?

Campus/Facilities

- Is the campus safe and secure?
- Is there a blue light system or a late-night escort system available?
- Is there a library on campus that is open 24 hours?
- How many bookstores are on campus?
- Is there a post office on campus?
- How accessible is the campus for students with disabilities?

TIPS FOR VISITING MILITARY ACADEMIES, WOMEN'S COLLEGES, AND HBCUS

Certain types of schools—such as all-women's schools, military academies, historically black colleges and universities, technical colleges, and sports-crazy schools—have readily identifiable distinguishing characteristics. You'll want to explore the issues associated with those characteristics during your visit; here's some information to get you started.

Military Academies

Federal military academies educate and train officers for the Army, Navy, and Air Force. These institutions require recommendation and appointment by members of Congress. There are certainly benefits associated with attending a United States military academy. In addition to free tuition, military academy students receive a top-notch education, a prestigious degree, and access to an unparalleled alumni network. Private and state-supported military institutes, however, accept applications from students interested in attending. They all offer degree programs in engineering and technology with concentrations in various aspects of military science. When visiting a military academy, these are some of the things you should ask about:

- What is the length of the post-graduation commitment?

- What percentage of graduates receive their first choice assignments after graduation?

- What is the attrition rate for freshmen? How many leave because they "can't take it?"

- Is the campus coeducational? How fully are women integrated on campus? How are women treated by male classmates?

- Will the school accept your high school ROTC credit?

- To what extent do students get a "free ride?" Does the school charge tuition? Room and board? Other fees?

- What sort of extracurricular student activities are available? Does the average student have time to participate in these activities?

Women's Colleges

Women's colleges were originally founded in the nineteenth century to meet the educational needs of women—needs that had, up until then, largely been ignored. Independent nonprofit women's colleges were created as a counterpart to the liberal arts colleges that existed for men. Others were affiliated with religious denominations and open only to white women, while still others were founded as historically black women's colleges. While their numbers may not be as great as they once were, women's colleges have experienced a new popularity over the last several years. Competition is fierce at the most selective women's colleges, with many women choosing single-sex education not because it was the only option available to them, but because of the opportunities an all-women's college offers them.

According to the Women's College Coalition (WCC), students at women's colleges "report greater satisfaction than their coed counterparts with their college experience in almost all measures—academically, developmentally, and personally." In addition, the WCC states that women's college students "continue toward doctorates in math, science, and engineering in disproportionately large numbers." In fact, women's colleges confer a larger proportion of bachelor's degrees in traditionally male-dominated fields (mathematics, science, and engineering) than coeducational, private colleges do. Women's colleges also have a larger percentage of female faculty and administration. While many factors go into making a college choice, women's colleges are definitely worth considering. Here are some things to inquire about when you go visiting:

- What is social life like? Many women's colleges have relatively quiet campuses, which may or may not appeal to you.

- If you're interested in dating men, where are the closest men's and coed schools? Does the women's school traditionally have a strong social relationship with these schools?

- What are the advantages of attending a single-sex school? Your tour guide and the leader of your information session will be more than happy to tell you!

- Remember that most women's colleges are relatively small institutions. As with any small liberal arts college, check the availability of programs in areas that interest you. Does the school have extensive offerings in the liberal arts? Fine arts and performing arts? How about science and mathematics? Is cross registration at other schools available to make up for absences in the school's curriculum?

- Is there a visible LGBT population on campus? Are there organizations supporting these communities? Is there a visible heterosexual community on campus? Are there indicators of strained relations among these communities?

- What support and advising resources are available for students interested in graduate school and/or other pre-professional programs?

Historically Black Colleges and Universities (HBCUs)

For a little more information about HBCUs, please visit **www.princetonreview.com** and search for "historically black colleges and universities."

An HBCU is, by definition, a school that was established before 1964 with the intention of serving the African American community. There are more than 100 HBCUs in the United States, and they come in all types and sizes—public and private, two-year and four-year, single-sex and coeducational. Few, if any of them, are all-black and some, such as Lincoln University of Missouri, actually have large white populations. The size and involvement of the African American community at any college is a factor you should weigh carefully before you apply. Dig beneath the perceptions and stereotypes to discover for yourself which environment is best for you. Visiting the schools you are considering is a great way to assess their environments. Start by asking these questions:

- Does the school have extensive offerings in the liberal arts? What about fine arts and performing arts? How about science and mathematics?

- Is cross-registration at other schools available to make up for absences in the school's curriculum?

- What is the social life like here?

- How strong is the alumni network? (This has historically been one of the great strengths of HBCUs.)

- How widely available is financial aid?

- How many companies recruit on campus? (HBCUs often excel in job placement for graduates.)

Part 4

The Right College for You

18 FACTORS THAT DO & DON'T MATTER

Finding the right college for you is an exercise in matchmaking. You should begin with a thorough self-examination that will help you consider your options and keep track of those colleges that do and don't satisfy the various needs or wants you've identified. You can decide exactly how to build out your personal inventory—whether in a spreadsheet, chart form, or simply mentally—but you will find that in the course of your college search, you'll confront an amazing array of statistics and other data related to every college you consider. In order for all of this information to be helpful, you'll need to have some sense of how to interpret it, which is why a chart or table can play a helpful role in evaluation and comparison. Remember that choosing a college is a personal decision, so data is only one aspect of how a college should appeal to you. To get you started, we've listed eighteen factors that do and don't matter.

Money

A lot of colleges cost a lot of money. If your parents aren't rich, the cost will make a big difference. Even when colleges say they don't pay attention to applicants' financial need in accepting and rejecting students, they really do. How much money your parents can afford to spend on college is going to affect not only where you go to school but also what your life is like once you get there. Do you mind juggling a job (or several) with your schoolwork? Do you mind graduating with a heavy debt? Do you want to go to a school where virtually all of the students come from fairly wealthy families? There's a lot of financial aid out there, but few scholarships pay the entire bill, and most have strings attached. One of the important things you have to do is sit down with your parents and talk honestly about the bottom line. At the same time, don't rule out a college based on cost entirely—you haven't yet applied for financial aid, and grants and loans can make a big difference.

Distance

How far away from home do you want to be? Going away to school will definitely help you broaden your horizons, but you'll have to be outgoing enough to build a whole new social circle. And when you're calculating college costs, don't forget to add in the cost of transportation. Flying back and forth between school and home can cost a few thousand dollars a year, particularly if school and home aren't located on heavily traveled air routes. However, if the tuition somewhere further from home is much cheaper, then it might be better to go "away" to school. Be realistic: Don't decide that you'll save money by staying at school during all your vacations.

Students stranded on empty campuses during big holidays are among the most depressed people in the world. Spending holidays away from home may sound like a great idea to you now, but a rough first semester as a freshman could change your mind.

Location

Is there an area of the country you want to be in? City or country? Do you want to be in an urban setting? A rural setting? Something in between? Do you want access to mountains? A beach? Is there an outdoor activity you love to do that requires you to be in a certain geographical setting? Do you mind living in a town that has no good restaurants? These questions have nothing to do with education, but they are not frivolous. Again, you're selecting not only a school but also a place to live for the next few years. Be sure you want to (or at least can stomach) living there before you sign up to go. Also remember that if you're going to have to work your way through school, a big city will probably offer more employment opportunities than a small town. It will also make it easier to find jobs that won't bring you into constant contact with your schoolmates, if such a thing would bother you.

Climate

Does weather influence your decision? If you grew up in Florida, you may have trouble adjusting to winters in Maine. You're also going to have to buy a lot of new clothes. Weather can make a big difference to your state of mind. If rainy days make you feel gloomy, you may want to think twice about going to college in a place like Seattle. Though most schools aren't in places where you'll never see the sun, you'll still want to keep climate in mind.

Living Arrangements

How you live is just as important as where you live and colleges differ greatly in the housing they offer. Some offer none at all. Some don't permit off-campus living. Do you mind showering in a large bathroom with a dozen other people? Are single rooms available for freshmen? If it matters to you, find out. Your living arrangements will influence who your friends are, how you spend your free time, how early you have to get up in the morning, and how late you can stay out at night. Here's how one of our former students puts it: "The best thing about college for me isn't college, it's my apartment. After freshman year, you're allowed to live off campus. My parents give me what they would have spent on room and board, and I use it to pay my rent and buy my food. I sleep in a bed I bought for ten dollars, I make my own breakfast and my own coffee, [and] I feel like an adult. And my grades are better too." You might be a lot happier living in a dormitory around other students, but this particular student's college experience would have been much different if he had attended a school that didn't let sophomores live off campus. Life in virtually all freshman dormitories is alike in some respects: It's loud, messy, crowded, uncomfortable, and usually a lot of fun. There are important differences, though, and understanding them before you make a commitment can lead to a happier few years.

Where Your Friends Go

Going to college with high school friends can be great or terrible. On the one hand, going away to a college where you don't know anybody is one of the few opportunities you'll have in life to wipe the slate clean on the person you used to be. Even better, it comes at a time when many people are very eager to do just that. On the other hand, having a close friend nearby can make the first weeks of freshman year less frightening. Nevertheless, we feel you're probably better off on your own. You'll make more new friends if you don't have the old gang to fall back on. Feelings of freshman alienation usually don't last beyond the first couple of weeks. People also change at college. The kind of people you like to hang around with won't necessarily stay the same.

Where Your Girlfriend or Boyfriend Goes

A fair number of people marry their high-school sweethearts but many more of them don't. Before you decide to attend a certain college to be with your current boyfriend or girlfriend, think through the consequences. Freshman year in college can put a huge strain on a high-school romance. Dormitory life is fun and liberating. Even small colleges offer temptations that high schools don't. It takes a strong relationship to survive the dramatic change in lifestyle that freshman year in college means to most people. We knew two students who had been going steady since eighth grade. They ordered catalogs together, picked colleges together, filled out their applications together, and enrolled in the same school. Then, a week into freshman year, they broke up. They spent most of the first semester just trying to avoid each other on campus, which was hard because they were at a small school. He ended up transferring. Also, having a steady boyfriend or girlfriend nearby can limit your ability to make new friends of both sexes; you may want to consider attending college a few hours away from your significant other. You know the saying about how if a relationship is meant to last, it will last; though that might not necessarily be true, a strong relationship will survive some distance.

Trends

Every year a few hot schools emerge to which everyone seems to apply. Hot schools are usually good colleges that are suddenly perceived as being easier to get into than the very best colleges or are schools that have seen a sudden increase in national exposure and attention. As a result, they attract a huge number of applications. But the more people who want to go to a school, the more people who are going to be rejected. This doesn't mean you shouldn't apply to a hot school; it just means you shouldn't depend on getting in, even if your credentials would ordinarily make you a strong contender. Use your judgment. If you decide to apply to a certain school because you read an interesting article about it in *Time* magazine, remember that millions of other people will have read about it too.

Student/Faculty Ratio and Average Class Size

While you should acknowledge these statistics (often found in a college's informational material), course quality is much more important than class size (although it's also much harder to assess, unfortunately). Huge courses taught by great teachers are more rewarding than tiny courses taught by below-average teachers. In small classes, you could end up spending an excessive amount of time listening to the opinions of your classmates. Some professors who shine in big lecture courses are unbearable in small seminars. One of our students summed it up for us nicely: "I came from a big high school where there were never enough desks, and one of the things I cared about most when I applied to college was class size—I wanted them small. But the funny thing was [that] my very worst class freshman year was an English class that only had six students in it and that usually met in the professor's living room … and my favorite course was a freshman science course that met in an auditorium and had about 500 students in it. The professor was like a great actor, and every lecture was exciting." Also remember that student/faculty ratio and average class size mean even less if the courses you plan to take don't fit the usual pattern. If you are planning to major in Greek and the university to which you're applying only has seven Greek majors, many of your classes are going to be small no matter what the overall university statistics say.

Course Catalogs

Some students try to compare colleges on the basis of catalogs of course offerings. As college freshmen soon discover, course catalogs are works of fiction. Courses that sound great in a catalog can be very different in reality, and the course that makes you want to go to a certain college may be canceled by the time you get there. Who the teacher is usually makes more of a difference than what is being taught. Of course, if you have special academic interests, you need to be certain that the colleges you are considering can satisfy them. If you want to major in Russian, be sure the schools you apply to have Russian departments.

Campus Culture

Does the idea of Greek life frighten you, or is that something that you'd be interested in participating in? Do you want an environment where students spend a lot of their free time in the library? Are lots of clubs and extra-curriculars important to you? Do you want an active social life with large crowds gathering at a huge sporting event every weekend in the fall? Do most students live on campus and congregate in dorms, or are there a lot of com-muter students? Do you want a campus that is a hotbed of political debate? Do you want to live in a place where students are focused on environmental initiatives? Do you enjoy a more artistic environment or a technical environ-ment, perhaps? All of these things should be taken into account.

Viewbooks

Many colleges supplement their catalogs with viewbooks, brochures, and other publications. You can get some idea of what a campus is like by look-ing at the pictures, but no college in existence looks as good as it does in its viewbook. Let's face it: A viewbook is an advertisement. The college hopes it will put you in the mood to buy. You should be just as skeptical of a view-book as you are of the claims in a television commercial. You will never find a college that has the same proportion of happy students, magnificent scen-ery, and beautiful weather that it depicts in its brochures. Colleges also use their viewbooks to spell out their educational philosophies. Most colleges have interchangeable philosophies—"a firm commitment to the liberal arts," and so on—but some colleges do have unusual programs or other special-ized approaches to education. These will always be explained in the view-book or other brochure. Colleges may have a five-year co-op program or an expanded Experiential Learning Programs that expose first- and second-year students to outside-of-the-classroom course work. There may be online courses or required study abroad so when you look at viewbooks, focus on the programs and not just the pictures.

What Your Parents Think

The truth is that you're probably going to need your parents' help in financ-ing your education, so don't alienate them by saying that you don't care what they think. If you want to go to an Ivy League university but they want to economize by sending you to the local college, see if you can find a compromise. Try persuading them to at least let you apply to some local colleges and an Ivy League school or two. If you get into the school of your choice, your case will be strengthened, but if you don't, there's nothing to fight about. If there's substantial overlap between what you want and what your parents want, that's great! If you are determined to do battle with your parents, make sure you're fighting over a school that genuinely means something to you. If you fight with your parents and win, you may find it difficult to back down later, so make sure you really want to go to school three thousand miles away from home!

What Your Guidance Counselor Thinks

Most counselors are knowledgeable and really do care. Listen to what they have to say. That said, many counselors are overworked (in a budget crunch, the counselors are among the first to go), and some are, well, just bad. A counselor may have to advise hundreds of students about personal, career, and academic concerns, not to mention college planning. Moreover, even the best counselor cannot be expected to know about all of the programs and departments at the colleges around the country. If you are applying to a college or program outside your counselor's experience, you'll have to do your own research. If you feel you cannot talk to your counselor because he or she is overworked, you should consider seeking the help of a good independent college adviser.

SAT/ACT Averages

One of the first things students do when they begin to think about college is to read through a college guide and then eliminate schools whose average SAT or ACT score is higher than their own test scores. While your high school transcripts and admissions exam scores are not the be-all, end-all, they do provide good guidance in terms of the academic challenge(s) you would want from a college or university. Do you want to apply to a school that will provide you with the right level of academic challenge and growth? Are your grades and scores on par with what the school requires? Are they too high? Too low? Don't scratch a school off the list just because you think the scores are out of range, but make sure you're aware of how your scores compare to those of students who get accepted.

School Size

The size of the college you attend can have a big effect on your experience there. Big schools have more activities, more facilities, more students, more everything. It's easier to stand out at a small school, but harder to melt into the crowd. At a big school you may also have to take a greater responsibility for planning your own education and securing your own living arrangements than you might at a small school. You shouldn't have any trouble thinking of plenty of differences between big and small schools—think of the differences between living in a town and living in a city—you'll find an equivalent for each pro and con on campus. Size is important, but it's sometimes not as important as most high school students tend to think it is.

There are benefits to both a small school and a large school, and the strength of what you will get out of that small or large environment depends on what you want and what you know about yourself.

Library Size

The number of volumes in a college's library can make a difference, but think about this carefully. It is not unknown for a high-school student to cross a college off his list because its library is "too small," then go to a college with a bigger library and not set foot inside it during four years except to use the bathroom. For most students, computer labs and dorm Internet access are far more important than the number of volumes in the library.

Computer/Internet Access

Computer labs are often located in residence halls and libraries and are sometimes open 24 hours a day. "Hot spots" for free Internet access also cover the grounds of many campuses. Increasingly, professors post syllabi, assignments, and additional reading materials online, while internal college websites allow you to schedule classes and apply for financial aid efficiently and securely and maybe even take online courses. Still, even though virtually all colleges have integrated technology into the college experience, they have done so to varying degrees. Some colleges expect you to use technology daily. Others make it available but don't necessarily expect you to use it, other than to write your papers. The best people to ask about the use of technology at a college are the students at that college. Most students will have well-developed opinions regarding everything from Wi-Fi access and how easy it is to find a printer on campus to how annoying the college's internal website is to navigate.

COMMON MISTAKES TO AVOID
WHILE CHOOSING A COLLEGE

The college admissions process may seem like a minefield of advice. College counselors, parents, teachers, friends, and even representatives of the colleges themselves all have admonishments to "be sure to…" and "don't ever…." Unfortunately these tidbits, while intended to be helpful, can often contradict one another, giving students a picture of the process that looks more like a booby-trapped labyrinth than a map of a clear and straightforward path to success. In order to avoid adding to the confusion of the college selection process, here are just a few very important mistakes to avoid.

Get Started Now!

The biggest pitfall is probably the most obvious. Don't procrastinate! Getting started can be difficult, and there are plenty of places where you can get hung up or feel overwhelmed. Procrastinating can create undue stress and probably won't allow enough time to visit a campus so that you can get the most out of each college visit. And of course, there is also the ultra-last-minute procrastination of the applications themselves, which can cause you to make careless errors that could jeopardize your admissions chances. The bottom line here is that being prepared in advance for each step of the process can make the whole college admissions timeline much more manageable.

You have to take this project seriously. Which school you end up attending is the biggest factor that will shape your college experience, but many students don't put that much time or effort into this consideration. Don't make a decision without spending time researching colleges and finding out what you want. Because students don't often invest much time in exploring their options for different colleges, they can fall into the trap of assuming the best colleges are the most familiar ones. If you don't spend enough time thinking about the kind of person you are so that you can come up with a more appropriate "fit" instead of just getting in to some "brand name" institution, then you may not be able to realize your full potential, or you may just end up switching colleges after the first year because the experience wasn't what you dreamed it would be.

Schedule A College Visit

Part of taking this process seriously and doing your research properly is visiting as many colleges as you can. Often students and parents put this off, thinking it's either a waste of time or too expensive, but visiting at least a few schools is almost always worth it. Nothing can give you as much information about how a school "feels" and how you'll feel at it as actually walking around campus and getting a sense of its atmosphere. If you have the time and ability, visiting multiple schools early in your application process can help you narrow down which schools to apply to. If your candidate schools aren't local or you have limited means, it can be helpful to wait until you've received acceptances and weighed aid offers, and visit only your top two or three schools to aid in your final decision. We have multiple strategies and tips about planning an effective college visit in Part 3.

DOs	DON'Ts
Do it early, as soon as possible, or right now.	Don't procrastinate.
Do consider many schools you haven't heard of.	Don't choose a school based on name recognition alone.
Do listen to professional advice.	Don't neglect school visits.
Do it yourself!	Don't let your parents make all the decisions.
Do your research.	Don't let a school's "sticker price" scare you.

WOULD YOU RATHER?

Now that you know some of the key factors and some of the mistakes to avoid, it's time to really start figuring out what you want from colleges. Read through each question and write down your answer without thinking about it. You might be surprised what you learn about your college expectations.

Would you prefer a school that…

1. is big (10,000+ undergrads), medium (4,000–10,000 undergrads), or small (fewer than 4,000 undergrads)?

2. is close to home, or as far away as you can get?

3. requires you to live on campus, or off?

4. has an ivy-covered campus, or looks modern?

5. has a set, structured list of academic requirements, or grants total academic freedom for all four years?

6. is in a city, the suburbs, or a cornfield?

7. is warm and sunny 340 days a year, or cold and snowy from October to April?

8. has many of your high-school friends as students, or is full of total strangers?

9. has plenty of fraternities and sororities, or no Greek scene at all?

10. has a dry campus, has somewhat of a social atmosphere, or is a party school?

11. has 400 students in lecture classes, or six kids in a small class?

12. is populated with liberal hipsters, or young Republicans?

13. has professors who will know your name, or will refer to you by your social security number (in paperwork, since they probably won't call on you in their large classes)?

14. has mostly students who live on campus all four years, or is mainly a "suitcase" school where people travel to and from campus?

15. assigns lots of homework and readings, or hardly any of the same?

16. is bureaucracy central, or a well-oiled machine?

17. has a politically active student body, or one that never reads a newspaper?

18. has tons of things to do off campus, or where the school itself is the center of all fun activities within a 20-mile radius?

19. has a diverse student body, or has a fairly uniform student body?

20. is very accepting of gay students, or has a "don't ask/don't tell" policy?

21. is a "jock" school, or is full of students who rarely participate in sports?

22. enrolls mainly pre-professional students, or kids who will "figure it out after we graduate"?

23. sends almost every junior abroad for a semester or year, or where everyone stays on campus all four years?

24. doesn't consider environmental issues as a top priority, or recycles everything possible?

There you have it: A few ideas about how to start your search for the college that will fit your needs. But you're not quite finished; we have a few more activities for you.

FINAL THOUGHTS

It's important to remember that most students end up liking where they go to college. The student who is crushed to have been rejected by Princeton ends up loving Oberlin and being happy that the fate kept her from being accepted by what had once been her first-choice school. In many ways, the most important thing about college is the one characteristic that virtually all colleges have in common: They are communities of young people living on their own without many serious responsibilities. You'll never get another chance to live this way, and you'll probably enjoy it almost anywhere you get the opportunity. In addition to determining where you spend the next four years of your life, where you go to school can determine where you work after graduation, whom you marry, where you live, and who your life-long friends are. A degree from Wharton really can make it easier to get a good job after graduation; however, spending four years in a sunny locale such as Hawaii really can be a lot of fun. You should make your college decision carefully and with a clear head. Don't make your decision simply to please (or infuriate) someone else. If you begin to think that you won't be able to go on living unless you get into Yale, get a hold of Yale's faculty directory and see where its professors went to college. You'll see that some of them went to Yale, some to Harvard, and some to other Ivy League schools, but that many of them went to exactly the sort of colleges that you may think are "beneath" you. If those colleges are good enough for Yale, might they not also be good enough for you? You should approach college selection thoughtfully, but not with a conviction that your entire life hangs in the balance.

Because, let's be honest, it doesn't. No matter the college, the education you will get out of it largely depends on what you put into it. No one can tell you what you want or need. Not your parents, not your guidance counselor, not your teachers, not your older brother or sister, not us. Students who end up enrolling in colleges based on the wants, needs, or expectations of others often regret it. You should certainly listen to the advice all these people have to give you, but you need to do your own soul-searching and research because only you can figure out what attributes of college are most important to you.

No matter where you go for your college research help or where you end up actually going to college, we sincerely hope that it's the right school for you. Best of luck!

NOTES

NOTES

NOTES